Cambridge Studies in Cultural Systems

The Untouchable as himself:
Ideology, identity, and pragmatism among the Lucknow Chamars

Cambridge Studies in Cultural Systems

Clifford Geertz, Editor

1 The anthropological romance of Bali 1597–1972: dynamic perspectives in marriage and caste, politics and religion
James A. Boon

2 Sherpas through their rituals
Sherry B. Ortner

3 Literature and violence in North Arabia
Michael E. Meeker

4 Knowledge and passion: Ilongot notions of self and social life
Michelle Z. Rosaldo

5 The Lumbee problem: the making of an American Indian people
Karen I. Blu

6 Human spirits: a cultural account of trance in Mayotte
Michael Lambek

7 Rank and rivalry: the politics of inequality in rural West Bengal
Marvin Davis

8 The untouchable as himself: ideology, identity, and pragmatism among the Lucknow Chamars
R. S. Khare

The Untouchable as himself: ideology, identity, and pragmatism among the Lucknow Chamars

R. S. KHARE

Department of Anthropology
University of Virginia

CAMBRIDGE UNIVERSITY PRESS

Cambridge
London New York New Rochelle
Sydney Melbourne

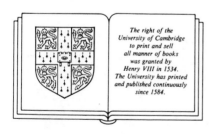

Published by the Press Syndicate of the University of Cambridge
The Pitt Building, Trumpington Street, Cambridge CB2 1RP
32 East 57th Street, New York, NY 10022, USA
296 Beaconsfield Parade, Middle Park, Melbourne 3206, Australia

First published 1984

Printed in the United States of America

Library of Congress Cataloging in Publication Data

Khare, R. S. (Ravindra S.)

The Untouchable as himself.

(Cambridge studies in cultural systems; 8)

1. Chamars. 2. Lucknow (India)—Social conditions.
I. Title. II. Series.
DS432.C48K48 1984 305.5′68′09542 84-7016

ISBN 0 521 26314 X hard covers
ISBN 0 521 26926 1 paperback

Tohī mohī, mohī tohī antar kaisā

Ravidas

[Between thou and me, me and thou
How can there be a difference?]

Contents

Dr. B. R. Ambedkar: Bābā sahib

Preface

To study the contemporary culture and condition of the Indian Untouchable is to learn something about the problems and perspectives of those who have been a classic example of social deprivation and oppression. It is to know about those experiences and perspectives of Indian society that only the Untouchable can provide. Although such information most often is swept aside by the dominant caste-Hindu viewpoint, the voice of the Untouchable is neither incoherent nor insignificant. It encourages reflection on certain fundamental issues of self and society. However, such a study requires a careful handling of the diverse Untouchable thoughts and experiences, including those localized and scattered. Unless pursued with care and suitable encouragement, the local knowledge tends to be easily disregarded. It hides behind diffidence. Genuine cogitation is also usually lost unless the local Untouchable thinkers are accorded full, unqualified attention, and without presumptions. As educated urban Untouchables often remarked in Lucknow, they are served better by genuine inquisitiveness and criticism rather than by unqualified pity. Because they think they represent suffering on behalf of a "frail humanity," they claim that they deserve more than mere condescension.

Facing each other, the Untouchable and the caste Hindu exemplify the characteristic relationships of the dominated and the dominant. As the dominant impose their ideas and will on the dominated, they offer a scheme of justification to maintain their position. The dominated, on the other hand, either accept such schemes or refute them in a way suitable to social circumstances. Although this has been the standard social script for the Untouchable, the everyday reality of independent India is altering it in important and unexpected ways. The clear traditional notions of dominance and privilege are becoming blurred as democratic law, politics, and economics release new forces in India. Urban centers usually show this effect more, where the weaknesses of the strong and the strengths of the weak are constantly uncovered in new ways. In this circumstance the dominant feel threatened and the weak emboldened for new reasons. The ground rules of social demarcation and distance are renegotiated, though haltingly and with apprehension. The new phase raises the expectations of the lowest and the fears of the highest.

In this ethos, the Indian Untouchables, especially in the cities, begin to argue that they are much more than their abjectly low status in relation to the caste Hindu reflects. They dare to question the schemes of the Hindu social precedence. They insist that they are not merely "the signified"; they signify as well. Despite their long-standing dependence on the dominant Hindu social system, they offer evidence that they are alert and sensible about themselves and the larger society in which they must live. If they must face numerous concrete problems in everyday life, they seek survival with social dignity. They challenge tradition as they test the promises of Indian democracy. Thus, compared to the first decades of this century, much has changed for them – more than ever before perhaps; but compared to what they should have in a democratic society, these changes are hardly enough.

The issues of positive self-image, social fairness, and practical effectiveness engage the contemporary Untouchable in India. The changing politics of culture, especially in this century, shape his expectations and strategies. To survive in today's political culture, therefore, the Untouchable must have not only a positive cultural ideology but also an ideological voice; he must have an effective cultural reasoning and not merely a tenacity for daily survival. The urban Untouchables studied here display such a tendency. Their resentment of traditional deprivation and dependence finds a sympathetic ally in democratic politics and its version of social justice.

A fundamentally positive ideology and assertive identity are therefore indispensable to the contemporary Untouchable but, as this study shows, they are much harder to achieve, except in ideas and values. Yet as certain civilizational categories provide genuine value formulations, the categories do not stop there; they also evade static value oppositions to raise a truly Indic – holistic and cosmological – lexis and praxis. As Derrida has said, "To deconstruct the opposition is first . . . to overthrow [*renverser*] the hierarchy" (quoted by Spivak in Derrida 1976: lxxvii). The construction and deconstruction of differences actually go hand in hand in indigenous thought and experience; each must not only culminate in the other but also transcend itself and the other. As I indicate in the text, a Derrida-style erasure, dispersal, and indeterminacy may help capture the presence and meaning of such "differences" within the Indian scheme. Obviously all such interpretations refer to a configuration of critical Indic notions (i.e., dharma, karma, *māyā*, and *saṃasāra*) that guides the recognition and passage of all distinctions and differences between the self and society.

The Indian Untouchable, though increasingly estranged from the caste Hindu, continues to share this civilizational framework. But it produces wrenching paradoxes for him in independent India. His radicalism begins to dissipate before it can take a clear direction; his ambivalence becomes confounding; his political assertion harbors self-doubts. Traditionally, this is how the Untouchable has sublated his own existence. Still, the present story does not stop there. Actually, the most important sociological developments appear when the Untouchable is found comprehending and responding to this deeply rooted framework in the context of this century's initiatives for social reform and democratic change. Throughout this new turbulent phase, the educated Untouchable wants to be sensible and intelligible and expects the caste Hindu to be unprepossessed and just in response.

Larger questions frame this picture of the Untouchable. For example, how do the severely deprived symbolize? To know how they use the given symbols is useful but not enough. We should know the changes as they occur in cognition and symbology under severe and prolonged deprivation. How do the deprived compose a tenable, coherent voice from within their dependent culture? How do the Untouchables forge viable relationships between "self-grounding," "self-assertion," and social odds? Moreover, how do they view "self-worth" with changing social reality and employ it to expand their practical reasoning to take up the matters of comparative social evaluation and accountability? There is a further question: How do the Untouchables transform social dependence into a strategic political resource, claiming compensatory social justice and inalienable self-worth not only from the caste Hindu but also from Indian society and humanity at large? But, then, how far can they proceed toward such objectives by controlled alienation (i.e., by following the civilizational values of moderation and tolerance)?

Such conceptual questions are at present embedded in a social paradox. As contemporary Untouchables stake claims for social improvement, their dissatisfactions mount alongside those of the caste Hindus. This is because the democratic premise of "free and fair play" clashes with the traditional concept of karma-dharma, of "cosmic fair play." Hence, whatever the Untouchables gain threatens the established notions of caste privilege and justice. More dilemmas must appear, however, when tradition and democracy bare their own intrinsic weaknesses in the heterogeneous social reality, leaving each disillusioned and insecure.

Such a situation escapes any simple theory, any clear social classification, and any essential structuralism. Yet all is not confusion. Ideas and actions interrelate in new ways, with new significance. In the Untouchables' case, speech, writing, and action instigate each other by the force of the abject social dependence. If their speech and writing often have originated in social crisis, and have been very poorly preserved, they also have helped germinate the idea of individual and group search for redress. The Untouchables' speech and writing do not only mean action; they are complete acts in themselves, especially for the reformer. Seeded with an innate sense of moral justice in the cosmos, such acts must yield the intended consequence, argues the reformer, "sooner or later." This cultural axiom of the Untouchable thinker energizes ordinary Untouchables in their daily struggles; it also offers a perspective for understanding social differences.

At present both Untouchables and caste Hindus concentrate on their social differences, each for separate reasons and in separate ways. Each repels the other for fervid politico-economic reasons. Yet both remain ambiguous and uncertain beyond a point; they depend on each other by civilizational constraints and human geography. They have yet to discover ways to move beyond these forces. Still, both have changed significantly in this century. Thus if there is the conceding Hindu on the one hand, there is also the Untouchable consolidating a *positive* self-grounding and social worth on the other. The latter must refute and reject the assigned social difference and engage in his own individuation. Issues of self-definition confront him more directly and urgently than perhaps any other Indian group. To reconstruct self for him means to realign social presence and responsibility from scratch. Sri Chandrika Prasad Jigyasu, the Untouchable thinker, repeatedly underscored this point in his interviews and writings. For example, he concluded his account of Achchutananda by quoting a Buddhist sutra:

Attā hī attāno nātho attā hī attāno gatī,
Tasmā samyattānam assam bhadram vā vaṇijā.

(You are your own master; you are your own destiny. Therefore keep yourself as restrained and ready as a trader keeps his beautiful horse.) Achchutananda called self-reliance (*ātmanirbhartā*) the climax of reformed ideology; he emphasized self-respect, self-assurance, and self-reliance as the bases for all political and economic improvements.

Though this study has considered several interrelated themes of Untouchable thought, many remain unexplored. Some obvious contributors to the contemporary ethos also remain unaccounted for, especially the women. During the course of this inquiry, their critical role was repeatedly evident. Some Chamar women, like men, had an acute awareness of, and clear opinions on, changing social circumstances. I met women who were interpreters, dissenters, skeptics, and imperturbable housewives. In most cases both men and women helped me understand what social dependence meant to them; what "loss of face" is for the "faceless"; and what self-reliance means when social conformity and consensus give way to endemic conflict. Obviously, of what one learns in the field only a small segment gets reported in print. However, my appreciation of those I studied (and of those who, in turn, studied my efforts) is abiding, for they helped me learn something both as an anthropologist and as an Indian.

My systematic work on the Lucknow Untouchables, especially the Chamar (traditionally a leatherworking north Indian caste), started in the summer of 1974. However, in 1972 I came in contact with Sri Jigyasu and a whole range of reform literature. I met some local Chamars in 1974 with the help of a young anthropolgist, Mr. Nadim. Several initial encounters took place during this summer to help me formulate the stance of the present inquiry. If the Chamar youths reflected a social restlessness the reformers took me to their *mohallās* to listen to a wide range of opinions, and to meet diverse people. Such exposure was critical to enable me to reach Chamars of diverse backgrounds, whether a shoeshop owner, a politician, a teacher, or an ascetic, who made me aware of their immediate and ultimate concerns. They also freely stated their doubts, concerns, and apprehensions – sensibly insisting on anonymity – often by context and issue. They sought my assurances as I sought their understanding. Consequently, I have tried to honor their wishes for anonymity as carefully as I could.

My acknowledgments must start with these anonymous informants, friends, and commentators. This is a study done *with* them, not of them. Considered alongside the ordinary Chamar and the reform literature, they often lighted up the known issues in a new way and put me on the road to a civilizational perspective. The critical contributions of Jigyasu, Achchutananda, and local thinkers are evident throughout this study. To them my sense of gratitude is deepest. The late Sri Jigyasu was that rare intellectual bridge who ably connected the national with the local, the ancient with the contemporary, and the profound with the popular. He was a reformer, thinker, and critic all rolled into one. Next, I am most appreciative of all the local leaders and reformers of the three Lucknow neighborhoods; they were reasonable even when time treated them unkindly. Dr. Agney Lal of Lucknow University, the priest and the associated officers of the Ravidas temple, and certain political leaders also gave me the benefit of their advice and comments. The local libraries and archives helped me collect and verify empirical information on the Lucknow Chamar, giving me access to records at short notice.

Several institutions and individuals facilitated this research from my workplace. The American Institute of Indian Studies awarded me their senior fellowship to support my fieldwork among the Lucknow Chamar during 1979–80, and the American Philosophical Society gave me a grant-in-aid in the summer of 1976 to conduct interviews on religious and ritual aspects. My summer trips of 1974, 1976, 1978, and 1981 were partially supported by the Center for Advanced Studies, Summer Grants Committee, and the Center for South Asian Studies, all of the University of Virginia. A Sesquicentennial Award of the university supported my stay at Wolfson College, Oxford University, during the spring of 1980, when much of the preliminary writing was done. Among all these sources of help the consistent support of Dean W. D. Whitehead, also director of the Center for Advanced Studies, stood out. As an academic administrator Mr. Whitehead does best what matters most: He fosters faculty development with a truly catholic view of human knowledge.

Aspects of this study were discussed at the Institute of Social Anthropology,

University of Oxford, and during colloquia and seminars on the Indian Untouchable and asceticism at the University of Virginia. Two anonymous reviewers with Cambridge University Press helped me improve this study in several ways, but without forcing their own views on the analysis. Susan Owen read the penultimate draft for clarity with her usual keen eye. As before, when all else failed, Sudha, Manjula, and Gopal came through as helpers, and much more. Always caring and near, they are my "little India" in America.

The book would defeat its sense if it were dedicated to any other idea than the intensional "us," a notion integral to an Untouchable saint like Ravidas, and a conception critical for anthropology of social differences.

Note on transliteration

Although almost all Sanskrit and Hindi words in the text are transliterated in a standard style, the book must also accommodate rural Avadhi, Hindustani, and Urdu, as well as Persian words currently used in everyday language in Lucknow. Consequently, transliteration is not uniform for all non-Sanskrit words. Some words are characterized by the context of usage (e.g., *sāhéb* and sahib), whereas others are distinguished for clarity (e.g., ''Brāhman'' for the caste member and ''Brahman'' for the Absolute). Common words such as Chamar and achchuta retain their anglicized form throughout the text. ''Ravidas'' rather than ''Raidasa'' is used to reflect Chamar reformers' preference. Most of the vernacular terms are spelled phonetically (with a minimum of diacritical marks). Further, most of the Hindi or Sanskrit proper names, and those words found in the *Oxford English Dictionary*, are also spared transliteration. In this way the reading becomes less forbidding. To facilitate comprehension of the names of Untouchable authors and their works, I have supplied appropriate diacritical marks in Part A of the Bibliography.

Introduction:
The inquiry and its context

Approach

The Untouchable symbolizes several critical social dilemmas of independent India.[1] Whatever he is reflects on the larger society and its values. Although he is now more studied and talked about, he himself remains a social enigma. This is so because he is too readily stereotyped by others while he himself often remains remote and silent. His social voice is still too weak. We should nevertheless record the content and character of his voice at this time because it comments significantly on his transforming ideals, social priorities, and practical strategies. Once we prepare ourselves to consider the Untouchable on his own terms, after penetrating certain stereotypes, his arguments for alternative self-evaluation begin to surface. And as we do so, we learn that he displays a piercing seriousness about his social lot, a seriousness often marked by disarming integrity, insight, candor, and humor. We also come to know about the Untouchable's self-image, shaped both by long-standing Indian civilizational forces and by daily events.

The Untouchable for us will be a cultural construct under some circumstances and a concrete social group (the Chamars of Lucknow) under others. The general and the particular, the ultimate and the proximate, the symbolic and the empirical, and the shared and the unique, all will be indispensable for our view of the Indian Untouchable. The Untouchable's varied relationships with the Hindu system, whether of consensus or conflict, or conciliation or alienation, will be important for our study. Though diverse social conditions and regional cultural concerns characterize the contemporary Untouchable, we will converge on that urban, often educated, segment that influences others by its social thought as well as action. The rival counterpart often follows its lead in matters of cultural ideas, changing lifestyles, and political strategies. The educated, urban Untouchables, in turn, try to face and fathom the diverse legal, economic, and political forces that contemporary India and its government release.

We will be interested in a cultural analysis of the ideas and actions of the Lucknow Chamars, an urban Untouchable group, to see how they organize and express their ideology for self-identification and how this ideology is then related to some concrete social contexts and conditions. Although our exposition will help show interdependencies between cultural values, symbols, and practical social action, an overall emphasis will remain on explicating and understanding the symbolic ideas and strategies that the urban Untouchables at present pursue to cope with changing social circumstances. The Untouchable's "symbolic," we must clearly recognize, penetrates as well as binds and transcends "social" and "personal" realities. This enunciation stands at the center of the Untouchable's cultural ideas, perspectives, and expressions. How do the deprived symbolize? How do the symbols work when questions of privilege and justice are concerned? An explication of such questions may be helped by previous studies but they need to be studied and understood on their own terms to derive larger imports. (For references useful to symbolic analysis, see Whitehead 1927; Langer 1974; Geertz 1973; Schneider 1976:197–220.)

The urban Untouchable's symbolic formulations will inform us about certain deeper issues of the hierarchical caste society in India and its assumptions about equality, freedom, justice, and utopia (for a sociological discussion of these concepts, see Dahrendorf 1968; also compare Weber 1963: 95–117; Sigrist 1971: 240–56). We will let the competent Untouchables tell us their own interpretations and arguments regarding these issues, which will allow us to discover their internal sources of knowledge as well as doubt and disaffection. For example, if the classical Indian lawgiver Manu alienates them and Gandhi breeds ambivalence, Ambedkar enlightens as well as revitalizes them. Thus their own sense of moral placement will be as important to us as their perspectives about the dark past, the ambiguous present, and perhaps a better future.

The urban Untouchable that concerns us will often present himself as an active subject. Though obviously a part of the larger, Hindu-dominated social order, this Untouchable is seldom merely a passive, voiceless, and unchanging object of caste domination. He is a product of accelerating social change in democratic India; he strategically exploits the changing socioeconomic constraints as he now translates his past social deprivation into a political resource and seeks an immediate advantage from it.

In general, the urban Untouchable seeks compensatory equality today. He expects it from two sources – Indian spiritual idealism and Western-introduced democracy. This is also his way to challenge caste-ordained inequality in democratic India. Sociologically, an equalitarian ethic is proposed by the Indic "cosmological" order, and it is recurrently expressed via ideal, mythical, symbolic, and reformist formulations. For example, one quickly cites in this context the ideal polity of *Rāmarājya* (a condition free from want, deprivation, and dominance); the spiritual equalitarianism (for *ātamika samānatā* and *samadṛṣṭi*) of the Bhakti movement; and the recent liberal reform movements culminating in twentieth-century humanism (*mānavadharma*). Hence, as the Untouchable thinker engages himself in a serious debate with the Brahman, he illustrates a scholarly position of radical revision that is neither spurious nor unknown to the Indian tradition.[2] If it remains unconventional, it is no less real or less pressing for him.

Sociologically, the Untouchable thinker hopes that a weakening of the caste Hindu's privileges will automatically mean social gain for the Untouchables in general (Laski 1934). Whether it actually happens this way in India is another matter. But we will not underplay the role of diverse social developments in independent India. Most important, such developments have encouraged the Untouchable to push to acquire a social "voice" for improved self-image and social position. He has been engaged in a cognitive remapping of his cherished values within the immediate surroundings; he is articulating a positive moral (and spiritual) ideology from within the Indian civilization. In doing so, the Untouchable confirms some expected criteria of the sociology of the "nonprivileged."[3]

If such efforts make it necessary that we consider in detail the work of some Untouchable thinkers, even those who claim an Aristotelian *vita contemplativa*, we will do so. We will discuss such a thinker's position in relation to other reformers, protesters, and politicians, examining how he may be revitalizing some symbolic complexes and weeding out others. He might also give some classical complexes (e.g., *ātamika samānatā* and *saṁyama*) new political meanings, to be used as springboards for social assertion and protest. We will examine the effective feedback relationships among these symbolic complexes to show how the Untouchable now revitalizes his thought, speech, and action with help from those cognitive processes that the changing society yields.

We will develop our discussion in terms of three sociocultural processes critical to the Untouchable's contemporary social condition and its characterization. The first process concerns his "articulation" of the contemporary social situation in terms relevant to his immediate needs as well as larger aspirations. Such an expression, his "voice," gives us an idea of the deeper changes in his values, symbols, expectations, and actions. Since his voice concerns both ultimate and proximate goals, it is encountered in a discursive ideological text as well as in the ordinary Chamar's struggle to provide for his family. The second process, called "evaluation," represents the Untouchable's efforts to compare and weigh his present-day social odds as well as advantages. This process works as he recognizes social options, establishes practical priorities among them, develops a strategy for concrete action, and assesses the result (see also n. 7, chap. 4). "Accountability," the third process, concerns the Untouchable's image of self and society as he renders others accountable to himself (and his group), and himself to the society as a whole. We detect that he is developing a sense of relative accountability. He weighs the caste Hindu's rights and responsibilities in relation to his own; he does so by context, as well as on the whole, and seeks adjustments in them until they are congruent with his notions of a fair society. He aims to acquire a genuinely positive social accountability for himself, combating deeply entrenched negative roots. However, he recognizes that such a change demands a realignment of certain major civilizational values; merely superficial change will not do (see n. 6, chap. 4, and also chap. 9).

Previous Studies

When we examine the treatment accorded to the Untouchable within the scholarly traditions of the Indian subcontinent, two types of studies become readily evident: those in which "others" have considered him in the ancient, medieval, and recent past, and those in which he has had something to say about himself – mythical, intellectual, and descriptive. Obviously, the first type predominates. Within India, Hindu thinkers, reformers, and writers have variously "explained" the Untouchables' social lot. Ideologically they bring into focus the classical Brahman – Untouchable polarity, yielding version after version of moral justification for why the lowest, exterior position was assigned to the Untouchable. The *Laws of Manu* continues to be a locus classicus – scholarly, mythical, and divine (for the Hindu) – within such discussions. What it ordains on the issue continues to influence ordinary caste Hindus. If a modern Hindu criticizes Manu it is only half-heartedly. It is no wonder therefore that twentieth-century Untouchable reformers attack (and sometimes even burn) this book in protest (see Zelliott 1972: 69–95). Manu also may have been variously attacked by some recent Hindu social reformers but seldom totally repudiated in social practice. From the Untouchable's position, therefore, all the powerful waves of social reform, radicalism, and revolt must finally crash within the same old Manu-ordained parameters.

This study will explore only the contemporary phase of this age-old issue. Although a firm factual ground may be available to us to investigate the issue only during this century (and perhaps in even the last few decades of the previous one), there is, however, little or nothing known with certainty about any of the Untouchable's efforts to protest and reform the situation. For over a century, based often on indirect evidence, one could surmise that the Indian Untouchable has been slowly but surely responding to the British-introduced "seeds" of present-day administration, economy, law, and politics. Such developments seem to have received greater attention from those regional and local Untouchable reformers who were literate, and had inherited the broad-minded devotional culture of the medieval reformist heroes, saints, and ascetics.[4]

In the contemporary period, the Untouchables are increasingly studied by "others," whether the results are poems, novels, research studies, or bureaucratic government reports and statistics. Also, the Untouchables now increasingly write about themselves to raise a polemic, a political protest, or a philosophical and ideological argument. However, the two types of studies seldom communicate with each other, and they tend to pursue their own separate analyses.[5] A comprehensive and reliable bibliography usually reveals best the distinct themes and emphases of previous studies. Fortunately, a readily useful bibliographic survey is available to us (see Zelliott 1972: 431–86; see also Rao 1978: 233–43). Several entries in Zelliott's bibliography have repeatedly informed the formulation and conduct of this discussion.[6]

Because this study's aim, emphasis, scope, and conduct will engage us on their own terms, the purpose of an occasional citation of this background literature is mainly to recognize and reiterate some necessary analytic distinctions and to institute suitable precautions. For example, the previous anthropological literature on the Untouchable cautions us to avoid (1) a hasty imposition of any a priori doctrinaire or theoretical schemes of explanation, (2) an uncritical and unsubstantiated acceptance of any exaggerated or extreme social formulation, and (3) a simplistic dichotomy of either practical or ideological constraints in everyday life. Most important, the Untouchable's indigenous thoughts and actions, we are reminded, need careful explication in their own context, and in that of a specific social circumstance.

This requires us to approach a specific group like the Lucknow Chamars from up close, allowing them to surface as fully and uninhibitedly as their own cultural ideas and social experiences will permit. We will study them for what they symbolically express and what they do as a part of their daily social life. Both of these frames of reference will be helpful to us. If the social frame views the Lucknow Chamars as belonging to a specific household (*ghara*) of a particular lane (*galī*) located in a particular neighborhood (*mohallā*), the symbolic frame offers schemes of shared ideas, images, and representations. The Chamar ideologist thus easily puts on the face of the Indian Untouchable and begins to speak on behalf of the whole. He then draws upon a whole range of conceptions, experiences, and personages representing different symbolic aspects of the Indian Untouchable.

The Lucknow Chamar will similarly also present to us two more faces at once, one old and the other new, one frozen within the massively institutionalized caste order and the other congealing with encouragement from Indian democracy. The two faces of the Chamar currently interact as symbolizations of the past and the present, and of a possibly hopeful future. A preindependence description of the Indian Untouchable, even fictional (e.g., Anand's *Untouchable*) could be helpful as a comparative background for deciphering the cultural significance of what one encounters today within such a group as the Lucknow Chamars.

These urban Chamars will offer us several deftly interwoven portraits of educated as well as uneducated leaders, heads of households, prominent residents, and ordinary members of the community. The young and the old, the successful and the unsuccessful, the achievers and the failures, and the happy and the oppressed all will illustrate a range of ideas and experiences. Their language will at once express their social hope and frustrations mostly in relation to the pre-Ambedkar and post-Ambedkar developments (for a comparable sketch, see Miller and Kale 1972: 317–59). Not unlike "the man inside," the burden of Beatrice Miller's (1972: 361–73) sensitive account of the Mahars, the Lucknow Chamars will be found matching values, ideals, expectations, and emotional responses "*to communicate with other members of their society*" (p. 361; Miller's emphasis).

One of our main purposes in approaching such data will be to discover the Untouchable's general "lexicon of signification." We will recognize how the Lucknow Chamars put distance between themselves and the caste Hindu by distinguishing between what we shall call the "Indic" and the "Hindu," that is, those civilizational configurations of values of which the Hindu is only a part. Thus the Chamars may identify themselves as ideologically different from the Hindu on the one hand, and yet control the resulting cultural divergence with centripetal civilizational forces, on the other. This property is rooted in certain Indic philosophical perspectives; it also resonates with subtleties captured within *différance* (a concept of Jacques Derrida, the French linguistic philosopher; see, for example, this study's Conclusion; see also Culler 1979: 154–80).

The Untouchable thinker often presents his case this way: He considers his group to be simply neither Hindu nor outside Indian civilization; neither merely consensual nor entirely alienated. He claims a positive and different civilizational place for his kind essentially on the same lines as did the Buddhists and the Jains. Recently he has illustrated the two positions available to him; first as neo-Buddhists (an Ambedkar-led option), and the second as a distinct community of the *ādi*-Hindus (i.e., the original Hindus of the subcontinent). Such points about self and society are critical for the Untouchable's ideological position.

Assumptions and stipulations

We will devote the first part of this study to a discussion of the Untouchable's cultural ideology, concentrating on its cultural principles and constitution. We will analyze the version of this ideology that the Untouchables themselves offer, keeping its internal cultural symbols intact and its logical relations undisturbed. Our method will consist of a series of steps: It will distinguish a fundamental axis of cultural categories, illustrate its alternative orders of arrangement and significance, draw upon the explicit and implicit messages that these orders release, and culminate in ideological reformulations and practical strategies.

We will further assume that the Untouchable is innately as capable of responding to his social conditions as any caste Hindu. Both are now subject to intensifying secular social forces and both learn by trial and error. There is no evidence to support the premise that the Untouchables, even when given the chance, cannot learn from or respond to changing social aspirations and conditions as quickly as the caste Hindus can. After over thirty-five years of political, economic, and civil involvement in independent India, the Untouchables show repeated signs of conscious social estimation and decision making. This social acquisition, often unconscious and informal, is neither merely incidental nor limited to a select few (e.g., see the cases cited in chaps. 7, 8, and 9). Secular democratic forces are challenging their passive approach to social deprivation. Newly acquired social ideas and actions are being discussed. Many urban Untouchables now challenge and attack their social disadvantage, rather than unquestioningly accepting it as a social given.

However, recognition of this widely shared awareness does not demand that we disregard the specific empirical differences among the Untouchables. Thus, though it is necessary to recognize that the Indian Untouchable, despite his social deprivation, carries the same basic *potential* for rational action as a caste Hindu, not every Untouchable is a philosopher, a saint, or an adroit politician. Although only a few can be any of these at any one time or place, most others are ordinary (yet reasoning) people. Finally, those who are leaders still show divergence among themselves in their stated aims and concrete actions, and in promise and performance.

This social heterogeneity means that the Untouchable must be examined from several interrelated vantage points – from symbolic and empirical, and from near and afar, from above and below, and from side to side. Such steps are necessary to complete the Untouchable's picture from those directions the predominant caste-Hindu system hides or obscures. Such a stipulation might help reveal the overshadowed, correct the distorted, and restore the misplaced structures of significant relations. Thus anthropological procedures, when studying the Untouchable's case, have to examine not only the dominant social viewpoint, but also the countervailing, the spontaneous, and the resurgent. They must be alert to the subtle and subliminal biases usually embedded in the dominant Hindu system.

Such a perspective demands, most of all, that we examine carefully the indigenous schemes of cultural categorization, construction, and interpretation. The indigenous categories should be considered for their multiple meanings and interrelationships, whether classical, popular, or conjectural. (For example, see n. 1 for a discussion of the term "Untouchable.") The Untouchables' ideological schemes will be especially appropriate for such an exercise, since their approach to asceticism and to the ascetic-Brahman contrast posits different distinctions and helps reinterpret certain classical cultural categories for wider sociological significance (e.g., see chaps. 3 and 4). Properly handled, these categories need not breed noncomparability and obscurity. The categories a study converges upon most must also reflect the conceptual focus of the study.[7]

Simultaneously, the Untouchable's categories and conceptions rarely exhibit an unconditional and unequivocal opposition to the caste Hindu's. This is obviously because the Untouchables ordinarily absorb so much of the Hindu, and are so dominated by the Hindu, that their recent politics of reform and emancipation remains ambivalent in thought as well as deeds. The nature of this ambivalence will be repeatedly evident here. But now it is not without a polarizing rhetoric and an increasing demand for separate but equal social status in relation to the caste Hindu.

For identifying the Untouchable's ideological categories, it is crucial that a distinction be maintained between "the Hindu" and the earlier "pre-Hindu" roots of Indian civilization. The pre-Hindu (i.e., the Buddhist, Jain, and other ancient ascetic traditions; for an overview, see Bhagat 1976) categories are indispensable for the Untouchable thinker. We will call this segment of the civilization "Indic," distinguishing it from the "Hindu" (i.e., the later *smṛti* versions) and from the "Indian," which would embrace all major indigenous and foreign contributions to India's heterogeneous culture.

Finally, we urge caution in passing quick judgments on the Untouchable's present initiatives. The final outcome is still unpredictable; the current situation shows widening social gaps and rising conflict between the caste Hindus and the Untouchables. Thus though the caste order resists all structural change, it must now face unremitting social pressure from democratic forces. However slowly and reluctantly, it must strike compromises with the changing social reality. And as such leeways appear, the Untouchable discovers a ground from which to consolidate his positive self-definition. A positive cultural ideology and identity are always very precious gains for the socially deprived. The more pronounced the deprivation, the more socially sensitive, coveted, and contested are these gains generally.

The context and range of data

I have so far mostly employed the general type, the Indian Untouchable, to contextualize my formulations. I do so purposely to offer a generalizing picture that my data sustained and also that a review of Untouchable writings corroborated. However, now we can be empirically specific: The people under study in this book are almost exclusively the Chamars living in Lucknow, the capital of Uttar Pradesh, a state in northern India.[8] I have called them Lucknow Chamars. However, only three neighborhoods of the Lucknow Chamars were studied through intensive fieldwork, where each neighborhood followed a weakening traditional organization by *thoks* and *ṭāṭs*.[9]

A count of these traditional clusters was usually mentioned when asked, though the Chamars' lane- and *mohallā*-oriented social life was more important to them on an everyday basis. Identifiable further, and much more relevant to us, were the informally named *galīs* (lanes and bylanes) within a named *mohallā* (an informal urban "neighborhood"). Though seldom coextensive with any administrative city ward, a neighborhood had several lanes, named either for a prominent resident or on the basis of numerically dominant occupations (e.g., Ram Prasad *ki galī; Mehetron kī galī*). At the level of the lanes, the Lucknow Chamars usually offered several tightly knit clusters of houses within the city. A *thok*, in comparison, rarely forged a stronger residential bond, and its members usually showed declining traditional cooperation and interdependence. A *ghar-galī-mohallā* cluster nurtured their everyday social life, including daily problems, secular aspirations, and political activism.

The empirical data on which this study is based are drawn from three different Lucknow neighborhoods. One neighborhood was at the center of the "new city," virtually under the shadow of the state legislative assembly buildings, and the other two were in the "old city." One was located along the two sides of a 25-foot-wide bricklined open drain, and the other was on the western fringe of the old city, linked to villages of the area. These three neighborhoods reflected distinctly different cultural profiles, an aspect of central concern to this study. These Lucknow localities represented the cultural diversity of the contemporary Chamar. They also presented a reasonably wide-ranging and heterogeneous occupational picture of these people in independent India and exposed the social processes of their everyday struggle in the practical world.

Since these aspects will claim more of our attention than a plain enumeration of the ranked social relations and the details of the *jāti* praxis, the three urban localities, selected after a search during the summer of 1974, will yield ethnographic data on the changing Lucknow Chamar.[10]

Our attention was on the ordinary, as well as the active (or the "awakened") Chamars, whether an illiterate shoe-making "commoner," an educated thinker, a hero, a leader, or a militant. However, since only with considerable perseverance did I shed my own upper-caste blinders allowing the Chamars to present themselves uninhibitedly, this exercise was for me much slower and harder than I had expected. My learning increased as I was exposed repeatedly to self-effacing as well as radical Chamars.

In the "new-city" neighborhood lived that Chamar who was often literate and who invariably sought employment in urban surroundings, whether in factories, labor gangs, small vending businesses, or government offices. With accessible schools and colleges, and with government subsidies and encouragement, this Chamar neighborhood was populated by, among others, a prestigious railway driver (earning in four figures every month), a high-ranking postal employee, a state assembly leader, a poet, a fully qualified physician (of Western medicine), a university-educated philosopher, an engineer, a draftsman, an architect, a photographer, a three-star hotel employee, a chef, a chauffeur, and a contractor. Members of thirty-five of the two hundred households in this neighborhood were found to have decidedly "prestigious" work, that is, employment that *both* Chamars and caste Hindus would consider a "good placement." This proportion significantly increased when mechanics, car drivers, and small "businessmen" (i.e., shopkeepers, vendors, masons, and painters) were included. As it represents a "better-off" Chamar locality, this neighborhood will be called "Modernganj," a pseudonym but one that aptly reflects the overall cultural ethos.

The second neighborhood, spread along a major old-city drain, was bleak by comparison. It had more Buddhist householders, several reformers, and a visible group of radical ascetics. We will call it "Baudhabagh," because its prominent residents repeatedly longed for urgent reform along the views held by Ambedkar as a Buddhist. These people were also often those most visible and vocal. They were partly a legacy of a group of earlier reformers (Chamars and others, including a nonresident Buddhist monk) and political (including the Republican party) leaders, and were partly shaped by the need to express their acute social and economic discontent. The daily wage-earning laborer, the leather worker, and the vendor of small items dominated the neighborhood. They could not make the local municipal functionaries protect their (tin-covered or thatched) dwellings from the easily swollen open drain, which in the past had swept off houses with loss of life, health, and property. They complained that the local officials and politicians, even those from their own community, had turned their backs on them. Radical rhetoric and protest, often a safety valve against open militancy or violence, were therefore easily generated by the gathering discontent.

As this neighborhood represented a brink, it also graphically embodied the enormous strains and dilemmas of the deprived Chamar (see Chaps. 5–7). Wanting ever more but unable to change or move away from the "exploiting social order" (as they put it), these Chamars encapsulated the ethos of a dispirited neighborhood. The reforming, radical Chamar, whether a follower of Ambedkar or Ravidas, found here ample grist for his mill. Modernganj, being smugly content, had turned away from genuine change, according to this Chamar. The Baudhabagh radicals argued that they could "liberate" themselves only by discovering the true nature of caste-Hindu exploitation, and by combating it every day.

The third neighborhood, practically a hamlet, almost villagelike on the western outskirts of the city, was still different. It was, as we shall call it, "Karampura." The accomplishments of Modernganj and the Baudhabagh rhetoric of an inevitably radical reform faded before "the givens" (i.e., the karma of the Chamar) emphasized in this settlement. Gusts of the *shahrī havā* (urban "ethos") were intruding into several homes, however, as evidenced by handpumps, bicycles, electricity, radios, cameras, tape recorders, motorcycles, and even a scooter. The urban employed, about a dozen in seventy-five households, pulled Karampura toward the city. This group was also drawn toward the new, the "reformed," and the glamorous, whereas the rest, as field laborers, saw themselves as struggling within the given unfavorable social lot.

Here the urge for reform was mild, largely within their traditional social scheme, and with a firmament full of deities from the Hindu pantheon. The "Buddhist alternative" was largely alien, even unwelcome, to them. Yet, not surprisingly, caste-Hindu discrimination and exploitation were increasingly less tolerable to all. The young, urban employed advocated radical social reform; the older generation favored accommodation over alienation as long as some social improvement was occurring. However, the youth found this stand naive and delusory.

These three neighborhoods also often supported Chamar or low-caste ascetics. A few of these were always found in each neighborhood, either passing through, or staying for a few months, or on a regular quarterly or half-yearly visit. A highly varying lot among themselves (see chap. 7), some were reformers, others were informal leaders and tacticians, and still others were regular devotees of Ravidas (also spelled Raidasa) or Buddha or a Hindu god. The "monist" ascetics (*advaitavādin* or *śūnyavādin*) were relatively rare. During the entire period of fieldwork, I encountered seven monist ascetics out of a total of fifty-two, and they were interviewed in all three localities. Karampura and Baudhabagh entertained the most ascetics on a regular basis, whereas Modernganj had several itinerants of a shorter duration, facing keener competition from their low-caste (Hindu) counterparts. However, despite the presence of the Chamar ascetics, it was often the householders, especially those who had "awakened" and were educated, who put forth the ascetic basis of their reformist ideology and led me either to appropriate written sources or to what were known as the "knowledgeable ascetics."

Jigyasu, a reformist writer from yet another neighborhood in the western part of Lucknow, was a householder, not an ascetic. For my study, he stood out as an important source of ideological data. But before he consented to participate in the study, he committed me to refrain from publishing his biographical details – not yet at least. I shall honor his wishes. I interviewed him several times before his death. Not unlike those of the higher caste groups, such prominent householders kept themselves in close intellectual and personal contact with prominent as well as promising ascetics, and they often helped each other articulate thoughts before the larger society. Social interdependence between the householder and the ascetic was critical for increasing the social impact of such an ideology as the Untouchable's.

The field data offered by the three Lucknow neighborhoods were also suitably augmented by documentary and published evidence. A number of publications, documents, and handwritten (family-held) accounts were made available to me by a reformist publishing house in old Lucknow. This body of evidence, most often written in Hindi, with a sprinkling of classical texts in Sanskrit, was most helpful in examining the structure of the cultural ideology (see Part A of the Bibliography).

Thus, this study draws upon the four main indigenous sources, namely, the three Chamar neighborhoods, the neighborhood ascetics, the reformist writers, and the informal documents. These sources also determine the empirical scope, direction, and limits of this study. However, by deciding to admit this particular combination of data for cultural analysis and interpretation, this study will not seek to offer a monographic discussion of a particular Chamar group. Instead, it will present an analysis of a selected series of socially significant issues upon which the Lucknow Chamars (and hence also the Untouchables) converge in contemporary India. A juxtaposition of the Untouchables' cultural ideas and social actions is critical and unavoidable because that is where the real struggles are.

Data collection

Reliable sociological data on Untouchables are still hard to obtain, and what one has is often insufficient. A non-Brahman Hindu investigator like me, or even an Untouchable investigator, I would venture to suggest, faces the same obstacle. Many complications are often due to the Untouchable's strained social placement and its perceptions by the investigator. If the Untouchables were simply either the lowest or not the lowest, clearly within or outside the Hindu caste order, or uniformly deprived or not deprived in the larger society, the investigator's problem would be easier. Then, we would know where they see themselves standing, and they would know how to place an unfamiliar investigator and his purpose – in their own scheme of concerns. But since this is not so, and they are in the throes of a deep and disorienting change, they must subject the investigator to their distrust of the times, putting him to an unexpectedly critical test. The investigator is required not only to adapt and empathize with their social conditions, but also to develop a credulity and sensitivity suitable to their whole range of changing moods, motivations, and purposes.

The Lucknow Chamars, who fuss over a stranger, and who have been almost endlessly scrutinized, are no longer humored by an inquiry. They become instead suspicious, drop distancing mental devices, and probe in return. They ask why, what for, and so what, and withdraw. When the investigator is persistent, they rationalize as they have many times before: "We are studied to no end; it is a part of being the disadvantaged in the society. Your job is to inquire, so inquire" (a school teacher from Moderngani in the summer of 1974). Another Chamar, a local leader, said: "I may talk with you but not inform, and may inform but not really share my mind. I may inform as well as misinform you until I am sure that you are honest in your intentions." The problem thus emphasized is that the investigator usually does not know how to demonstrate the required honesty and sincerity. The clever Chamars readily present the picture the society expects – ignorant, crude, and passive; they thus easily escape the inquiry as well as the investigator.

Over time, the investigator may be watched and repeatedly tested, first of all for his intentions and motivations, and second, for the sincerity in his attempts to understand the Untouchables' position. But their demand may hide a conflict. Although the initial approach of an investigator raises their suspicion, interacting with him eventually becomes a pleasant diversion. But the investigator's presence remains an enigma for the ordinary Chamar; they find it hard to believe that somebody would *earnestly* want to learn about (and from) them. Wanting to understand them and their mind therefore means assisting them in overcoming their own deep-seated doubts about others. The uncontrolled pragmatic ethos – where everything is related to (and is caused by and for) some practical purpose, whether obvious or latent – may be one of the culprits. "Why will somebody want to know what we really think? The longer the inquiry the more sinister could be your motives. Even if I trust you this moment, tell me how can we really be sure about you in the future?" (a shoe-shop owner from Baudhabagh in the summer of 1978). Deepening distrust seems to be part of the contemporary ethos; people promise too soon and forget equally easily. "Words of honor are there but flouting them makes a better practical sense and politics. In these times why would somebody (especially an Indian) like to know the Chamar in depth? Nobody enquires these days simply for the sake of knowledge. It could be another Brahmanical trap" (a relative of a Chamar political leader from Baudhabagh). Such spurts of scorn, irony, cynicism, and distrust continuously put a social distance between the investigator and the Chamars, making their study difficult.

On the other hand, like any fieldwork, there was threshold after threshold (from crude to subtle) of communication to be crossed as familiarity increased. The Lucknow Chamars displayed their own, some quite distinctly. For example, their harsh social experience, including decades of exposure to social and political reformers, had made their repertoire of evasive devices unusually rich, resilient, and finely tuned. They were all too ready to "reveal" what a local politician or a municipal functionary or a social welfare officer wanted to know. The triter the inquiry, the "better" the Chamar's response. In less trodden areas, evasive devices – deflection, postponement, containment, cliché, rhetorical questions, and feigned ignorance – were deftly employed.

In my experience, I found it helpful to understand the reasons behind the Chamars' aloofness. Merely to wear them down by sheer persistence was seldom enough. It was not hard to make them protest, but to have them communicate from up close, from where they and I could comfortably lose our defensive postures, was difficult. Although at first generally eager to share food and drink with me at their doorstep or inside the kitchen (for well-known hierarchical reasons), they were most reluctant to share their minds. Their interpretations, practical actions, and decision-making tactics had to be carefully deciphered, for they were critical for this inquiry in order to learn as they tried, competed, and protested daily in the society.

However, once the Chamars do open up and communicate, they bring home a realization: It is impossible to bypass their cultural argument (see Part I) and understand them as they are at present. This argument may very well be imperfect, based on selected myths and favored interpretations and carrying a response to the "tilted reality" of the Hindu system. It may be fed and shaped constantly by an antagonistic bias, exaggerated distinctions, and sharp rhetoric, but it is most authentic and real to them. Actually, the Lucknow Chamars' everyday social experiences vindicate the worth of such an ideology. It is *their* ideology, fashioned and constantly tested by them.[11]

More recent fieldwork among the same Lucknow Chamars (from July 1979 to March 1980) extended considerably my previous contact of the summers of 1974, 1976, and 1978. My exposure to them deepened. I had more opportunities to hear them express their developing social sense and sensibility, and to observe them live their daily lives with diverse ups and downs. The range of their social strategies became evident for routine as well as critical social situations (see Part II). Their attitude toward me also began to relax, once they were sure that I belonged to a family long resident in Lucknow, and openly hospitable to the Untouchables. Some skeptical Chamars insisted on visiting me at my family residence early in the summer of 1979 to ensure that they knew enough about me. Implicitly, the purpose was twofold: first, to discover some common social acquaintances, however remote, and second, to assure themselves that there would be no discrimination from me or my household members. Once I or my family members suggested some common references and acquaintances, and once they checked out satisfactorily, the Chamars' attitude toward me changed distinctly. If, however, they maintained distance in some ways, it was not for reasons of basic distrust or social strangeness. I had been accepted as a *bhaiyā* (a wide-ranging term of endearment) by older Chamars and as a *bhāī saheb* (brother) by those my age or younger. The relatively distant *bābū jī* was given up uniformly after the initial phase.

In the second and third phases of the fieldwork, the sharing of "everyday joys and sorrows of life" (*jīvan ké sukha aur dukha*) began to occur. It was then that the real fieldwork, and real learning, started for me. It was the time to think with them, explicating their ideas about their symbols and categories. It was also the time when the ordinary Chamar would open up with his successes and failures, including his complaints toward the caste Hindu. Speaking to a caste Hindu, they complained, chided, rebuked, explained, and afterward apologized. Toward the end of the fieldwork, we agreed that our parting was going to be an interruption in, rather than termination of, our contact. It was natural that we would meet again, since my home was in Lucknow and since we had uncovered some common acquaintances. In retrospect, my study of the Lucknow Chamar was, I think, desirable as an ethnographer and necessary as an Indian.

The Untouchable ideology: a rationale

Since this study will devote considerable attention to the cultural structure and significance of the Untouchable's ideology, we should comment briefly on the reasons for this ideology's inclusion in this study, and on the anthropological merit of such a step.

Though its ethnographic merit was never in doubt, my decision to examine in detail the Lucknow Chamar's version of the cultural ideology of the Untouchable posed several difficulties. I propose to use the phrase "cultural ideology" to distinguish the ideology of cultural principles and values from political, economic, and militant ideologies. I want to draw attention especially to the former and its properties, though its interrelationship with other ideologies cannot be denied. Initially, there was the problem of availability of reliable, suitable, and sufficient data, both field and documentary. But once in touch with appropriate sources, I was insufficiently prepared to recognize that the topic, not merely a political rhetoric, could be culturally so complex and finely developed. Once Lucknow Chamar and Untouchable (i.e., other than the Chamar) thinkers, leaders, and reformers had opened up sufficiently and shared systematically their written and oral cultural formulations, the topic became not only approachable but increasingly serious and valuable for an anthropologist.

Much more persistent, however, were the issues of reliability, verification, and validity of what the Chamars said to me or wrote. Their ideology was evidence of serious scholarship to them, but conceding them genuine scholarship, however uneven and rare, was generally a serious partisan issue, I found out, for caste-Hindu scholars. A standard orthodox argument: Since the Untouchables did not (because given the denial of educational opportunities, they could not) have a "tradition" (*paramparā*) of scholarship, they could have neither reliable scholarship nor accredited scholars. Another, somewhat more conceding, position: If they have any scholarship it could be only from the times of Ambedkar, which is too recent to have taken widespread intellectual root, and is already ineffective beyond an initial impact. Yet another contention, politically leftist: The values and schemes of the cultural ideology were still too subservient to Hindu obscurantism and domination.

Lending an ear to such skeptics, my doubts were initially overwhelming, even crippling. Some of my upper-caste informants had recommended a full range of precautions – from dismissing what Untouchables said and asked me to read, to an outright suggestion that I stay away from their fabrications and handle only the "authentic" caste-Hindu version. But an important common characteristic of such advisers was that few had ever cared to hear (much less read seriously) even a single full statement of the Untouchable's or the Lucknow Chamar's side of the story. Rarely did one of them know where to even look for a suitable source. On the other hand, this situation perhaps showed how ineffective the Lucknow Chamar has been in making his cultural side known. But having a genuine ideology and its dissemination and acceptance among the opposed groups are two different issues. We shall claim that the Chamars in fact have a significant cultural ideology, consequential to themselves, and comparable to the ideologies of other deprived groups (e.g., see Rao 1979).

However, the larger and more difficult questions of verification of the Chamar's categories of the ideology remained before me. These problems were essentially of three kinds: first, those that arose from an almost total absence of authentic social history; second, those resulting from the Chamar's scholarly weakness and waywardness in his central argument; and third, those emerging from the Chamar's circular interpretation and dilation of the basic ideas. If the first problem meant that I should severely confine myself to the later decades of this century for a few empirically reliable social footholds, the second one meant a closer inspection of the basic cultural categories (besides the logic and style) of the ideological argument, and the third one, a separation of confusion, exaggeration, and diffusion from the Chamar's core formulations. (For examples of such points, see chaps. 2 and 3.)

The message therefore was clear: If this cultural ideology were to be studied it would have to be chiefly for moral, symbolic, and logical plausibility and significance. Obviously, historical verification (or falsification) could be of high priority for its own sake, but our inquiry, because of its methods, could be held neither incomplete nor dependent on such a step. Rather, it must base itself on the internal cultural veracity of the ideology, tracing its transformations under idealism as well as practical action.

The symbolic structures, in terms of their civilizational priority and fundamental logical coherence, will offer us a basis for testing the cultural genuineness of this ideology (e.g., see chap. 1). When the Chamar's symbolic schemes and ideological postulations run far ahead of the reform achieved socially, the ideology begins to work like a road map (see Geertz 1973: 218). The Lucknow Chamars, especially those who are educated or articulate, find that the ideology offers them a new ground to stand on; it influences and motivates them; and it is now them in an ultimate sense, that is, they are renewed without being uprooted. When a radical Chamar ideologist like Achchutananda (see chap. 6) said that history follows, not precedes, the Untouchable's ideology, he transfigured (*aufgehoben*) myth in fact and value.

Their ideological constructions reflect the larger social dilemma of being the incomplete non-Hindu, the bind of trying to become a non-Hindu by employing cultural principles and products shared by the Hindu, and, in some cases, even the wrenching puzzle of remaining the incomplete Hindu and the incomplete Buddhist. Their new cultural identity is born from such halting and hesitating forces, adding irony to the radical Chamars' claim of being the original Hindus (*ādi*-Hindus) of India. However, the ideological contrast offered by the Lucknow Chamar is unambiguous. He rejects the Hindu's idol worship; gods and goddesses; Vedas and law codes; belief in rebirth; Brahmanic rites, ceremonies, and sacrifices; and the entire *varṇa* and *jāti*-engendered hierarchical relations (for further details, see chap. 3).

As we shall see, the Chamar's ideology, essentially symbolic and moral in character, is found to be at once deeply connected with certain Indic philosophical issues, and to practical and concrete contexts. Its main purpose is to show to the hierarchical person an equalitarian mirror that the Indic civilization offers. If this ideology has yet to yield *uniformly* higher education, income, and social status to the Untouchable, it has neither uniformly failed in the Untouchable's eyes, nor does it preclude doing better in the future.

The intellectual style of most Chamar thinkers has been populist rather than scholarly, but their thoughts – dissuasive as well as persuasive – show a penetration that comes only from a lived mediation between the Indic and Hindu traditions, and between the recognized (*śāstrika*) "intellectual traditions of reasoning and argument" and a popular handling of knowledge (Gombrich 1978: 23). These thinkers are given to overblown contrasts and express themselves through the metonymic and the metaphorical. The esoteric and the exoteric are made to communicate with each other. Parables, legends, stories, political rhetoric, and poetic afflatus are considered helpful devices, allowing them to gather, generate, and spread their knowledge. They carry a *Weltanschauung* that is found deceptively weak by the larger society.

Actually, one could contextually discover faint analogues of, for example, a Hobbesian, a "ghetto Nietzschean" (Feuer's phrase), a Hegelian, a Marxist, a pragmatist, and a libertarian lurking among some regional Untouchable and Chamar thinkers, and we may sometimes allude to them for appropriate analytic reasons. The allusion will be analogical (on the limits of analogy, see Burke 1954: 97), and in relation to Indian thinkers and philosophers. If the Untouchable ideologist must discover an innately shared (i.e., a metonymic) intellectual genealogy with Nagarjuna, Sarhapada, Kabir, Ravidas, and a host of other medieval (low-caste or Untouchable) ascetics, reformers, and thinkers, he must also develop what Burke called a "planned incongruity" (i.e., a metaphoric subversion of the caste ideology) by linking himself to agreeable Jain and Buddhist spiritualists. We will focus on such cultural roots of the Untouchable ideologist, since most of his creativity has been concentrated in this domain (both before and after the Ambedkar phase). Such an approach offers the anthropologist another way to study Indian society, but this time in the company of the Untouchable thinker.[12]

Part I

Untouchable ideology

1. The moral basis

Sociological background

We will initiate a discussion of the Untouchable's ideology in the general background of Weber's handling of Pariah religion and intellectualism (1963: 95–117; 118–37), and move toward the central ascetic–Brāhman axis that embodies the contemporary Untouchable's cultural aspirations, identity, and paradox. Weber's sociological characterization of asceticism (1963: 166–83) will also be directly relevant to our discussion. However, we will be mindful of Weber's empirical limitations and simplified assumptions on India.

Weber finds the Indian Pariahs bereft of an ideology for two major reasons: They lack both the "communal feeling of an urban citizenry" and "emancipation from magic." Even if we do accept these as necessary and sufficient conditions for the possession of a cultural ideology, Indian Untouchables can no longer be considered an apt example. They now have a definite urban citizenry, are more cohesive, and have undergone various religious reforms. In any case it is difficult to concede Weber's point outright: We can find cogent historical instances of Untouchable thinkers and ideologists who have occasionally flourished, yielding cultural creativity and a significant social following. The Indian Untouchable provides such evidence despite an uneven dependence on magical beliefs. Moreover, Weber did acknowledge (1963: 126) that a Pariah group could enjoy certain conditions of intellectual freedom:

> It may be noted that pariah intellectualism . . . derives its intensity from the fact that the groups which are at the lower end of or altogether outside of the social hierarchy stand to a certain extent on the point of Archimedes in relation to social conventions, both in respect to the external order and in respect to common opinions. Since these groups are not bound by the social conventions, they are capable of an original attitude towards the meaning of the cosmos; and since they are not impeded by any material considerations, they are capable of intense ethical and religious emotion.

Though somewhat overstated for the contemporary Chamar, this characterization remains essentially true, especially for the Chamar ascetic.

Asceticism as a sociological phenomenon underscores, among other things, two distinct principles for Weber: "rejection of the world" and "flight from the world," allowing him to propose a whole set of useful distinctions between ascetic and mystic. The "worldly ascetic" remains involved in "rational ethical conducts" as a part of his "vocation," whereas contemplation and inaction characterize the mystic. If the first is the "gods' instrument," the other is "the gods' vessel" (p. 171). If the first is more typical of the Occident, yielding also what Weber noted in various contexts "ascetic Protestantism," the second is identified with the Orient, including Buddhism and Hinduism. Closer to our requirements, he also finally remarks, albeit in passing, that "the distinction between world-rejecting asceticism and world-fleeing contemplation is fluid" (p. 170).

The ascetic–mystic distinction remains unnecessary in Indian civilization in both idea and history: Religious personages are allowed to bridge diverse spiritual goals, "worldly contradictions and compromises," and practical (i.e., economic and political) needs. An ascetic in India, in principle, acquires maximum authenticity – legitimate social power – by maintaining a genuinely world-fleeing stance. The more he cultivates this tendency the more he is able to "pierce through" what Weber (p. 171) calls "insoluble tensions between violence and generosity, between empirical reality [i.e., social inequality in the Indian context] and love [i.e., spiritual equalitarianism]." In comparison to Weber's formulation, therefore, the Indian case places an inviolable cultural primacy on the "mystic" (yogi) and handles most of the ascetic–mystic dichotomy under moral and symbolic transformations. As we shall see, Ravidas, an Untouchable ascetic, illustrates this transformation in a manner meaningful (yet hierarchically paradoxical) to both Untouchable and caste-Hindu ideals.

Such an idealized ascetic is the crucial cultural platform from which the moderate Untouchable now launches his ideology and connects it with the recent radical Buddhist alternative. In doing so, he starts with a historically observed tendency whereby the "non-Brāhman status group of ascetics emerged [in India] by the side of the Brāhmans and competed with them" (Weber 1958: 269). But in order to meet his goals, the Untouchable accentuates the value differences and ideological contrasts between the two, managing practical interests and social conflicts in terms of the Brāhman–non-Brāhman symbols. If Weber, following Marx and Nietzsche, establishes a correspondence between "ideas" and "interests" without overlooking tensions between them (see Weber 1958: 61–5), the Untouchable thinker's major concerns and strategy echo the same approach: "Not ideas, but material and ideal interests directly govern man's conduct. Yet very frequently the 'world images' which have been created by 'ideas' have, like switchmen, determined the tracks along which action has been pushed by the dynamic of interests" (Weber 1958: 63–4; see also chap. 2). Finally, after all, it would be intriguing, but not impossible, to have "plebeian mystagogues" and "civic 'pariah people' " (to use Weberian phrases) articulate such ideas for different practical reasons.

Indian asceticism

Asceticism in ancient (e.g., Kane 1941: vol. 2; Holck 1969; Bhandarkar 1950; Bhagat 1976) and more recent (e.g., Ghurye 1964) India is such a deep, complex, and continuous cultural current that any oversimplified view is easily disputed.[1] Our approaches to Indian asceticism will be highly selective: We will focus on the controlled cultural antagonism between the caste Hindu and the Untouchable, considering broader logical and symbolic characteristics only in the context of the Untouchable's ideological concerns. The non-Brāhman, the low-caste, and the Untouchable ascetics must loom large in this picture, where the Untouchable reformer would like to claim that the non-Brāhman ascetic is also the anti-Brāhman ascetic, and that he alone is the "original" ascetic, the supreme mystic, the true visionary, and the savior, since he alone could be the messiah of social equality, hence also of love and social justice.

As he alone represents the Untouchable's hope for equalitarian idealism, the ascetic has also been a master "switchman" in Indian society. He can power the Untouchable's utopia because ideally he is a moving utopia himself (Dahrendorf 1968). Nonetheless the ascetic remains the Untouchable's ideological linchpin. He continues to represent a forceful moral critique of a caste-ordered hierarchy "and its excesses" and subverts unjustified inequality by launching alternative symbolizations (for example, consider the ladderlike versus the concentric versus the rising spiral models of social hierarchy). Ambedkar, the most recent "savior" of the Untouchables, perhaps a Nietzschean "reflector" of the accumulated Pariah resentment, only widened and strengthened the position of this ascetic as he linked himself to Buddhist asceticism and contrasted the non-Hindu genres of Indian asceticism with those of the caste Hindu.[2]

As a cultural construct the ascetic is the symbolization not only of ideological contrast or controlled difference, but also of sharing. Whereas ordinary Chamars admit this fact ("for it is within us," as one Chamar Ravidasi reformer remarked), the Untouchable reformer does not. For to do so would be to weaken his own distinct argument. Thus, as we will admit all the three relationships (i.e., of contrast, controlled difference, and sharing) during the course of this study, we must focus here on the first relationship, for the ascetic–Brāhman contrast offers the Untouchable reformer a fundamental axis from which to articulate his ideology. (Compare Das 1977, on ascetics for certain caste-bound distinctions.)

It is essentially with the help of this reformist ascetic that the Untouchable determines what he spiritually is; what the moral nature of his deprivation has been (i.e., the identification of moral issues, paradoxes, and sources of resentment); and what the cultural bases of his ultimate moral individuality and identity are, establishing his responsibility toward himself as well as others. These three dimensions of his idealism and ideology will engage us in this and the subsequent three chapters.

Asceticism and the Chamar ideologist

The Chamar ideologist we will consider is articulate; he expresses his concerns under ideal as well as practical conditions: "Our definition, organization, and reading of the 'ascetic tradition' are, as expected, strongly influenced by our ideological aims and purposes, just as the caste Hindu's perspective is by the Brāhman's interests and caste viewpoints." So observed a Baudhabagh Chamar thinker, who also claimed that the cultural principles of asceticism and austerity (*tapas*) must ultimately contest the principle of birth-ordained purity. Another prominent thinker (Jigyasu 1968a) asserted that the Indic (the pre-Vedic, Buddhist, Jain, and the monist) tradition remained ascetic, while the caste Hindu tradition remained Brāhmanic (cf. the evidence offered in Bhagat 1976: 103).

The Untouchable thinker's phrase for this Indic tradition is *saṅta-śramaṇa-siddha-saṃskṛti*, and we will gloss it simply as "ascetic" tradition or culture. The Untouchable thinker emphasizes the pre-Vedic *yatī* over all other varieties of holy beings, and he calls today's ascetic *yogī*, *sādhū*, *saṇta*, *paramahaṃsa*, *śramaṇa*, and *ātmavādina* according to the context of the discussion (Bhagat 1976: 9–13). Unfortunately, the cultural richness of the original categories will have to be encapsulated by "ascetic," a manageable English gloss. Coming from the Greek *askeosis* (meaning "training"), ascetic stands, in spirit, nearer to the Indic conceptions of *yatī* and *yogī*, keeping austerity (*tapas*) as the central cultural value all along (see Bhagat 1976). I prefer "ascetic" to "saint," since the latter is influenced by a host of Christian theological notions (see the *Concise Oxford Dictionary* 1976: 54, 995). The Untouchable ascetic thinkers generally distinguish a culture of the deprived, as we shall find, from that of the upper-caste Hindu's by such devices as making the socially near distant, overlapping ideas separate, ambiguous social relationships antagonistic, and the ancient and the mythical images of the illustrious Untouchables living. In this way they free the genuine content of Indian asceticism from the caste Hindu's distortions, and make it the center of their attention and efforts. (For examples, see Jigyasu 1968a in comparison to *Bhaktamāla*.)

We may note, however, that they start with a cultural background shared with the caste Hindu. For example, as the Indian ascetics represent varied configurations of celibacy, austerity, concentration (meditation), and ecstasy (see Ghurye 1964: 15, and compare Weber 1963: 166–9, and Bhagat 1976: 13–61), they become moral guideposts for the common person's society and its changing moral character. They form a moral locus for raising social issues and for initiating and influencing change within Indian society. Under ideal abstraction, the ascetic is that cultural construct that undertakes to represent critical relations between relations (e.g., between such cultural categories as "soul," "society," and "God," the Moral Absolute), and critical values between values (e.g., as between austerity and its ultimate renunciation [*śūnyavāda* or nirvana]). However, in order to understand the Untouchable thinker's emphasis on asceticism, we must note the ascetic's five cultural positions that are generally recognized within the Indian system.

The first three of these positions are easily shown and are traditionally recognized by the Hindu society as well (see Ghurye 1964). These appear when the ascetic locates himself either within, at the fringe of, or "beyond" (*parê*) the society (cf. these points with Weber's ascetic–mystic distinction). Ascetics living in a dense forest, or in an unknown and inaccessible Himalayan cave, offer examples of the third kind, whereas the wandering ascetics and leaders of sects, monasteries, and innovative spiritual centers illustrate the other two. The secluded ascetic is, however, held to be nearest to the ideal: He is seen by the society as a self-controlled individual who strives toward spiritual oneness with the Absolute. He becomes a model of spiritual monad (*ātman* as *Ātman*), which is amoral (but obviously not immoral), asocial (but not antisocial), and unconditionally equalitarian. He lives the values the larger society idealizes.

Once this ascetic attains this state, the fourth location, a spiritual summum bonum (whether a *siddhi* or self-realization or nirvana) is reached. The ascetic is then regarded as being one with the master spiritual construct (like Ātman or Brāhman or God or Śūnya). He becomes that ascetic (perhaps à la Buddhism and Jainism) who alone can reveal, the Untouchable thinker argues, that root of morality that upholds the length and breadth of the entire Indic civilization. Although the philosophical significance of this formulation for the Hindu may vary (Bhagat 1976), the Untouchable ideologist accords it the most fundamental and invariant meaning.

The fifth location is in fact an extension of the first, where the ascetic is treated as a moral image immanent in all humans. "The yogi and *bhogī* [hedonist] reside within everybody," repeatedly observed both my Chamar and Brāhman informants. The ascetic here represents for the householders (both men and women) the spiritually cherished goals of renunciation, self-control, and austerities. All are expected to inculcate this ascetic image within themselves, strengthening it with old age. We may call it "essential asceticism." It is available to the Untouchable as well as the caste Hindu and normatively consists in a personal, conscious *control* of breath (*prāṇa*), food (*āhāra*), sex (*kāma* and other desires), and possessions (*aiśvarya*). A Brāhman worth his name cannot disown or dismiss this essence if he is a real Brāhman, asserts the Chamar ideologist.[3]

Jigyasu characterized in an interview the place of asceticism. As an ideologist, his concerns were to formulate distinct cultural propositions for the Untouchable; as a local thinker, his observations were comparable, whether implicitly or explictly, to the Hindu schemes.

Ascetics as gurus have always been very important to the Chamar. We have lived in their company in villages and cities for centuries. For the people whom the Hindus had systematically isolated and excluded, the Untouchable or low-caste ascetic was a guide, a doctor, a teacher, a benevolent companion, and a true friend. We, the Chamars, did not have ambivalence toward the ascetic. He was always more on our side than any Brāhman. Even if we did not dislike the Brāhman, he did. A Brāhman ascetic, on comparison, was congenial only out of his benevolence; if he did not care for us, there was nothing that we could do to change his mind, except try to win him by our genuine devotion to a Hindu deity. The common Chamar is still too much in awe of a Brāhman ascetic, though it is unnecessary and out of ignorance. The awakened Chamar should suspect the Brāhman ascetic, especially these days. He could do so only if he put distance between himself and all things Brāhmanical. The Chamars routinely bring their families in close touch with a sympathetic ascetic. Again, unlike the Hindu, they do not know ambivalence toward him. The Hindu householder fears the ascetic's wrath but craves his miraculous blessings. He is caught forever in his own doubts about the nature of the sacred. Actually, this is a trap Brāhmanic thought has produced and maintained. Spared of this, the Untouchable ideally approaches the ascetic with full, unwavering faith. The householder interiorizes the ascetic. The Untouchable has little difficulty in doing so, for both the Untouchable and the ascetic receive little from the society, the first under denial and the second under self-denial. But both the Chamar householder and the Untouchable ascetic impart critical lessons to each other: The Chamar reminds the ascetic of worldly reform and of restoring will within the oppressed; the ascetic reminds the Chamar of his true spiritual heritage and individual worth.

Such an articulation of Indic asceticism raises the sights of the Untouchable thinker toward an alternative, and not merely a surrogate, cultural ideology. He strives to make the ascetic *the* independent variable within the Indian spiritual and social order, for the ascetic reveals to him the roots of all his caste-engendered deprivations. His tactic, through this procedure, is to work up a cultural radicalism powerful enough to help him transform his passive social placement and identity. As we will see, his cultural radicalism, uneven but persistent, has acquired a new and pervasive force in this century.

The ascetic–Brāhman axis

It is thus in this background of cultural inspiration and social transformation that the Untouchable juxtaposes ascetic and Brāhman, the two predominant and intriguing genres of moral power within the Indian system. Both constructs represent sacred power, and both apply to holy personages who have critically shaped Indian society and culture for millennia. The Brāhman is a close representation of Universal Spirit (*Brahman*), and the ascetic an "image of God" (*Bhagwatswarūpa*). One is a sacred fountainhead of divinity by birth; the other is a living example of how to approach, to live with, and to become the regnant Spirit by oneself. But this also introduces dissimilarity: The Brāhman predominantly orders and stays with the collective sacred whereas the ascetic stands for the spiritual and cosmological sacred and its transformations. Yet they are both constructs of the sacred, and they are probably much closer to each other in nature than the derivative construct of the Hindu king is to either of them. The three may carry different functions, significance, and purpose, but they are equally guided by the principle of self-control (*ātmasaṃyama*). Accordingly, I am more inclined to see the three of them as constituting a triad of sacred power, with three flexible but mutually adjusting sides. This adaptable but stressful triangle is perhaps a more complete and responsible (e.g., consider the regnant ascetic, ascetic king, Brāhman king, and ascetic Brāhman) model for the nature of sacred power within the Indic system.[4]

A sociological way to ascertain their status is to observe the ascetic and Brāhman working within the context of a caste-Hindu family and to compare this version with that obtained from the Untouchable. In this context, my field data on the Chamars and the Brāhmans in Lucknow fell into three categories: First, the Brāhman priest usually exerted distinct authority in rites of passage and protective rites (though obviously the reformist and radical Chamars would in fact reduce this role to a minimum). Second, the Brāhman priest and the ascetic were both consulted, but the ascetic (whether a guru or not) exerted greater, if not determinative, influence over the members of the family (e.g., concerning sickness, mental problems, everyday domestic problems, and "bad luck"). Third, the ascetic, not the Brāhman priest, was expected to appear and suffice on some occasions (e.g., for divine miracles, spiritual healing, and blessings). In fact, these spheres of influence and authority vary over time, because they reflect the strains of the larger society. During this century the Brāhman priest (but perhaps *not* the Brāhman as such) has been losing his traditional ground among the Untouchables as well as among the caste-Hindu householders of Lucknow. The ascetic is now slowly nudging out the Brāhman priest, as the calendrical and astrological rites attenuate and disappear in favor of the more general notions of personal devotion and sectarian religiosity.

Culturally, on the other hand, when the Brāhman and the ascetic appear in the same person, he becomes a formidable powerhouse, crisscrossing the entire firmament of Hindu mythology. This ascetic most often propels the mythology with a complex network of curses and blessings. The Brāhman ascetic, however, tends to defy his *jāti* ethic; he discovers that he cannot make asceticism privy to his kind and that he is dangerous to the householder unless he controls himself. Similarly, a non-Brāhman ascetic trying to become a Brāhman (or Brahman-like) conspicuously challenges the hierarchical precedence (see Bhagat 1976 for a variety of appropriate examples from Hindu mythology; compare my treatment of Ravidas in chap. 3). Crossing boundaries, we come to know, is common with the ascetic. They exist for him only to be culturally infracted, moved back and forth, and redrawn with more significance. Such devices perhaps become his mental technique for grappling with the new and the paradoxical.

From a normative perspective, the Brāhman, by and large, continues to occupy a winning (but not an unassailable) position within the institutionalized caste order. But reverse the emphasis from the social to the spiritual, devotional, and inspirational spheres and asceticism gains the upper hand. The ascetics control sectarian religion in India. The explanation for this is ideological and constant: Even the Cosmic Man can undertake creation only through asceticism (examples abound in the *Mahābhārata*; see Bhagat 1976: 204–5); "every aim can be attained by asceticism" (Gonda 1970: 118; see also p. 27). The tension between the two representations of sacred power is not merely situational; it is fundamental to the Indic order. It draws attention to two different sacred principles and their cosmogonic, moral, and social expressions. The ascetic, in principle, represents the unconditionally equalitarian world view, and the Brāhman upholds the conditional, the hierarchical.

Asceticism is an individual-based concept; it is devoted to a spiritual conditioning and lifestyle (i.e., through *tapas*, yoga, and *tyāga*) of the moral "individual" (as correspondingly reflected in "autonomy" of *ātman*) through a morally ordered cosmos. This moral individuation (see Coomaraswamy 1978: 72, 77) pervades and subordinates the competing construct of the hierarchical Brāhman at the level of "Kingship of Kingship." Even at the social level, when the Brāhman takes charge of the moral collective, the principle of asceticism attracts and shapes its constituents.

Asceticism is a fundamental property of the Cosmic Man, the same archetypal (ascetic) *Puruṣa* that awards the Brāhman his intrinsic moral status, and the *varṇa* order its ultimate cultural legitimacy (on *Puruṣa* as archetype, see Khare 1978). Yet when manifested within the Hindu social order the two principles are neither fully compatible nor equal. Actually, they are at best nonexclusively opposed: The Brāhman, despite his best efforts, cannot replace the ascetic, nor the latter, the Brāhman.

It is simultaneously useful to note that a milder form of tension is found between the Brāhman and the ascetic within the caste-Hindu society.[5] As this tension enables the radical Chamar ideologist to claim dissension among caste Hindus, it also reveals erosion in the general position of the Brāhman. Despite entrenched traditions, the Brāhman now has to increasingly depend on economic and political resources that are controlled by nontraditional institutions. He cannot depend simply on his traditional monopoly over the sacred power.

Instead, the antagonistic casteism and minority politics, once played against the full range of local economic and linguistic forces, produce that changing social matrix in terms of which *both* the Brāhman and the Untouchable, though each with distinctly different social resources, must adapt today.

The Untouchable ideologist does not deny this reality when he makes Indic asceticism the eye of his storm. Actually, he discovers in this development stronger moral footholds from which to articulate his ideological argument.[6]

Asceticism: a locus of morality

Jigyasu (1968a: 9–18) makes asceticism the foundation of his ideological argument and thus offers a larger picture of how the Indic ascetic remains the genuine locus of all moral improvement. In the next two chapters we will illustrate how the ascetic plank is actually employed for ideological reformulations. We will conclude this discussion with a few more remarks on the Untouchable thinker's general objectives and conceptual strategies.

The Untouchable thinker's general objective is to launch a genuine moral argument to combat his institutionalized social disabilities and deprivation. Since he must take on the caste morality in its traditional form, he interprets the ascetic morality as being uniquely stronger and deeper within India. Further, the more deeply fissured the *varṇa* platform is between the privileged and deprived groups, the more vulnerable it becomes to the ideological argument. The thinker systematically tries to recognize and build on the *differences* between the Untouchable and the caste Hindu. The Untouchable thinker we have been considering is critically concerned with launching such an ideological argument against the total caste ethic, rendering simplified questions of conflict or consensus shallow and situationally variable. Finally, we must note that to do so also means to stake a claim for the civilizational placement, to reformulate aspects of the Indian *Philosophia Perennis*, and to force the caste ethic to reexamine itself for morally compelling reasons.

Now to the ideologist's recurrent conceptual strategies. Jigyasu (1968a), for example, took a widely shared radical view of the ascetic tradition[7] when he associated it with the religion of "the original Hindu" (i.e., the pre-Aryan autochthons representing a precaste social order), treating the "Arya-Vedic" religion as *external* as Islam and Christianity. Indic asceticism was, he argued, "absolutely unique and *internal* to the land of Bharat [India]." It was the eternal (*ādi*) moral order, "one that antedated the Hindu caste order and would also survive it," Jigyasu remarked. Emphasizing "the quest for Truth," Jigyasu, the reformer, invoked the ascetic for his unyielding austerity, introversion, equanimity, fearlessness, and undaunted pursuit of social justice. He discussed how the ascetic rendered the Untouchable socially restrained but persistent in his goal. "The Untouchable must take hardships in stride, but no injustice lying down. In society what he is really after is not only this occupation or that, this isolated social privilege or that, but the true and complete equality that the Indic ascetic represents for all members of society'' (Jigyasu in interview).

The ascetic thus receives a subtler and more complex treatment from the Untouchable thinker. In this way the ascetic becomes a multipurpose figure – an operator, mediator, catalyst, ''bricolage,'' ''All-Worker,'' a role model for (and of) society, and more. He comes to symbolize a ''repossession'' of the Untouchable's own personal and social capacities. At the same time, however, this ascetic rejects the excesses of the caste collective and of the secular individual. Most of all, this ascetic encourages the Untouchable to be a true *owner* of himself. Accordingly, the contemporary Untouchable also wants to ensure that he is the inalienable, sole proprietor of his person and potentialities in all–sacred and secular–social spheres. His ideology may be after all a calculated cultural move toward this aim.

Overview

The Untouchable ideologist's first step is to articulate those principles and strategies that could give him a genuine cultural placement. The process of ideology formation starts when the Untouchable's own cultural rethinking becomes linked to and is empowered by a more widely shared sense of moral injustice. The Untouchable's ideology must be supported by a culturally genuine value order if it is to be convincing. To formulate an authentic and effective set of cultural principles and values, the Untouchable must not rest with the asceticism offered by the Brāhmanic perspective; his roots must come from deeper Indic sources. However, the Brāhman offers the Untouchable an axis of ideological and social contrast that he cannot ignore. The Untouchable ideologist's ideas begin to transform themselves into ''weapons of protest'' only when such a polarizing cultural view is taken. Only then do these ideas generate social action and enter the corridors of political power and strategy. Protesters turn into social activists, yielding a popular, ethnographically evident social awareness.

2. Formulations, categories, and procedures

An ideologist's formulations

The previous profile of asceticism has been modified during this century, first by the general impetus of Indian social reform and nationalist freedom movement, and second, as the neo-Buddhist alternative emerged with Ambedkar. Although Untouchable thinkers generally tend to shift by context in their allegiance to such influences, the position of the radical ascetic – the one who would come nearest to the Untouchable's aims – remains stable within the ideology. Though aspects of the Untouchable ideology are found in several writings (see citations in n. 8, this chapter), Jigyasu (1968a) offers perhaps the most detailed written statement from Lucknow. Jigyasu includes a crucial caveat: If somebody still discovers the influence of the "language of the Hindus, it is only a garb according to the practical needs of the time and circumstance but without any compromise in ideas" (1968a: 27–8). The following discussion is based mostly on Jigyasu's writings. It will be followed by an evaluation. (All major terms and concepts employed by Jigyasu will be offered within quotation marks, often with no further attribution.)

The ideologist's ascetic is identified by a set of distinct cultural characteristics. Most significant among them is his spiritual pursuit of the "Buddhist" doctrine of *śūnyavāda* (voidness of vacuity; for a range of meanings, see Apte 1965: 925). But as he pursues this doctrine, he is never free from the nondualists' Absolute (i.e., the Hindu monist's *nirguṇa* Brahman). This ideologist argues, as expected, that his ascetic "ancestors," whether Gorakhnath or Kabir or Ravidas or Nanak or Dadu or Namdeva, pursued these spiritual quests "under varied names and forms." This ascetic, as a model, mediates the "Nonexistent," practices yoga (particularly *hathayoga*), and remains free from all blemishes in his personal and social character (*viśuddha caritra*). He is always "inner-directed" to face toward the Absolute, displays an uncompromising social ethic of "human equality" (*mānava samatā*), and is averse to the birth-ordained orders of *varṇa* and *jāti*. He subscribes to *no* books of revelation and pursues only the goal of total deliverance (i.e., either of *moksha* or nirvana). He is freed from such delusions as believing in multiple gods or a personal supreme God (*Īśvara*) and "soul" (i.e., the Brāhman's version of *jīva* as distinct from the absolute *Ātman*), in "ritual exhibitionism" (*ādambara*), and in "violence-ridden Vedic sacrifices, rites, and ceremonies" (*karmakāṇḍa*). His ideal of social equality is grounded in "unbounded spiritual love" toward all, where everybody is congenerous, hence always inherently equal. His teaching is to love all "as a mother loves her lone son." It should be so whether one is "in front or not, above or below, far or near, small or big, or seen or unseen" (Jigyasu 1968a: 26–7).

In contrast are held the Hindu sectarian ascetics (*sampradāika santa*) who worship multiple personal gods and obey the Hindu scriptures (Vedas, Upanishads, Gita, and Brahmasutras) in hopes of ascending to their god's abode (e.g., Goloka for Krishna worshipers and Sāketa for those of Rama), their summum bonum, "seeking thus the enjoyment and luxury in this world as well as the next" (Jigyasu 1968a: 29–30). These ascetics, the profile continues, spend all of their time and effort on the fourfold devotion (through name, form, sports, and abode – *nāma-rūpa-līlā-dhāma*) to their deities, and follow the maxim of master (swami) and servant (*dāsa*) relationships in this life, and always. Actually, Jigyasu (p. 30) takes this to be a representation of "slave mentality" in these ascetics. "What caste Hindus try to do to other social groups, their gods and goddesses do to them."

These two genres of asceticism symbolize for him two distinct cultural orders: The first encapsulates the original and continuous order (called *śramaṇa saṁskṛti*; note the use of the Buddhist term, *śramaṇa*, for ascetic); the second is produced by the Vedic and Brāhmanical traditions (called *Brāhman saṃskṛti*). These two genres are not only contrary, but contradictory in the eyes of this Untouchable ideologist, particularly since he seeks to discover *independent* cultural foundations. Even if this case cannot be argued to a scholar's satisfaction, it remains a cultural ideal regardless of its form (assertion, axiom, premise, etc.). Ideal ascetic is *causa efficiens* for the cultural order. Ascetics, in this view, not gods, bring about and maintain all that is intrinsically significant in this world and the other. They bring justice and humanism to life, and such humanism emanates from the innate axioms of the cosmic (and thus also the social) equality. These features, and those we will consider later, are firmly grounded in the Indic ascetic – the "perfect" cultural foundation for the ideologist.

Jigyasu's ideal model moves toward the medieval ascetics through a discussion of Kabir and Ravidas. Jigyasu's descriptions and procedures are reasonably representative of a majority of renascent Untouchable writers and thinkers of this century (up to the middle seventies) and accommodate influences of local Buddhists and Ambedkar. He also offers us a spiritual theory of social reform, worthy of a detailed analysis in two overlapping ways: first for the scheme of cultural assumptions, contents, and distinctions he articulates and emphasizes; second, and more important, for the cultural structure and style of argument employed (or not employed) for the espoused ideological position.[1]

The first task of such an ideologist is to identify and trace the spiritual line of descent of the ascetics. He initiates this task by reconstructing the popular knowledge available on renowned ascetics, whether mythical or historical. He considers these ascetics according to his ideological position and maintains a cultural ambiguity whenever it is useful to the argument. Moving from the oldest to the most recent ascetics, he usually works with a highly selective list of renowned personages. The obscure ones are identified only when appropriate. Jigyasu, accordingly, opens his discussion by rapidly enumerating the twenty-eight Buddhas, the twenty-four Jain *tīrthāṇkaras*, the twenty-eight *bhāṛs* of the "archetypal Śiva" (as available in *Śaivāgama* literature; see Farquhar 1967: 384),[2] and the eight-four *siddhas* of Buddhist (*vajrāyaṇī*) order. Compositely, this is the "original" cultural foundation of the ascetic order on which the medieval ascetics are found to stand. Sarahpāda (a Buddhist *siddha*, according to Jigyasu), who is placed approximately twelve hundred years ago (Jigyasu's dating), illustrates a nodal figure within this scheme.

Jigyasu conjectures Sarahpāda to be of the Lohar caste, an ironsmith, because his family used to make iron arrowheads. However, "caste was inconsequential because he was a very knowledgeable ascetic," who had written a book of didactic verses that had, as Jigyasu observed, a surprising correspondence to Kabir's (*sākhīs*). "It looks as if both were conveying the same message; both [were] guided by the same [spiritual] aim" (p. 24). Sarahpāda thus offers to Jigyasu a link between the ancient and the early medieval saints. Accepted unquestioned, this single personage is seen as necessary and sufficient proof to show the "low-caste" base for a chain of subsequent Buddhist monks (*śramaṇa*), who, in turn, lined up with the medieval Hindu saints. A "genealogy" of successive gurus that is offered by Jigyāsu in support of this derivation is as follows[3]:

Sarahpāda siddha → Savarpāda → Luhīpāda → Darikāpāda → Ghantāpāda → Jallundharpāda → /break/ → Matsyendranāth → Gorakhnāth → Ganināth Triyambakanāth Pant (of Nepal) → Nivṛttināth → Jñānadéva.

This genealogy represents a bank of ascetic images and ideas that Jigyasu employs to demonstrate that the Buddhist ascetics not only stand at the back of the medieval (low-caste) nondualist ascetic, but also continue to shape their descendants up to the present. To do so for the Untouchable thinker is, however, to compose a new cultural strategy, for then the centrum – the Hindu-based ascetic tradition – is open to a displacement by the "pre-Vedic" and Buddhist cluster of values.

This tactic is radical even if the cultural history employed to accomplish it is not. In addition, we are told that the Hindu construct of the ascetic can only be a conglomeration of varied (yogic, tantric, devotional, sectarian, and even

Buddhist and Jain) cultural categories and relations during the medieval times. Viewed in this light, the aforementioned genealogy is a cultural statement with a hidden ideological agenda directed ultimately toward a creation and maintenance of the equalitarian spiritual monad.[4]

Aspects of what was highly condensed and terse in Jigyasu's writing became a topic of discussion in a later interview in which he had emphasized the necessity of realizing the distinct cultural relevance of ascetic tradition to the Untouchable ideology.

> The more I think and read about the [Indic] ascetic tradition the more I become convinced of the power and influence the ascetic wields over the ordinary member of the society. He symbolizes hope in despair and reminds us of social justice based on spiritual equality [*ātamika samānatā*]. But the ascetic tradition in India is so varied and complex that only a specific type could be most useful to the Untouchable's ideological goals. Those still dominated by the Brāhmanic rites and viewpoints are counterproductive; those unwilling to see a fundamental difference between the social justice of the caste system and of the spiritual order [*ātmavādi dharma*] are of limited value. The ascetics of the spiritual order clearly see how the Hindu weaves such a cobweb along castes, gods, Brāhmanic rites, karma, *māyā* [illusion], and *saṃasāra* [rebirth] that he begins to view social exclusion and injustice as a form of dharma.
>
> The ascetic tradition of true persuasion, however, needs to be carefully rescued from the surrounding Brāhmanic forms and images. The mentality of this ascetic, who is most often not a Brāhman, is best tested when he fights for the social justice denied to others. He does not believe in Hindu gods and their discriminatory rites, though he does not hesitate to practice yoga and other time-honored techniques for controlling his own mind and body. He is a true wanderer and a true renouncer. He is free himself and makes others free. He is a mystic and a well-wisher of everybody. He has more affinities with the Buddhist *śramaṇa* and the Jain *munī* than the Hindu *mahanta* [sectarian head]. The devotional movement suits him but only as a technique for the Quest of the Absolute. The Brāhmanic rites and ceremonies do not attract him for they are only a corruption of the spiritual core.

Jigyasu (1968a: 34–5) intensifies this definitional quest with the medieval ascetics – Kabir, Ravidas, Dadu, and Namdeva – who offer him a varying mixture of Vedantic monism, Buddhist nirvana, Sufist mysticism, and Vishnuite *kṛpā* (the unpredictable "divine grace"). These goals are variously approached by a melange of yogic, tantric, and devotional techniques, and sealed and sailed under a glittering polynomy of Hindu incarnations (as Jigyasu notes, via "Rāma, Kṛiṣhṇa, Murārī, Banwārī, Keśava, Mādhava, etc.").

Cultural procedures

How does an Untouchable thinker handle this puzzling but familiar Hinduist heterogeneity to get back to his main argument? The procedure proposed by Jigyasu, I think, is both ingenious and interesting. Much more so, because it remains at the same time, subtle but ambiguous, and intriguing but incomplete.

Jigyasu resorts to a Buddhist procedure. It is "*sarvastivādī mahāyānī* [great vehicle for 'all-things exist'], whose purpose is to change, without changing the exterior, the meaning [and content] of all things from the inside to turn them toward [Buddhist] nirvana" (Jigyasu 1968a: 35). This is his answer to a question that was raised in the previous chapter: How does one refute and bypass the Hindu cultural tradition when its numerous forms still seem to shackle the Untouchable ideas? Change the internally crucial assumptions and premises of the Hindu forms and their placement will also change in structure and significance. Historically, however, we can only wonder if both the Buddhist and the Hindu have repeatedly tried this procedure on each other with varying success. So also could significant social changes have come about over time.

Let us examine this procedure more closely, especially as it is used to formulate ideological goals. Two clear targets of change stand before the contemporary Indian Untouchable: removal of discriminatory social conditions (and institutions) and replacement of unjust moral values and attitudes. The ideologist (e.g., see also Sagar 1973) finds the Indic ascetic capable of directing himself to changing the second to effect a real change in the first. He continues to assert this claim though Indian asceticism has been unable to eradicate the caste order. His counterargument is first that it is a simplification and second that the ascetic never really applied himself to the task. He has been, so far, either too accommodating (e.g., Gandhi) or too nonpolitical (i.e., more of a mystic, recalling Weber's ascetic–mystic distinction) to let him test his full strength against the caste order. His major work has been, instead, to offer challenging moral positions, emitting undercurrents and countercurrents to chastise, limit, and correct the caste ethic.

Thus, as the general social "exterior" seems to remain the same, the moral basis for social inequality has actually been under periodic examination, argues the Untouchable ideologist, from the inside. The contemporary Hindu also may have been constantly influenced by the spiritual equalitarianism (*ātamika samānatā*) of the ascetic. This influence, argued Jigyasu in interviews, "made him agreeable to the democratic politics of this century." The ideologist argues therefore that if this indigenous development has prepared the way for democracy the next step will naturally be to strengthen a just social order.

In our analysis, although Jigyasu's recourse to the "realist" (*sarvastivādī mahāyānī*) procedure is contextually apt, it remains ironic and ambiguous. It is apt because it does direct us toward a fundamental Indic procedure for handling (and comprehending) change *within and between* competing moral orders and material conditions. However, it is ironic because the ideologist settles for much less than what is required. The ideologist should actually want his version of Indian asceticism to be capable of conveying (1) an *unequivocal* spiritual assumption for absolute equalitarianism from pre-

Buddhist times to the present; (2) an *uncompromising* confrontation of (and eventual victory over) the unjust and unfair social dimensions of the caste order (modifying the principles of karma and rebirth, which even Buddhism could not resist); and (3) an *ubiquitous* practical pressure to translate the spiritual and moral notions of equality into everyday social life. But Jigyasu's procedure must remain culturally ambivalent because he cannot rectify all the double allegiances of the ascetic as a cultural construct. The Indian monist ascetic, whether conceived in the Buddhist or the medieval Hindu ascetic tradition, cannot *simultaneously* serve two logically contradictory premises of equality and inequality. If it does, there will be an unavoidable equivocation, and thus a weakening of the ideological argument.

The spiritualist ascetic

The ideologist draws our attention, however, to certain subtler aspects of his argument. He stands between what is logically evident and what the civilizational proclivities mean to him. He regards ambiguity and irony as important properties of the Indian cultural forces. The ideological ascetic of the Untouchable must, accordingly, also remain ambiguous for culturally significant reasons. He must transcend and transform, back and forth, the hierarchical and equalitarian orders, and not merely confront one with the other. This way the ascetic would be strategically evasive, but never culturally irrelevant and ineffective.[5]

Jigyasu argued that, given the Indic ascetic tradition, the cultural formulations could not be otherwise and that the careful reader should not become confused on this point. He observed that this asceticism, despite several ambiguous transformations over the centuries (from *sthaviravāda* to *sarvastivāda* to *vajrāyanī* to hathayoga to Śaiva Nāthpantha to Vishnuite medieval cults and sects), had remained unchanged at its core, especially by pursuing the spiritual goal of "vacuity" or deliverance or nirvana (1968a: 40; for a brief summary of sectarian denominations, see Farquhar 1920 [Indian reprint 1967]: 103–18). As a protagonist of the spiritualist position, Jigyasu claimed that Indic ascetic values can transform the Hindu ascetic model from its foundations *without* undergoing any radical change themselves. In support of this position he offered a string of spiritual transformations characteristic of the Buddhist ascetic's renunciation and spiritualism. He noted the moderation, compassion, and detachment they exhibited. He also devoted a full chapter, early in his argument, to the assured continuity of the Buddhist ascetic tradition *within* Indian asceticism, though he conceded that the Buddhist ascetic had always been under pressure to disseminate his message according to the demands of the age (*yugānurūpa pracāra*).

This assertion faced unfavorable evidence and resistance from Indian historical, philosophical, and cultural studies. Jigyasu did not hesitate, however, to dismiss such unfavorable evidence as insignificant because he had to keep the ascetic model as ideal and pristine as he could. Most of the model's fundamental assumptions had to remain intact, uncorrupted by influence from the historical and cultural particulars of the Hindus. Jigyasu adopted a clearly partisan cultural focus, releasing new arguments, moods, preferences, and motivations with the hope that they would yield new seeds for social reform. A spiritualist–reformist construct of the ascetic was the core of such a focus, and an odd-looking but vigorous marriage of this ascetic with the twentieth-century pragmatic forces was its climax (see Part II).

Jigyasu's argument reached a climax as he articulated the ultimate spiritual principles of the Indic ascetic. In doing so, he often leaned heavily on the Buddhist version to evolve an Ambedkar-style alternative for the Indian Untouchable. Yet he could not be exclusively identified with it, for he also showed a discerning sense in recognizing the weaknesses of this alternative and the strengths of the medieval low-caste ascetic's yogic spiritualism. For example, he first placed a clear distance between the karma–rebirth complex and the Buddhist spiritual idealism (because he thought the first corrupted the second), and he then reformulated the Buddhist version to suit medieval spiritualism. We may compare Jigyasu's handling of Buddhism with acute observations on the subject by Bouglé (1971: 68–79). Buddhism, all in all, could not be egalitarian "exactly because it remained Hindu" (Bouglé 1971: 20), and it remained Hindu because "they worked at replacing the roof, [but] they never gave thought to changing the foundation," that is, the Hindu theories of karma and rebirth (p. 73).[6]

Jigyasu decried dependence on reincarnation and advised filling the gap with genuine yogic experiences of the medieval nondualist ascetic. He thought that the karma theory yielded "enslavement," whereas the nondualist spiritual doctrines awarded self-respect, equalitarian individuality, and freedom. He offered a brief but recondite discussion of the cultural order the medieval spiritualist ascetic represented (see his biography of Ravidas for the chain represented by such technical yogic categories as *deśa, bheṣa, surata-śabda-yoga, gatī,* and *sahaja samādhī*).

In contrast, Jigyasu found the Hindu and Brahmanic arguments tortuous and "mazelike" (1968a: 18). They produced "endless contradictions" (i.e., simultaneous *mandana* and *khandana*), revealing Hindu temperament that made a chain of blessings and curses the spine of all Hindu scriptures. The Hindus always attempted to corrupt and denigrate the "true" (i.e., *ātmavādina*) ascetic, in Jigyasu's view (1968a: 44–5), but could not succeed. In the medieval period, the same ascetic had to face resistance from another direction – the Islamic mullah. However, the ascetic not only survived the external challenge but also helped society to do the same, keeping the conscience alive and focused on social justice, reform, and equality. It is this spiritual spark, asserted Jigyasu, that kindled the nineteenth-century Hindu cultural renaissance and reform. For this spark alone offered such "a knowledge of humanism [*mānavatāvādī jñāna*] in which there was neither the extrovert Brāhmanic web of illusion [*Brāhmaṇī māyājāla*] nor the noose of Islamic law – *shariyat*" (1968a: 45).

This articulation of ideology, in essence, exemplifies what today's young and educated Chamar radicals call "a traditional position for reform." Its cultural foundation is pre-Ambedkar in size and shape, though its facade is Ambedkar-influenced in exterior design and appearance. This argument is not offered simply as a platform for counter-Hindu politics, we are reminded by a reformer like Achchutananda (see Jigyasu 1968b), but as something deeper – a resurrection of spiritual transcendentalism "which powers *all* forms of Indic social orders, including the caste system."[7]

An evaluation

We have presented the ideological formulation mostly as the Chamar thinker writes and talks about it. He asserts that his ideology should not be treated as a social relic. It is a part of his life and a basis for social hope. If we were to dismiss it out of hand, we would lose, I think, not only a significant and fragile segment of Indian social ideas, but also miss the major sociological clues such an ideology carries for a better explication of the Indian social system. Most of the urban Untouchables retain aspects of this ideology as a heritage of post-Ambedkar India. The Lucknow Chamars use it as a pliable cultural background for understanding their self-identity and social goals. They try to narrow the gaps between the passive (and resigned) Chamars and those labeled as awakened, progressive, radical, and militant radical. This is so even if we find the ideology to be flawed, with incomplete assumptions, logical ambiguities, unsupported propositions, shifting meanings of critical categories, and exaggerated claims.[8]

Yet the ideology exhibits the critical dimensions of the necessary category separation, systematization, and contrast. Achchutananda (see also chap. 6) and Ambedkar are useful to the Chamar in this exercise. Their resentment-filled theses help him show how the *varṇa-jāti* order is unjust, avaricious, economically exploitative, and socially impositional. He finds that Hindu values, gods, and personages relentlessly exclude and dominate the weak. Equally important, Chamar ideology specifies not only what the Untouchables are not (and what they do not get from the Hindus), but also what they have positively been, and now are (e.g., see Sagar 1965). They are, the ideology asserts, the autochthons of India, at once freedom loving, reasonable, modest, adaptable, and accommodating.

A general point is worth mentioning here. As the ideology is extended to contemporary India, and as the Untouchable controverts the ideal relations of the caste order by juxtaposing the ascetic and the Brāhman at the most fundamental level, the ideologist's goal is not to stop at mere polemics, protests, and imitation of a few secular political styles. Rather, his goal is to summon all such efforts, first to realize a spiritual indivisibility and then to start negotiating a civil personhood. Ravidas and Kabir appear in this task as stewards of the World Spirit (to adapt a Hegelian phrase). Past saviors of the Untouchable receive new social interpretations as they are now increasingly paraded up and down the country for political purposes. The Untouchable reformer argues that spiritual equalitarianism is now being resuscitated because it is sustained and echoed by the democratic ethos.

If we were to characterize the foregoing ideological formulations of the socially deprived in terms of a general sociological theory (e.g., see Feuer 1975: 1–16), they mostly uphold "the Mosaic revolutionary myth." In this myth, as with the Indian Untouchable's picture of his own social journey, the oppressed (with their leaders) appear to be upheld by ascetic heroes and reformers and their intervention. Promises and demands of freedom are made, but the tenacious tyrannical "ruler" (here it is the Brāhmanic order) does not give up. Thus appear initial defeats and repeated struggles followed by brief periods of renaissance and reform. Repeatedly reformed and new time-suited doctrines are launched until a final spiritual and moral effort for the total removal of the oppression and the oppressor is successful.

This ideological profile continues to express the goal of gaining "freedom from dependence on the will of others." The ideology encourages the Untouchable to renegotiate his relations of social interest under a compensating equalitarian ethic and to assert proprietorship of his "own person and capacities."[9] This brings us to the next step in our exercise, that is, a cultural evaluation of his ideological categories and structures.

3. Evaluating an ideal ascetic

The previous chapter sets the stage for discussing that medieval ascetic who would represent the Untouchable's ideological issues. We will pursue these issues à la Ravidas, especially as Jigyasu (1968a) interpreted his life and mission, and also because the Ravidas story helps illustrate the direction of our discussion. Ravidas exemplifies the medieval ascetic central to the formation of the Untouchable's ideology and at the same time illustrates some critical properties of a Hindu ascetic. The selection of Ravidas is culturally significant because he remains enigmatic, immediate, fresh, and most representative of the dilemmas and aspirations of contemporary Untouchables in northern, central, and western India. His occupation, domestic life, and subtle estrangement from Hinduism all reflect the Untouchable's dilemmas better (than perhaps Kabir), and he is more easily worshipped and politicized than stern Kabir. Though a householder-saint, Ravidas is now a temple-enshrined "deity," a saint who is spiritual yet humane. Since he is unashamed to be an Untouchable, he immediately illuminates the depth of the Brāhman–Untouchable divide. He is uniquely unexpected, regal, miraculous, moderate, and exceptional for the Untouchable, and also equivocal, anomalous, and yet clearly an outstanding devotee (*paramabhakta*) of "Rāma" (i.e., Rāma as Vishnu's incarnation) for the caste Hindu.

Jigyasu (1968a) wants to protect Ravidas from the "equivocating" upper-caste Hindu because he considers Ravidas to be non-Hindu (but not openly anti-Hindu).[1] In spirit he is, for Jigyasu, so clearly antihierarchical and anti-Brāhmanical that he should be recognized for what he really is: an ascetic in the true tradition of the "*ādi*-Hindu asceticism." However, as we consider this position further, it will be instructive to bring up the two distinctly different versions the Untouchable and the Hindu award to Ravidas. The cardinal Hindu principles that the Untouchable ideologist variously refutes or rejects in his version are a faith in and/or the pursuit of (1) God as deified *Īśvara*; (2) rebirth; (3) Vedas and subsequent Hindu law codes; (4) Brāhman-presided personal and collective sacrifices, rites, and ceremonies; and (5) the "divine" *varṇa* and *jāti* (caste) order of social status and authority (see also chaps. 5 and 6).

There are few readily available and reliable textual sources on the Hindu and Untouchable treatment of Ravidas.[2] I select the reputable Nabhadas's *Bhaktamāla* (1969) for the Brāhmanic model[3]; Jigyasu (1968a) for the Untouchable's version; Briggs (1920) for an external perspective on this ascetic; and a popular, several-volume collection of devotional songs – *Bhajan Saṃgraha* (1972) – for cross-checking Ravidas's poems as shared among the ordinary Hindu. We will focus on the first two sources, giving special attention to the dominant patterns and meanings of value relationships.

Ravidas also gets the following entry, as an introduction, from Bhandarkar (1965: 74):

> Ravidas, a pupil of Ramananda, was a founder of a sect the followers of which are to be found in the caste of Camars, or leatherworkers. Nabhaji in his Bhaktamāla tells many legends about him. Under the name of Rohidas he is known and revered even in the Maratha country, and Mahipati, the Maratha writer on saints, devotes a chapter to him.

On the other hand, Farquhar (1967: 328) mentions 1470 A.D. as the only approximate date in connection with the sect of Ravidas, giving very little historical or sectarian detail for this specific group. (Kabir received his primary attention.) Culturally, therefore, these sources are not very helpful, leaving little choice but to turn to the legendary and the mythical data on Ravidas.

Ravidas: the *Bhaktamāla* version

Nabhadas's text on Ravidas, as recorded in the current version (1969: 470–1) of *Bhaktamāla*, may be sequentially broken up in the following major cultural strands and their dominant values:

	Cultural strand	*Significance*
1.	Having pure (*vimal*) speech (*vāṇī*)	Enlightened ("pure") word and speech
2.	Being deft in resolving ("knots of") doubt	truly knowledgeable (*jñānin*)
3.	Uttering words in agreement with Vedic and scriptural injunctions	Concordance with the Hindu tradition
4.	Carrying deep, clear discrimination (*nīra-ksīra-vivéka; or sārāsāra*) emulated by the highest ascetic (*paramahaṃsa*)	Highest reflection, wisdom, and understanding
5.	Ascending into heaven with his body by the grace of God	A celestial soul (*divyātmā*)
6.	Announcing his *real* caste (*jāti*) even as occupying the throne (*rājasiṅghāsana*; i.e., as a sect leader)	Truthful, fearless, and successful

7. Receiving veneration from those of high *varṇa* (e.g., Brāhman) and *āśrama* (e.g., *Saṃnyāsin*), who had to leave their pride behind	Highest veneration despite low birth

This list of cultural strands is sufficiently symbolic and representative for our purposes. It calls attention to a number of dilemmatic cultural relations that reflect the paradox Ravidas represents to the regular hierarchical order: He was socially low yet spiritually exalted. Thus, we cannot mistake the central structural issue, namely, how does a "lowest" (*atiśūdra*) person acquire a position venerated by, and sought among, the Brāhmans? Is asceticism alone, even of the best kind, sufficient to achieve this position? The *Bhaktamāla* version offers us an interesting if indirect and equivocal cultural answer, one that cannot satisfy the Untouchable ideologist. However, examined in terms of the Hindu cultural system, the *Bhatkamāla* version tries to offer a culturally consistent approach to the preceding two questions. Let us first see how this is done within the Hindu scheme, reserving for later a consideration of the Untouchable version.

In the foregoing list, items 3, 5, and 7 are worthy of special attention. If item 3 establishes the cultural backdrop against which to view Ravidas's life, mission, and work, item 5 accords him a mode of "death" reserved for gods, demigods, and only liberated souls. Simultaneously, under the ascetic model, this very feature stamps Ravidas as superior as an ascetic can become: He is the ultimate Indian representation of the triumph of spirit over physical body, and of the perfect, "unbounded" ascetic (i.e., the Individual of the Indic scheme, see chap. 4) over social order. Items 1, 2, and 4 elaborate what is good for those following Ravidas; from the ascetic's point of view they reflect the properties of a celestial soul. Such a soul, the cultural assumption goes, effortlessly exudes deep wisdom, miracles, enlightened words, good deeds, and exemplary lifestyle. Power and influence (see item 6) come automatically to such a person. We will see why (and how) Ravidas's lowest social status could become problematic, especially when items 6 and 7, probably the most crucial of all, clearly juxtapose the relations of the two important Hindu orders (i.e., *varṇa* and *āśrama*) to the placement of the ascetic. Does the ascetic overpower the social order? Can he really do so?

An answer to the last question is found in the legends surrounding Ravidas. These are recorded by the commentators of *Bhaktamāla* alongside the main entry by Nabhadas. Briggs (1920: 207–11) also mentions most of the same legends, but without catching the Hindu's dilemmatic approach to basic conflicts between the ascetic and the social order. In contrast, Jigyasu's (1968a) account of Ravidas carefully eschews Hindu apologetics as if it were either a totally irrelevant or superfluous "concoction." Several Chamar informants, drawn from each of the three Lucknow settlements, remarked repeatedly, "They are the Hindu devices to treat Ravidas Saheb [note this long-standing honorific the northern Untouchables consistently apply to their leaders and heroes] in terms of the caste Hindu excuses." "He was not a Chamar ascetic but an ascetic Chamar," offered a reformer from Baudhabagh.

It is significant in the *Bhaktamāla* narrative that Ravidas was, in his previous birth, found to be a *celibate Brāhman* disciple of Ramananda, a reputed saint-reformer of the Vishnuite sect. The disciple Ravidas had once committed an unpardonable lapse in his worshipping duties. He had collected alms in the form of uncooked food (*sīdhā* or *cutkī*) from a Bania shopkeeper who kept business relations (*kārbāra*) with a Chamar, and offered it to the deity worshipped by Ramananda. The deity, Ramananda "saw" in his meditation, did not "eat" the food that day, leading to Ramananda's inquiry about the source of the food (for the impure source necessarily lends impurity both to the food and to its eater). When told the truth, he cursed Ravidas to be born a Chamar in his next life.

The culturological commentary hidden behind the legend is now clear: Ravidas was not "really" a Chamar. He was instead a "Brāhman soul" (note how here the "soul" is considered indivisible), given to asceticism and Vishnuite devotion continued from his previous life. He was neither truly a Chamar nor a Chamar ascetic but a Brāhman ascetic in the temporary "garb" (for a body is considered to be clothing for the soul) of a Chamar. If any doubts remain, the second legend, immediately following the first one, tries to resolve them.

Upon rebirth in a Chamar house, Ravidas, as an infant, would not suckle his mother's breast, thinking "if for one lapse I am born a Chamar, what would become of me if I take her milk?" Ramananda, however, was instructed by his deity to be compassionate to his cursed disciple, now born a Chamar. Ramananda consequently initiated the infant, and the latter accepted his mother's milk.

What is sociologically important is the procedure of status reinstatement (again through food) in Ravidas's case. For what appears here occurs rather repeatedly in such cases in Hindu culture and society. We may observe that the two principles of karma and reincarnation weave a basic pattern from which these (or other such) "corrective legends" derive their explanatory meanings. Notice how, for example, a bad karma in his previous life condemned him to the Chamar's status and how the cumulations of the good karmas in the low birth (beginning with rejection of the Chamar mother's milk) started his journey upward *in the same life*. If the principle of rebirth were subtracted, Ravidas would be a truly inexplicable cultural anomaly for the Hindu system. How else can one really explain a Chamar (a lowest-ranking person) becoming an ascetic of the highest order? The legend of his rebirth (from high to low) must, however, steal Ravidas's thunder as a Chamar saint; it compromises the ascetic's spiritual principle, making him fall within the established order of caste precedence. In the preceding list, items 3, 5, 6, and 7 describe

Ravidas's position as a Hinduized ascetic: Here he obeys the Vedas and other scriptures, shows signs of a vestigial sacred thread on his body, is venerated by the Brāhmans and the *saṃnyāsins*, and bodily ascends to heaven. What initially seemed highly contradictory is now rendered ideologically tame and culturally understandable. It thus becomes apposite to Hindu cultural ontology.

Several other aspects are hidden in this legend, but we shall emphasize one aspect a little more: True to the Brāhman's form, Ramananda's deity refuses to eat food obtained from a Bania shopkeeper who does business with Chamars. This indirect defilement of food is so strong that it meets refusal from the same deity who, later on, after the fulfillment of the curse, sends Ramananda to initiate the Untouchable infant (an abnormal case, of course) with a mantra most sacred to all the Rama-worshipping Vishnuites. And Ramananda, with no qualms, works as an "instrument" of divine mercy (and boons) for a Chamar infant. (Note the Hindu ethic of spiritual and undeniable equalization.)

Untouchable thinkers (Jigyasu 1968a; and 1965, summarizing Bodhananda) characterize this response, whereby the deity on one occasion upholds the rigorous Brāhmanic injunctions for food purity, and on another reverses itself by reaching out to the lowest to lift him up "like a Brāhman," as emotional and contradictory. ("Brāhmans' deities are as volatile as are the Brahmans," was the comment of one Chamar informant.) However, what is contradiction for the Untouchable is a subtle, ultimate arm of "justice" (*dharma-saṁgata nyāya*) for the established Hindu moral order. A Durkheimian sociologist, in yet another view of the same property, may discover qualities of hierarchical interdependence and holism between those high and low. Alternative (but all singly incomplete) cultural interpretations are perhaps at the heart of such a story.

The *Bhaktamāla* version of the Ravidas story contains several more legends, classifiable in distinct ascetic themes. For example, Ravidas's detachment from the world forms the core of one legend in which he, rejected by his family, lived in poverty in a small hut with his wife and followed his traditional occupation – shoe-making. Allured by God to accept riches for himself, he remained undaunted until he was sure to employ it in His service (i.e., on temples and devotees). But such a use brought him repeated confrontations with Brāhmans – the second theme of these legends. They would grow jealous of his devotion, fame, and riches and would either complain to a regional raja, refuse meals from his kitchen, or repeatedly and publicly test his asceticism and devotion to God. However, without exception, it was of course Ravidas who would win. How is this moral consequence to be justified?

Again, it is significant that the *Bhaktamāla* commentator attributes responsibility for this anomaly to the equivocating deity, who would, for example, *test* Ravidas by offering him a philosopher's stone, force him to handle conspicuous riches and social gatherings, and then would turn the Brāhmans against him. Social resistance and opposition, we are told by implication, are not without divine purpose. What looked like the Brāhman's ignorance is in fact a divine design.

A crisis for the caste ethic, for example, was reached when at the invitation of a queen (named Jhali), Ravidas went to Chittaur (Rajasthan) and received her food offerings where the Brāhmans, present for a sacred occasion, were also eating. However, seeing Ravidas, they refused to accept even the fried (*pakkā*; impurity resisting) food and asked for only uncooked provisions so that they could separately cook and eat. But the legend holds that when they sat down with their plates, they found Ravidas sitting "between every two Brāhmans." "This opened the eyes of these Brāhmans . . . and several of them became his disciples" (*Bhaktamāla* 1969: 479). However, this could not properly be the climax, since "for the reassurance of everybody," Ravidas also related the story of his previous life and, "peeling off his skin," showed his vestigial "golden sacred thread" to all!

In this narrative, Ravidas is thus again selectively but variously (see items 3, 5, 6, and 7) incorporated into the Hindu fold. This process of successive cultural neutralization and incorporation, a process widely recognized as a characteristic of Hinduism (though perhaps not unique to it), must aim to contain, deflect, and disperse oppositions to the established priority of Hindu values. Jigyasu (1968a: 88ff.) calls this process *Brāhmaṇīkaraṇa* ("Brāhmanization") and, as expected, he wants to see Ravidas freed from the applicability as well as results of this process, for it is, in his view, extraneous to the "real identity and significance of Ravidas." (Compare this handling of higher caste values to Srinivas 1966, for Sanskritization.) Jigyasu would be suspicious of any explanation fabricated from *prasthānatrayī* (i.e., Upanishads, Gita, and Brahmasutra). These were to him storehouses of contradicting personages and equivocating divinity.

Before we consider the Untouchable's version of Ravidas's story, let us note how the Untouchable thinker interprets the principles of karma and rebirth. These dominant Hindu principles may illustrate what the Untouchable reformer calls the "heads-I-win-and-tails-you-lose" (*chit bhī apnī aur pat bhī apnī*) reasoning. For if somebody is born low in this life but was high before, these devices offer a means, usually with the help of a network of curses and blessings in myths and legends, to prove, whenever necessary, "that he is really not as low as he appears to be." Additionally, if somebody is born high, the same devices may offer equally effective means to prove that his previous low birth need not matter. For example, if an Untouchable is born a Brāhman in his present life, this is of course sufficient to make him a Brāhman. But if a Brāhman is born an Untouchable (and if there are circumstances as compelling as in Ravidas's case), birth alone will still be *insufficient* to wipe out the vestigial highness of the previous birth. In this way the supremacy of the top-down view of the hierarchical order must remain incontrovertible and completely dominant. Further, as Jigyasu remarked, somehow the "souls" of upper-caste members are considered "in-dividual," but divisible and scattered of those low.

Ravidas: the Untouchable's version

Confining ourselves to the ideological level, we shall once again examine significant symbolic features the Untouchable ideologist awards to Ravidas. A caveat is necessary at this point. Since this ascetic is variously worshipped by the Ravidasi Chamars in northern India, and there are internal sectarian or localized interpretations, we do not intend to evaluate this empirical heterogeneity. Jigyasu (1968a), Briggs (1920), and my Chamar informants from the three Lucknow localities, which include Ravidasis, will remain my main guides, lending uniformity to what has been and will be discussed.

One quick yet reasonably accurate way to characterize the Untouchable's Ravidas is to confute and reject those crucial items from the *Bhaktamāla* list that we have already pointed out. For example, Ravidas did not obey the Hindu Vedic and scriptural constraints (item 3); he did not literally ascend to heaven with his mortal body but achieved the highly desired goal of nirvana, as provided in Buddhism (item 5); he revealed his real spiritual identity as a Chamar without any camouflage or pretext (item 6); and he encountered resistance and opposition from the Brāhmans (and the caste Hindu) – householders and ascetics – throughout his life and overcame them like a true Chamar (item 7). On the remaining properties (items 1, 2, and 4, which award Ravidas exceptional intellectual penetration and powerful speech), the Untouchable version would agree, because these are the signs of any true ascetic, and the exclusive property of neither the Brāhmans nor the Brāhman asectics.

As would be logical to expect, Jigyasu's (1968a) profile of Ravidas significantly agrees with this reformulation. Actually, his first full chapter on Ravidas (chap. 6 of the book) is entitled "Were Sant Ravidasji's Words in Agreement with Veda-Śāstra?" and starts with the same quote from *Bhaktamāla* discussed earlier. However, his translation differs in some important respects (especially item 5) from that of the *Bhaktamāla's* commentator. He finds Ravidas unhesitatingly announcing his Chamar social status (p. 46). Jigyasu's several succeeding chapter headings are equally revealing: "Was Sant Ravidasji an Idolator?" (chap. 7); "Sant Ravidas on False Beliefs and his Contemporaries" (chap. 8), which is given to establishing a greater reliability and veracity of ascetic experiences (*anubhava*) over the Vedas; "Four Sectarian Saints of Brāhmanic Culture" (chap. 9), which compares Hindu sectarian asceticism to that of the *ādi*-Hindu (illustrating it with four low-caste medieval saints in the succeeding chapter); "Four *Panthīya* Saints of Ascetic Culture" (chap. 10); "Opponents Burned the Sayings of Ravidasji" (chap. 11); "Ravidasji and the 'Abode' of his Contemporary Saints" (chap. 12), which discusses yogic, philosophical, and sectarian distinctions within the ascetic culture; "'Rama' of Ravidasji" (chaps. 13–16), which dispute the common notion that Ravidas worshipped the incarnation of Rama rather than the formless, attribute-free God through yogic practices; "Fish, Ant, and Bird" (chap. 17), which analyzes three successively superior paths of the yogi-ascetic (and shows Ravidas to be of the last – highest – kind); Jigyasu concludes with a discussion of Ravidas's death, anniversaries, and memorials (chaps. 18–19), and "Ravidasji's [didactic] Sayings and Aphorisms" (chap. 20).

The foregoing is a thematic summary of the second of two volumes on Ravidas, which evaluates and carries forward to its ideological climax the biographical description of the first volume. The first volume is dedicated to establishing that Ravidas was *not* a disciple of Ramananda (also 1968a: 102); the second widens the base of its argument by presenting it in terms of the aforementioned chapters. The first theme of the second volume establishes a philosophical, mythical, historical, and sectarian dichotomy between the ascetic (*śramaṇa saṃskṛti*) and Brahmanic cultures. The second theme demonstrates that Ravidas belonged in word and deed to the first, not the second, culture and that the differences between the two cultures "prove" to us that the ascetic culture has "moral superiority" because it emphasizes spiritual equality in yoga as well as social life. The third theme presents "the most complete" assembly of Ravidas's sayings (ten *Sākhīs* and 102 *śabdas*), with an epilogue.[4]

The Chamar ideologist converges on Ravidas either to discuss or controvert the following: idolatry, the order of the four sectarian (*Panthī*) saints, the disappearance of Ravidas's work, and his spiritual and yogic pursuit. Each of these features, we will see, either represents an important point of ideological difference with the Hindus or points toward a way of life that ascetic ideology envisages.

Idolatry, the hallmark of Hinduism, comes under particularly sharp attack by the Untouchable ideologist. Such a repudiation allows him to reject what the Hindus deny the Untouchable (e.g., temple entry) and to substitute Hindu devotionalism with the Buddhist doctrine of "voidness" (*śūnyavāda*). In contrast, Hindu legends repeatedly depict Ravidas as one who showed his miraculous powers of devotion by being a devout idolator. Tested by the Brāhmans for his idol worship, he is known to have publicly "summoned the deity into his lap for accepting his food over that of the Brāhman." Jigyasu offers Ravidas's own sayings to refute this attribution. (We may note, however, that these sayings would be persuasive if Jigyasu were at the same time sure about what is genuinely Ravidas's work and what is not.)

Jigyasu (p. 55), in one place at least, notes that Ravidas may have kept up "the idol worship more to secure a right [denied] than as a believer." But he finally rejects this "halfway formulation" as yet another Brāhmanic invention and propaganda, and he offers in support of his own position *two* poems by Ravidas, appended with an ideological interpretation. One of these two, I have discovered, is also freely included in popular Hindi anthologies and demonstrates Ravidas's devotion to "Rāma" (*Bhajansaṃgraha* 1972: 107–8). Finally, it is quite revealing that Jigyasu (pp. 7, 149–50), although reviewing the varied modes of celebrating the Ravidas anniversaries and memorials, approves rather than condemns the idol of Ravidas himself in ornate and larger temples. He commends Ravidas's worship and "Ravidas Kathā" (i.e., recital of the Ravidas story), offering it in place of the popular *Satyanārāyaṇa Kathā* (i.e., the story of the Hindu god Satyanārāyaṇa), which only a Brāhman priest can recite.

This mode of treating and discussing idolatry in Indic civilization has been endemic, and there seems to be little new that Jigyasu has been able to offer us in this context. It is probably the weakest segment of his argument. He yields most easily where he should have resisted most staunchly. However, this lapse, though important, is not sufficient to destroy the credibility of his ideological argument, especially since he confines Ravidas's deification to the less reflective, making the Ravidas temples a symbol of protest religion and politics. He refuses to admit that Ravidas represents any ultimate cultural principle other than absolute, unqualified spiritualism. This axis also remains at the core of his criticism of the Hindu Sectarian philosophers like Śaṃkara ("the one who crafted a new Brāhmanic garb for the Buddhist ascetic values"; Jigyasu 1968a: 71), Rāmānuja, Madhavāchārya, and Vallabhāchārya. He finds them torturing the selected ingredients of autochthonous asceticism to sustain the Brāhmanic culture.

This Hindu exercise could not succeed in diluting the principles of the ascetic culture, argues Jigyasu; instead, the latter became more widespread. The four "true ascetics"[5] from the medieval period (Kabir, Ravidas, Dadu, and Nanak), observed Jigyasu, "demolished the philosophical fort of the Brāhman's culture by denouncing unequivocally the distinctions of caste, sect, sex, and special privileges, and by downgrading sacrificial rituals, temples, and bibliolatry." Ravidas was on this difficult mission, according to Jigyasu, in the company of these three "roughly contemporary" ascetics. He notes that three of the four came from low castes (Kabir, a Julaha; Ravidas, a Chamar; and Dadu, a Dhunia), substantiating the point that the notable ascetics of this period were most often drawn from the low or lowest caste groups (e.g., Namadeva was a Chipi; Nabhadas, a Doma; Bulla Saheb, a Kurmi; Parmesthia, a Darzi; Sena, a Nai; Dhana, a Jat; see Jigyasu 1968a: 50–1, 78, for more examples) and that they were highly influential reformers of the Indian society. He finds Kabir influencing and converting Ramananda to his liberal view, controverting the usual information that Kabir was a disciple of Ramananda. Historically (whatever little is known), this position is untenable (Westcott 1953). But then we are not considering history alone, but rather an interpretation of the historical that must shape a whole range of notions from socially shared cultural innovations to intended meanings to mythic formulations.

Overview

In summary, a basic outline of the ideologist's argument is now clear. As he reflects on the dilemma of being the deprived and the lowest, he finds that his traditional cultural as well as social options must remain narrow, limited, and ambiguous. If the task has been to propose a radical cultural alternative, the result, although structurally neither illogical nor symbolically inconsequential, is mixed. The tactic is logical in seeking the alternative from a quarter most promising – asceticism. Asceticism's unquestioned cultural depth and pervasion are the ideologist's best hope. Accordingly, he begins to piece together his version of asceticism and its immediate and remote implications. He also tries to cut through obstructions by emphasizing the spiritual (i.e., the symbolic and abstract) ideas and relations of the sacred. It is a movement basically opposite to the Brāhman's, allowing the ideologist to try to limit and devalue the socially established Hindu icons, rituals, and institutions. The higher the stakes set by the concrete caste-Hindu relations, the more strongly felt is the ideologist's need to enunciate a contrasting spiritual scheme. From the outside, spiritualization may look like an escape, and perhaps the only one available, but from within, it is culturally the most direct, genuine, and powerful procedure to opt for. It is also the one that the caste Hindu can never dismiss or reject without damage to himself.

The foregoing evaluative argument progresses first by examining an ideological plank that stresses a *sharing* with, rather than exclusion from, mainstream Hindu values (e.g., of yoga, austerities, karma, and dharma); second, by recomposing the principal ideological categories and relations from within; and third, by trying to put Hindu ideology on the defensive.[6] The post-Gandhi caste Hindu in India, for example, has increasingly shown a mixture of resistance and guilt, though this has to appear in response to a far more varied social condition than the preceding ideological formulations alone can point toward. Yet this slow change in conscience of the caste Hindu is now indeed a part of the new social reality. It shows, most of all, to the Untouchable thinker a way to launch his own evaluative schemes by creating a relevant cultural platform for himself and his people.

The function of this ideology could either remain cathartic or mediating, or become antagonistic; the foregoing ideological exercise also means engaging in comparative social judgment, that is, evolving one's *own* cultural standards and measures, and evaluating others against them. It is a procedure that violates an absolute of the hierarchical caste ethic and promises potentially significant cognitive and practical consequences. To judge this way also means to claim freedom to plan, to respond, and to learn from social experience; it is also to make such a judgment serve one's own ultimate, as well as proximate, hopes for a changed identity and existence. The Untouchable thus announces his conscious entry into decision-making processes and his participation in the domains of comparative social responsibility (especially as between the Untouchable and the caste Hindu). It also means refuting the total-dependence model.[7]

Although we may not want to read too much at once into the comparative evaluation of Ravidas, it does encode, as we will see, such a transition in a germinant form, and Ravidas is found to play a heroic part in it. He is a medieval hero who, after Merleau-Ponty (1964: 183, and his quotations of Hegel), would stand, in the Untouchable's view, among "'the individuals of world history.'" This hero has "a presentiment of the future" and strikes "'against the outer world as against a shell and cracks it because such a shell is unsuited to such a kernel.'"

4. Moral individuation: A climax

The cultural basis and significance of this entire ideological exercise lie in the fundamental conceptual work that the master Indian construct – the ascetic – must represent. Most important, the ideology claims that this ascetic has worked to provide an indissoluble and unchanging moral "essence" for the Indian person. In doing so, the ideology follows, rather than invents, some well-recognized cardinal principles of Hindu or Indic philosophy and cultural principles. The ways in which it selects aspects for reformulation and attaches to them a distinctly different meaning and priority are its own contributions, however. It may illustrate a sociologically expected hypothesis: If the body, person, and self are the most central constructs in terms of which the deepest moral (hence social) deprivation is formulated, these will also be the most critical domains to be reformulated by the ideology. Untouchable reformers and thinkers, whether ascetics or householders, demonstrate this pursuit mostly by positioning themselves *within* the Indian civilization.

To achieve this goal, the Untouchable ideologist may quickly raise or lower the levels of cultural abstraction over that wide field of signification offered by classical concepts and principles. He approximates spiritual and philosophical presuppositions on one occasion, and lowers sectarian and practical filters on another. He also makes full use of cultural ambiguities, the "open endedness" that the classical culture as a whole has inherently reflected. We may discover the nature and scope of the Indian Untouchable's exercise once we superimpose on each other all such varying profiles and evaluate them in the context of the Untouchable's long passive history and tempestuous present.

In philosophical and spiritual terms, the ideologist must do so because he finds the classical Indian ascetic closely involved in the construction, representation, and consolidation of a moral individual "who is fully autonomous, having a self-contained identity and function" (Jigyasu in interview). This individuation is held to be spiritually indissoluble and always immanent in all creatures. This line of enunciation, where a creature, whether a human person or not, is defined by this spiritual individuation, is "patently indigenous" (see Potter 1980, and Larson 1980, for some *advaita* and *Sāṅkhya* principles and constructions, which, for the neo-Buddhist Untouchable, culminate in vacuity). Death normally means a continuation of this individuality in a different form. The same individuality translates into humans as consciousness (*caitanyatā*), "fixed intention" (*niśćaya*), and "inalienable worth" (*tathya*). However, as the Indic tradition gives great emphasis to knowing this reality, we are told that this reality is hidden behind the illusion (*māyā*) and ignorance (*ajñāna*) that pervades the "seen" (*dṛṣṭa*) world. This last point is important: Spiritual individuation is socially latent rather than manifest, and special efforts are required to reveal it.

Such characterizations are the backbone of the Untouchable's ideology. But as we take these up here in the context of a sociological discussion, and with the knowledge that they are seldom so directly considered, the question must arise whether such cultural formulations are sociologically analyzable. I argue that Indian sociology and social anthropology must acknowledge these formulations. They are best treated as powerful symbolic constructions of the civilization, which get reflected into, and respond to, firm sociocultural categories and contexts. Spiritual individuality is reflected by the Indic notions of personhood, personal duty, and personal and familial circumstances (*vyaktitva*, *karatavya*, and *paristhiti*). It thus translates into that moral individuation that each human being is awarded within the society; it also accounts for one's own actions within the society. Those normally good (i.e., persons, *jīva*, and *ātman*) become distinguished from those normally bad, though both record their presence within the society and both remain responsible for all their karma, past and present.

Thus translated, *ātman*, an esoteric and asociological formulation, becomes linked to exoteric, social formulations, whether living within the caste or outside. As long as such social translations are available, the abstract, esoteric formulations remain open to a sociological analysis. They become people's collective representations and social apperceptions. The Untouchable (with the Hindu) often makes his *ātman*, the spiritual individuation, a locus of all the moral causes and consequences within the world and beyond. Accordingly, he argues that any genuine moral and social revolution for justice must touch the *ātman* of the Hindu.

This Indic individuation (and individual), however, need not be an apology for Western development, nor need it await historical replacement by the Western construct to become truly sociological. Though the full evidence still awaits systematic scrutiny, the data at our disposal support the view that the orders of Indic individuation have their own systematic character, with social processes translating these orders into the everyday social life of the learned, the commoner, and the illiterate. Sometimes highly discursive, sometimes spiritual and mystical, and sometimes endlessly popularized, the construction of the moral individual is highly pervasive. Ideally and popularly, it (as *ātman*) is noncontingent; it is never a symbol *of* something, but rather always its genesis, offering an archetypal and uniform basis for self-identity. Under this scheme, the Indic person and society, whether caste bound or not, must represent this moral unit in order to authenticate themselves in a manner that is culturally genuine, full, and complete.

Indigenous construction of individuality

Since there is no place here to consider most of the foregoing general characterizations except as related to our discussion of the Untouchable ideology and its cultural consequences, we must return to certain specific concepts of moral individuation. We will ascertain how, for the Untouchable, the representation of individuality comes variously from "soul" (*ātman, jīva, jīvātman*) on the one hand and "person" (*vyakti*), "body" (*deha* or *śarīra*), and "birth" (*yoni*) on the other. When one's fieldwork seeks to explore different modes of moral individuation in everyday expression and usage (e.g., as in the contexts of birth, death, ascetic's discourses, and scriptural exegeses), and when interviews and observations cover wide groups of Untouchables and caste Hindus (the learned as well as the ignorant and the illiterate), some clearly *shared* "givens" emerge. If, however, such formulations must also mix up or "deform" or "innovate" certain Indian philosophical categories, they should be treated as a part of the popular cultural ethos. A cluster of the critical formulations, translated and quoted from the field data, is as follows:

1. We have in mortal life a body as well as a "soul" [*ātman*].
2. A body [*śarīra*] results from a particular *yoni* ["womb," representing the entrapment of a *jīva* by his karma into a particular *jāti*].
3. A person [*vyakti*] has a body and may thus also belong to a *jāti* [caste] but that person's soul does not.
4. A person can be without a caste but neither without a soul nor a body.
5. A person's body and caste are his exterior [*ūparī*] and temporary [*naśvāna*] sheaths [*cāddar*], while the soul is the imperishable one, which neither dies nor can be higher or lower, but always equally present in every live being.
6. You, I, and everybody are a "part" [*aṁśa*] of the same *Parmātman* [i.e., Ātman, the Universal Soul], hence all are intrinsically related and equal.
7. We are born as human beings and live in the society to realize this spiritual knowledge [*ātmajñāna*].
8. We as "original Hindus" want to live in its constant realization, within as well as among ourselves.
9. This ultimately remains the quest as well as the essence of our entire existence, whether we eat, sleep, and raise a family or go to work in fields, shoe shops, offices, factories, etc.

These formulations interweave a popular version of how the body, person, social existence, and cosmological truths reflect a spiritual principle and its translations. These cultural propositions offer a general cultural scheme against which the authenticity of different individuating Indic representations, caste-bound or not, is measured. The educated and the learned articulate these propositions in a philosophic manner, whereas ordinary people treat them crudely within everyday life. When the Lucknow Chamars are, for example, juxtaposed to the Kanya-Kubja Brāhmans (e.g., Khare 1970, 1976), both are found to carry refined as well as crude versions of these formulations within their own groups. The two versions also overlap in a limited way, but when the Chamar reformer and ideologist enter this picture, clearly position-specific contrasts are introduced and argued.

The sociological validity of the preceding propositions resides in their widely shared cultural representations. The illiterate Lucknow Chamar, for example, may initially plead ignorance in the affair, but opens up when reassured that he will be listened to:

> I am a soul [*jīu*] within a body [*dehī*]. When I leave [die], this body will be dead. My soul does not die; it cannot be destroyed; it is born again. My guru says that if I realize who I am, I shall become truly free. I believe him but I really do not know exactly what he means. I would like to know but my mind wanders in the worldly affairs – caring for my children, my wife, and my home.

This response of a footpath cobbler outside Baudhabagh is suggestive of the ordinary version. However, even this simple version remains faithful to the foregoing critical cluster; it also remains appropriate for the Untouchable reformer's needs. One's own guru, an itinerant ascetic, a reformer, an educated neighbor, a devout shopkeeper, and a passing mendicant routinely initiate and contribute to such formulations. Religious gatherings and performances enhance their effect. Familial events and older relatives – men and women – also bring home the value of moral individuation in various ways.

When such different versions of the "cultural givens" are read together they show how the nine propositions are articulated. These versions raise or lower the representation of ideal constructs on the one hand, and alter their distance or nearness from the social (i.e., often the "worldly," the *saṃsārika*) and the personal (*vyaktigata*), on the other. In conception, these formulations are of course a mixture of different philosophical, reformist, and sectarian influences. For example, the ordinary Chamar, though taking a detached view, may downgrade the body *essentially* the same way as does a caste Hindu, but will still treat the caste dominance as simply unjust. Similarly, though anticaste, he may be sympathetic to the Hindu-style devotional ethic and ceremonies. The ideological version abstracts and reduces individuation to an absolutist spiritual principle and makes the "ego" (*ahaṃkāra*) dissolve into Universal Spirit; the popular version brings it nearer to the societal domain by locating it within the person who faces the moral issues of everyday life.

The Untouchable ideologist specifically construes some of the cultural givens (e.g., see items 5, 6, 8, and 9) his way. He finds the person contingent and dissoluble, staying with the soul, the only primordial basis for all genuine representations of the moral (read cosmologically harmonious) individuation. As Jigyasu commented in 1974 in an interview: "There may be castes, and persons within castes, but there are neither persons without soul nor any conception like 'caste souls' [*jātātmana*]. But the Brāhmans have fashioned thousands of castes out of the people who are spiritually equal. I therefore find castes social ephemera. They will be so sooner or later even for the Hindus, but surely if Hindus will be true to their own spiritual heritage."

Jigyasu also offered (in the same interview) five cardinal properties he considered critical to the content of the Indic individual.[1] He had repeatedly heard them brought together by several ascetic reformers, including Achchutananda, Bodhananda, and Anantananda. The five innate properties (*svābhāvika guṇa*) of the soul (*ātman*) residing within every person were permanence (*nityatā*), consciousness (*caitanyatā*), indivisibility (*akhaṇḍatā*), free will (*svātantrya*), and unconditional completeness (*purṇataḥ*). Jigyasu initially justified them, one by one, against classical monist philosophy, followed by a Buddhist approach to annihilate the self to reach nirvana. His dependence on the absolute nondualism was greater, however. For our purposes, let us see how the Chamars employ these properties to conceptualize moral individuation and accountability – the constructs of strategic ideological significance.

It is an authentic, time-honored procedure within the civilization to extract moral individuality from the classical properties of *ātman* (so that "soul" comes to symbolize moral individuation), and to represent such individuality best and most by the Indic ascetic. Jigyasu and his cohorts were therefore neither inventing nor imagining anything artificial. They were, however, engaged in forging a more direct and total (i.e., noncontingent) connection between the spiritual and the social domains than the caste Hindu and his institutions normally permit. The caste order is obviously a contingent morality to the Untouchable ideologist, and a noncontingent one for the caste Hindu. The Untouchable thinker will not gain anything if he submerges the moral individuality of the person within the caste collective.

The ideologist's task is to retrieve this moral individuality to the extent allowed by the spiritualism of the civilization. He would also like to put this gain to diverse social uses. A Chamar ideologist like Jigyasu or Achchutananda did so (a) to secure a culturally "irrefutable" ideological position; (b) to bind together varied internal platforms for social reform, ranging from mild to radical, around an unconditionally equalitarian position; (c) to make, at the same time, a political statement in the context of growing twentieth-century developments in democratic representation; and (d) to legitimize their egalitarian protests for rapid social development and economic welfare in postindependent India. Accordingly, a construction of the Indic individual has to be a multisided social climax.

Chamar ideologists attribute a special value and sociological interpretation to each of the five innate moral properties of the individual. The first property, permanence or irreducible presence, is meant to convey that caste, however entrenched and pervasive, cannot reduce the primacy and power of the "soul" in human life. This presence is considered to be deeply moral and symbolic, hence socially regnant. Persons, whether alone or in a group, represent this reality throughout their lives. The second, consciousness, refers to the innately endowed, complete, and unconditionally equal mental faculties of cognition, discernment, and experience. Though the degree of "consciousness" may be a matter of training and cultivation, the Brāhman cannot claim to represent a different root archetype (i.e., the Cosmic Being) than the Untouchable. The third, indivisibility, is made patently representative of the noncaste morality, where "each and every soul is considered a complete and equal replication of the Prajapati [Cosmic Being], with no necessity of the *varṇa* divisions between head, hand, belly, and feet of the Creator" (Jigyasu in interview).

The fourth, free will, and fifth, unconditional completeness, follow up the consequences of the first three, where the caste-ordaining karma is subordinated to enlightened spiritual independence of the individual (*ātman*). The expression of free will is directed toward the upholding of dharma. A literal translation of this dharma: It is for the common good of all, affirming the cosmic moral order.

> True dharma is against all forms of social injustice. While the ascetic best represents all the five properties, they also reside in all of us, but need to be cultivated patiently. They are the basis of our true identity. In our view self-regulation [*ātmasaṃyama*] is superior to the caste-hierarchical regulation. The first one is internal [*andarūnī*, Jigyasu's Urdu word] and eternal [*nitya*], while the caste regulation is external [*vāhya*], hence subject to the fluctuations and fortunes of history [*itihāsa ké utār caḍhāva par ādhārita*]. The caste order must therefore remain prepared to disappear just as it appeared – as a necessity of special historical circumstances. [Jigyasu in interview]

In his writings (1968a, 1973a, 1973b) Jigyasu pursued his demonstration of Indic individuation through a discussion of "genuine" ascetics (i.e., only those who were nondualists – *nirguṇa brahmavādī*). For example, in one source, to support his point he listed forty-eight ideal qualities of these ascetics (1968a: 28–9).[2] Though found to be quite standardized in Hindu devotional and sectarian literature, Jigyasu reinterprets them to produce an ideal construct of the ascetic and also to give content to the moral notion of individuality. However, Jigyasu pursued this aim rather cryptically, making my task difficult.[3] I thus cannot approach it without some degree of my own exegesis and interpretation. To do so I will depend primarily on my interviews with Jigyasu, supplementing his remarks with the observations of several more Untouchable reformers (see Part A of the Bibliography).

Jigyasu's list of forty-eight properties (*guṇa*) of the ideal ascetic could be roughly divided into three groups: those for personal (i.e., spiritual) code of conduct, those for the society at large, and a third set for the management of both self and society. Entries within all three groups demonstrate how these properties remain strongly undergirded by a consciously cultivated self-control (*saṃyama*) directed to achieve the highest spiritual goal, whether it is nirvana or self-realization (*ātmasākṣātakāra*). The ascetic must pursue his goal with unwavering will, controlling his sensoria and desires.

Accordingly, he develops his social contacts only for the unrestricted universal good (*loka kalyāṇa* or *sarvahita*). How does the ascetic do so within the Indic order? It is by following comprehensive rules of social conduct (i.e., *yama, niyama, saṃyama, svādhyāya, abhyāsa, satsaṅga*, etc.) for training one's mind as well as behavior. His sensoria, perceptions, needs, inferences, and desires must also be equally trained to uphold these rules of conduct. For example, an ascetic distinguishes himself as he practices an unconditional equality (*samatābhāva*) toward different members of the society; absence of enmity; love toward all; freedom from coveting honor (*mānavihīna*); absence of social intrigue (*ṣaḍayantra*), harsh speech (*puruṣa vacana*), greed, desire, anger, and attachment (*kāma-krodha-lobha-moha-rahita*); and abundance of forgiveness (*kṣamā*). His pursuit of these behavioral qualities yields him a social and spiritual individuation; it lets him control, simplify, and minimize the influence of the social over him. Conversely, it raises his individuality socially, morally, and spiritually.

Simultaneously, to complete what he practices toward society, he must also subject his mind and body to a corresponding code of personal conduct. For example, he should always be courageous, honest, cautious, and truthful in his approach to *himself*. As a "conqueror of his senses" (*jitendriya*), he is a yogi; he is free from egoism (*ahaṃkārarahita*), enlightened (*bodharūpa*), and desireless (*ikṣārahita*). He must neither divert his attention from nor dilute his commitment to self-realization (*ātmasākṣātakāra*). He remains calm, composed, content, and disciplined in seclusion as well as before society. Further, his freedom from desire, greed, anger, and attachment; his pursuit of equanimity, truth, and honesty; and his moderation in speech, diet, and indulgence (*mitabhāṣī, mitāhārī, mitabhogī*) all work *both* ways – for controlling self as well as influencing society.

These properties also offer more clues about the ascetic's irreducible presence, consciousness, and indivisibility, the three primary qualities of moral individuation we have considered before. An ideal ascetic, for example, projects his irreducible presence within society by being an incorruptibly moral person who has taken complete command of his thoughts, intentions, and actions. This brings him charisma, which in turn exerts reforming social influence. He reflects an *unconditional* composure because he attributes an inherent "equality" (a poor gloss for the word *samatābhāva* employed in writing and speech) to all. Changing social contexts and conditions (*paristhiti*) cannot be expected to compromise him. (Such a formulation makes a basic sociological point recognized by Weber; e.g., see Weber 1958: 269–70.)

An old ascetic (seventy years of age), who was passing through Baudhabagh in the summer of 1974, remarked:

The qualities of an ideal ascetic [*saccā yatī*] are endless. The presence of a genuine ascetic is immediately known and the influence is tested in terms of his spiritual force. He is precious to this world because he is himself beyond it. He reduces all social differences and distinctions to the substratum of spiritual equality [*samatābhāva*]. His detachment helps him in this pursuit. Once this state is achieved, the society bows before him because he becomes the ideal of its members. Such ascetics are rare to find but they do appear in this world and lead ideal lives.

In comparison, an educated Chamar householder, a follower of this ascetic, interpreted this quality under social practice.

I consider a true ascetic like an anchor for a rudderless boat in this world. He offers us firm security and moorings and is always there when needed. When caught in the whirlpool [*bhaṅvar*] of this world, he secures us from it simply, immediately, and surely. What he does, nobody else can, for he reminds me what I am, and can be. He shares his virtues openly while the Brāhman must jealously guard his unjust ritual position and privilege. The Brāhman only knows to say how low I am, not how good I am or can be.

The Untouchable ideologist strongly resists any sectarian dilution of the principle of spiritual equality. An ideological ascetic therefore must not only exemplify equality but must also entitle each and every person to it. He is therefore found to be "enlightened" (*bodharūpa*) and is considered devoid of "egoism" (*ahaṃkārarahita*), "covetousness" (*viṣayalampata*), and "impurity" (*apavitratā*).

As Jigyasu observed during an interview: "All of us have the same goal, but each one of us has different inclinations and needs. Everyone is unique, alone, independent, and totally responsible for himself on this road. A guru is necessary and helpful but the final responsibility is always one's own. The Brāhman deviates from this truth when he tries to hide behind unequal ritual status and privilege."

This process of individuation (via the ascetic) yields some useful observations. First, though the ascetics are obviously better (and sometimes even perfect) examples of this pursuit, it emphasizes a cultural goal and a social practice that ordinary men and women may freely share and pursue according to their own potential. Second, genuine ascetics, as models, show how to practice such equality and they encourage the common person to follow suit. (The use of the word "model" in this context refers to the "living ideal" rather than to an abstract analytic construction.) Third, individuation is considered a conscious moral process for the common person, who participates in this process in everyday social life because he holds it to be the route to his ultimate spiritual identity. Finally, events like sickness, old age, misfortune, and death, which afflict everybody, high as well as low, intimate the innate equality of all human beings.

A comparative placement

I have presented an essential outline of how the Untouchable thinker expresses and substantiates his argument for an equalitarian, moral individual. He does so obviously because this moral individual alone can alter the foundation of his caste-based social classification. Only a new moral individuation could offer him a new self-identity that will be clearly meaningful; only a new moral accountability could combat his abject social dependency and disadvantage. Only this development, repeatedly argues the Untouchable thinker, can remove the ultimate moral debasement from which his soul suffers.

A brief comparative evaluation of this effort could be helpful at this point. What larger, genuinely unworked problems does this effort allude to, and how is it similar or dissimilar to certain properties of Western individualism? This comparison is inevitable to a certain extent, given twentieth-century political developments in India and the Untouchable's apprenticeship in them. However, it must remain by necessity cautious and controlled, clearly demarcated by, and limited to, the aims of this inquiry.

The Indic and Western schemes speak essentially two different languages, as it were, of locus, procedure, and purpose.[4] The Indic construct originates in the abstract notion of the Universal Spirit and returns to it after passing through the entire creation, including human society and the human body. Individuation is a process of symbolic identification and transformation within this Indic scheme, generally *classifying* as progressing toward the human condition (e.g., as in *vyakti, jāti, saṃasāra,* and *yoni*) and *declassifying* as returning toward the Universal (e.g., *jīva* and *ātman*). The spiritual individual, not the "person," is a commensurate construct within this scheme, for the *ideal* purpose of the Indic exercise is to show *within the society* an unconditional and complete transformation, back and forth, of the Universal Spirit into its "copies" (cf. the "no one" formulation of Burridge 1979: 4–6). In social practice it means maintaining individuality for oneself in terms of the spiritual essence one represents, remembering the moral properties of indissoluble equality and innate sameness. Juxtaposed to the caste order, this individuating scheme rarefies the caste person in terms of civilizational proclivities, challenging him to move beyond the nature of his birth-awarded properties. This scheme constantly critiques and corrects institutionalized caste morality. The Untouchable ideologist essentially radicalizes this corrective function by a suitable reconceptualization until it is transformed into a challenge to caste inequality.

The Western scheme, in a synoptic comparison, poses contrasting procedures and purposes, even if we keep finer distinctions out of the picture. If the Western scheme, for example, increasingly subjects its construction of the individual to historical experiences, the Indic scheme continues to subscribe largely to ahistorical, moral ideals. If the Western scheme must increasingly transform the originally sacred contents of the individual into those legal, political, and economic, the Indic order, until very recently, has almost solely thrived upon spiritual, ontological, and cosmological formulations. If the Western scheme must formulate the conception of the individual by securing him politico-economic rights and obligations from the state, the Indic order has continued to regard certain moral duties and spiritual states as necessary and fundamental for its individual. The worldly journey may be dilatory but not destructive to the Indic construct, for it is assumed to go through the social, historical, and secular domains with no possibility of being dismembered or dissolved. What the Western scheme verifies through history, the Indic counterpart accomplishes through symbolic verities, usually spelled out in moral paradigms and borne out by the myths and legends developed around model personages and values. It is as if the social experience is judged somehow to be an *incomplete and insufficient* basis for the Indic construct's necessary verification.

Even this crude comparison is better than no comparison, especially in the Indic case, which has otherwise remained hidden behind a seemingly, and sociologically, impenetrable but dubious curtain of the esoteric. Our comparative stance also implies that the "individual" (i.e., as morally responsible sociocultural unit) is in one sense a logical as well as cultural necessity of human societies; it cannot simply be treated as a historically unique and geographically limited development.

We will produce in the following table a few basic characteristics of the Indic (essentially Hindu) ideological scheme alongside their approximate Western counterparts, noting some primary cultural principles or propositions and their corollaries on both sides. (Dumont [1965] and Lukes [1973] remain my sources for the Western scheme.)

Although the comparison in Table 4.1 conveys several, only rough, differences between the two schemes (since the scope of our comparison is limited), we must also remark that they are not the inverse of each other, nor is one scheme more complete than the other. If each scheme has its own special cultural and cognitive grounds from which to formulate its version of individuation and individuality, both of them employ logical and symbolic devices to construct and define the individual significant to their own requirements. Individuation, in essence, may be a logical necessity for the recognition and representation of collective relations and facts.[5] Society manifests itself in terms of individuation because it offers a pervasive basis for establishing moral accountability for *all* the members within the society, whether it is hierarchical or not.

Table 4.1 Indic individuation and Western individualism: a comparison

	Indic individuation	Western individualism	Remarks
1.	The basic construct has remained moral and ethical, deriving from and returning to the sacred cosmology.	Religion and ethics originally had strong shaping influences but the focus has long moved to the secular – politico-economic – domains.	The conceptions of the moral, the social, and the secular so widely differ in the two schemes that it is hazardous to tamper with either one's independence. One cannot be reduced to the other. But we note roots of both in the sacred.
	Corollary: The "social," itself a product of the moral order, can contextually dominate, but not drown, spiritual individualism.	*Corollary*: The sacred roots must now compete and confront the secular development, one effecting displacement or replacement of the other. The social now shapes the moral and human individual and his apperceiving ability.	
2.	The introverted ideals of equality and *liberation* are constantly pursued through the social sphere, represented best by the ascetic.	The extroverted ideals of equality and *liberty* must increasingly be pursued within the secular, social domain.	Underneath the ideological contrasts, there is a strong logical and analogic similarity to be discovered in the way they employ the social domains to express themselves.
	Corollary: Cultivate the "moral monad" over and above the social if the ideals of equality and liberation are to be really achieved in this life and beyond.	*Corollary*: Cultivate appropriately the political, legal, and economic orders if equality and liberty are to be achieved by individuals in their lives.	
3.	The spiritual monad, one with the Whole, becomes the archetype par excellence, and a structural necessity. There is a total (seamless), reversible conversion between the unit and the Whole. (The secular individual of post-independent India is, however, introducing new pragmatic strains into this scheme.)	The Western individual, initiated by the sacred, has moved on to become a politico-economic ideology, a historical necessity, and an "organological" (cf. Lukes 1973) context. The Whole is considered *more* than the total of its parts.	The domains of critical emphasis between the two schemes now diverge on substantive historical and ideological grounds.
	Corollary: The caste-order ethic of inequality finds its limit as well as significance in the spiritual unit (*ātman*) and its equality and individuality. Both – caste and moral monad – remain, however, constructs of the overarching Indic dharma. All constituents develop in relation to the Whole.	*Corollary*: The dignity, autonomy, privacy, and self-development (see Lukes 1973: chaps. 7–11) of the individual must reflect the tensions between the parts and the Whole. Theories discuss tactics to selectively open or close parts to the Whole, or vice versa.	

Table 4.1 (cont.)

	Indic individuation	Western individualism	Remarks
4.	Individuation proceeds in terms of the moral principles of dharma (or *manavadharma*) and karma, which must assure justice and fairness under immediate as well as remote conditions.	Individuation, a process, proceeds as a historical dialectic, moving from singleness to uniqueness, where the latter must ideally remain grounded in legal justice, economic equity, and political voice.	Individuation is a necessary logical and cultural process that must actually manifest according to people's ideology and history.
	Corollary: Individuation is inherent within the Indic system as a moral requisite, including within the caste order. Cultural ideals and morals, together, inculcate this feature, making spiritual morality the rock bottom of the "social."	*Corollary*: Individuation is internal to this scheme as well but its process has been heterogeneous (drawn from ideological, historical, and politico-economic forces) over time. The substratum here is "social reality."	
5.	Unconditional abstraction of the individual is a high point of the Indic scheme. It makes the social a routine but not a fundamental or final domain. The "person" is a lower-level formulation in the chain of successively more abstract constructs (e.g., from *vyakti, jīva, jīvātman, ātman,* to *Ātman* in one scheme).	The abstract individual is variously elaborated in theory but it is now best described as follows: " 'Man is not an abstract being, squatting outside the world. Man is *the human* world, the state, society' " (Marx quoted in Lukes 1973: 75). The "person" is largely a social product.	If the abstract individuals of the two schemes may have originally carried seeds of some analogic similarities, the ideological divergence between the two has been increasing.
	Corollary: The word individual, in logic and effect, works to correct and stop the caste order (and its collectivism) from acquiring extreme social rigidity. The Indic order treats its individual construct sui generis, making it one with the cosmological principles.	*Corollary*: The abstract individual is an obstruction to historical verification; it is at odds with the "sociological apperception" (Dumon 1965; 1980: 5; also Lukes 1973: 150–3), and thus it must yield to the effects of the society, which is sui generis.	

Overview

In summary, emphasizing individuality over collectivity through the principle of asceticism, the Untouchable ideologist wants (a) to call the caste order to a fundamental moral account; (b) to create a tenable moral basis for freedom of thought and action for his own kind; (c) to register his claims for a positive social accountability of the Untouchable;[6] (d) to devise ways for the expression, identification, and evaluation of Untouchables' participation in democratic politics and equality; and (e) to renegotiate his institutionalized relationships to the society. Thus, societies seek radical change when they "redo" their conception and identity of the individual.

While doing so, the Untouchable ideologist, let us recognize, is moving analogously to a central thesis of Western thought (again recalling Macpherson, 1964: 264, on "possessive individualism"): "The individual is human only insofar as free, and free only insofar as a proprietor of himself." The first climax of such a development is reached when ordinary Untouchables, previously excluded from diverse social relations, enter "market transactions,"[7] involving identification of odds, evaluations of personal loss and gain, planned decision making, and competing accountabilities. Though what they have been able to do so far has not been enough by any means to alleviate all of their disadvantages, recent social gains are not insignificant. More important, an overall strategic consciousness is increasingly clear.

Some social gains are now empirically attestable and we will have to see if the foregoing ideological schemes of the Untouchable are reflected by selected social issues and relations. The resulting task therefore will be to see how the Untouchable's ideology might permeate those contexts that are increasingly pragmatic and political. As reforming ascetics and orthodox Brāhmans, both debased in their own ways, now stand face to face, *coram populo*, trying to cope with changing (and increasingly complex) surroundings, the Untouchables may be slowly but surely coming into their own. Their ideology is as much a statement of social deprivation to themselves as it is a commentary on the deeper issues of moral individuation and accountability within the social order of Indian civilization.[8]

In general, however, imprint and erasure, and gathering and dispersal, go on within the Untouchable's ideology. The Lucknow Chamars exemplify this quality in ample measure. Within the society, risks and apprehensions, experiences and meanings, and the "betwixt-and-between" conditions surround this ideology, making the idea of the individual supple but not weak, rarefied (i.e., "that goes around") but not evanescent (for comparable remarks, see Burridge 1979). To be a spiritual individual within the Indic scheme is to be morally accountable to oneself, to others, and to the Whole.

Part II

Pragmatic strategies

5. Transition I: The worldly ascetic

The previous ideological discussion reaches a conclusion that we must examine now in terms of practical – rational as well as realistic – social forces. From a moral construct and exemplar, the Indic ascetic must now translate himself into shared human incentives, needs, and conditions. Even as a renouncer he must face the world as a human being, and be so reckoned. If he is not secluded in a forest, analogues of market mentality (*saṃsārī vyāpāra*), however simplified or atrophied, must knock at his door, demanding from him appropriate social responses. The ascetic should not only be present in the world in this situation, but also must respond to social concerns and conditions of ordinary members of his society. He must morally affect, influence, and perform within the world.

We will discuss in this chapter and the next such ascetics, Lucknow Chamars, and their contexts that help demonstrate the sociocultural transition from ideological to practical concerns. That the concerns of the two domains are variously interrelated among the Indian Untouchables remains the overarching premise of this study. Although I will focus on the Lucknow Chamars, I will employ the term "Untouchable" in those contexts where the reference has to be either to other Untouchables or to the Untouchable as an all-Indian cultural construct. Essentially, the discussion will proceed in two contexts: first, as the Untouchable ascetic, following the Indic model of asceticism, transforms himself to address issues of Untouchable reform and welfare, and second, as the Lucknow Chamars now identify and approach their practical concerns in the company of their Untouchable reformers and leaders. If preceding chapters have considered an ideology for radical equality from within the Indic schemes, the following discussion will take up selected transitions and interrelationships that postindependent India has forged to create a political culture of social claims, organized protests, and practical gains among the Untouchables. The appearance of the "worldly ascetic" and his instigating role in the practical and political goals of the Untouchable (even at the local level, as among the Lucknow Chamar) are both the initial but critical links of cultural transition for our discussion. Because this is also the topic already discussed in sociology, we will take such aspects into account at the outset.

The worldly *ascetic*, more widely, represents a delicate balance between participation and nonparticipation within society. Though participation must always be controlled, and ideally at an absolute minimum, the social story of Indian asceticism (e.g., see Ghurye 1964) shows a wide and actually baffling range of cultural commitment and social activism. Although he should, by necessity, endure some form of worldly "involvement" as long as he has a "body" to feed and to maintain, he must also in fact experience wide-ranging social conditions and their consequences. The biological processes and the changes brought about by age, sex, physical abnormality, and sickness also remind him of his earthly existence, testing his spiritual equanimity. The popular view therefore is that the ascetic constantly faces worldly limitations that deflect him from his spiritual path. To transcend them, he must always be spiritually self-possessed, socially scrupulous, and morally committed to his ideals. In the words of a popular saying, his vocation is "like walking on the sharp edge of a sword."

The same popular view, however, also accords the Indian ascetic some inalienable moral and spiritual powers, which he may in fact variously hide and camouflage while living within the society as an ordinary ascetic. He is thus a puzzle to the ordinary person. He is always considered to be capable of enormous spiritual influence, social reforms, spontaneous conversions, and magical words. There is no social placement of the ascetic that could entirely deny him such intrinsic properties. The popular view thus renders the ascetic an ambivert mediator.

Sociologically, this configuration of the ascetic, relevant to the Untouchable's situation, recounts the earlier Weberian (1958, 1963) discussion of asceticism and the ascetic–mystic divide. As we noted earlier (chap. 1), we find no simplified divide between the ascetic and the mystic (Weber 1958: 324–6; also 1963: 166–83) within the Indian scheme. But Weber's general discussion of asceticism, under different doctrines of salvation, rationalism, and social activism, remains largely applicable. For example, his notion of the "Protestant ascetic" is relevant to the Untouchable's conception of reformist ascetic. If the Indian conceptions of austerity and related categories entail mysticism (e.g., *tapas, vairāgya, yoga,* and *saṃnyāsa*; see the summary of these in Bhagat 1976: 9–61), the practical ascetic would like to utilize them as a strategic commodity for increasing his social influence and managing practical problems. He would try to be mysterious to keep his followers and opponents guessing. Still, the ascetic's social activism must only subserve (not dominate) the mystic in him.

The Lucknow Chamars readily recognize the ascetic's miracles (*camatkāra*), charisma (popularly *karishmā* or *ojas*), and spiritual power (*ātmabala*). But they find the earlier ascetics (e.g., Ravidas) generally more authentic than today's counterparts because the contemporary ascetic is considered more worldly, hence less true to his calling. The Untouchable ideologist, however, gives a different interpretation to the ascetic's passage toward worldly participation. He discovers a general caste-Hindu politics behind the appearance and manipulation of miracles, charisma, and spiritual power. He is suspicious especially when ascetics support high-caste privileges.

The Lucknow Chamar's pragmatism and the Chamar ascetic

Let us now turn to the Lucknow Chamar to establish a frame of empirical reference for the entire second part of this study. We will repeatedly draw upon appropriate persons, events, contexts, and expressions encountered among the Lucknow Chamar. The worldly Chamar ascetic is a crucial node of the ideological *and* the practical; we will consider him in the context of the same three Lucknow Chamar neighborhoods described before (see Introduction). The materially most progressive Modernganj, the reformist Baudhabagh, and the tradition-bound and downcast Karampura offered us essentially three distinct but interrelated profiles of Chamar ideals and practice. The resident Chamar ascetics often involved themselves in the composition of each profile; sometimes they played a much larger role and conjugated the three local profiles together. They routinely mediated family quarrels, advised courage and perseverance in practical issues such as food, housing, work, progeny, and sickness, and resolved doubts about self-identity and social position. The Chamar ascetic thus often participated where most notions of the practical converged for interpretation, reform, and redirection.

An important feature appears in the background and it is necessary to mention it at this point to initiate a consideration of the Untouchable's pragmatic ethos. The Untouchable's "worldly ascetic" is most often in close touch with the Chamar householders of one or more neighborhoods. His diverse social contacts and knowledge about householders' woes generally increase his practical value within a neighborhood. The more he knows about them, the more he is able to influence them. We will assume this contextual role of the ascetic in the following discussion.

The Lucknow Chamar's pragmatic ethos now reflects crucially the unavoidable tension between tradition and democracy in India. The expectation of an egalitarian democratic society now enters into his social environs directly or indirectly, irrespective of whether he succeeds or fails in a particular social pursuit. It is also a hope that shapes his self-image and reformist idealism and renders even failures significant for new social reasons. This adjustment at present, however, involves a subtle and complex process of sociocultural interpretations. It starts with the Chamar himself. He is now in the habit of interpreting his life events (and their significance) in the context of the thirty-five-year-old Indian democracy and its promises to the Indian Untouchable. This first-level interpretation is neither always coherent nor evident, but it distinctly defines the Lucknow Chamars at present. The significance of this politico-economic development is never remote from them. The second-level interpretation of Indian democracy occurs with Chamar leaders and elites. They interpret the wider social ethos for their community members, and the position of their community in relation to the rest of the society, which includes politicians, caste Hindus, and government officials. The Untouchable ascetic complements this interpretation from his direction and he juxtaposes the indigenous values of social (and spiritual) reform and democratic rights. Obviously, he emphasizes the former over the latter and recognizes the democratic rights as a congenial social development. The third-level interpretation is the ethnographer's. It emerges as he converses with the people he studies and as he compares and explains their sociocultural differences (Geertz 1973: 5–7).

These multiple interpretations pervade the pragmatic issues and actions of the Chamar. What he does in the practical world is as important to know as what he means by it (and what it signifies to others). Postindependence political developments offer a necessary context for his practical issues; they influence the meaning and significance of his daily affairs. The Chamar, whether a modern physician, a political leader, a teacher, a mechanic, a painter, a cobbler, or unemployed, invariably discovers that the tussle between the traditional and democratic forces is a part of his everyday condition that he can neither escape nor ignore (nor does it ignore him). There are therefore traditional and new sides to the Lucknow Chamar but no purely traditional Chamar. If he might still be seeking, as in the past, suitable economic, political, and social justice, his present efforts neither follow the same old routes nor deny recent historical changes.

The primary loci of the Chamar's practical efforts, however, remain essentially unchanged — that is, acquiring safety, food, clothing, housing, employment, and education. But the last two portend important changes. The social resources for the pursuit of these goals are also changing in substance. The Chamars acquire new social rights under democracy while the caste Hindus must take on commensurate social obligations to let democratic justice prevail. Thus, observing how the Chamars acquire food, clothing, housing, education, and employment is often not sufficient for the ethnographer; he should also know how the significance of his social efforts is changing for the Chamar and for those "others" surrounding him. The webs of new sociocultural significance that the Chamar and the caste Hindu spin in relation to each other need to be understood as part of the practical domain. Without them, the Chamar's ethnography may come out flat and static, largely uninformative.

The preceding aspects of multilevel interpretations and of the webs of significance are integral to the Chamar's practical efforts. The following will illustrate some educational and occupational concerns among them.

The Lucknow Chamars covet modern education beyond high school. They look increasingly for modern white-collar occupations. Both modern education and occupation are considered to be sure routes to a better life, superior social position, and better social treatment. Modernganj clearly showed the multiple meanings education acquired among the Chamars. At least four social stages of education were readily mentioned: (a) government-enforced primary education of children, (b) high school education of boys and girls, (c) college or university education, and (d) professional or technical education. The first stage was considered largely inconsequential for a better job; it enabled one to sign rather than rely on the thumbprint. The second stage meant reaching a common social expectation. For the older generation, high school meant being educated (*paṛhé-likhé*); for the present generation, it was considered a common achievement, especially among the boys. College education, in comparison, represented personal advancement and family prestige. If one's daughter or sister was college educated in Modernganj, she was considered prominent within the neighborhood. People talked about her education – pro and con. Only three girls in 120 households were attending college during my fieldwork (1979–80). Since the previous generations could not recall any such instance, this change was locally dramatic (but still insufficient for comparison with upper-caste Hindus).

In Modernganj, the Chamars simultaneously awarded multiple meanings to education. It was increasingly a symbol of social comparison and competition with the wider Indian society. An unemployed laborer had vowed to provide his two children with a good education. Asked why, he pointed to his neighbors. Asked how, his answer was "by cutting back on our daily food." A railway engine driver had successfully educated his sons in the college and they were employed in government offices. A state bus transport mechanic had made it a point to teach his two primary-school children on Sunday afternoons. This he did to supplement the regular tutoring by a low-caste Hindu girl. A post office employee had sent his daughter to a local, Brāhman-founded college. He had done so despite the warning that highly educated girls were difficult to marry. He considered education essential to open up his own (traditional) community for his people's economic and political advancement. A clerk in the state government, a progressive song writer and musician, had joined an evening training course in accounting and shorthand. His ascetic guru had assured him that he was destined to rise much higher in his life and that greater skills acquired through education were the key. The clerk wrote inspirational songs to awaken the Chamar; he exhorted parents to educate their children in the name of Ambedkar. "Education – unlimited – is that democratic right of the deprived," he would proclaim, "that the caste Hindus also cannot deny anymore. Equality in educational opportunity is now the root of all other equalities." The clerk's guru interpreted the role of education a little differently: He evaluated its primary worth against the "spiritual awakening" within the ordinary Chamar rather than in social and economic terms, though he never denied their importance.

Yet another dimension of education was made clear to a Modernganj resident who, though himself a cobbler, had a son who was a physician of modern medicine, a graduate of the local medical college. Proud of his son's achievement and equally confident of his own traditional calling, he observed, "How can I fully explain my decision to give such an advanced education to my son? I can only say that my shoe shop sustained the expenses, though the government's quota policy on admissions and scholarship for the backward classes helped my son a lot. Beyond that, God gave us the courage and our son a good mind. He refused early marriage and I supported him. Equally important, my son strongly believes in Doctor Saheb [Ambedkar] and his social message. Though we did not become Buddhists, we take pride in his example. He asked us to educate our children the most we can. My guru also encouraged us. He is a very practical man; he considers a good livelihood necessary for mental and spiritual peace. He emphasizes that a son should not be married until he has a livelihood of his own, and there is no good livelihood these days without good education."

A Baudhabagh ascetic reformer labeled modern education "a key to the locked doors of the society. Once obtained, nobody can take it away in one's lifetime; nobody can either rob it or destroy it without destroying the person. Learning (*vidyā*) reforms sooner or later both the oppressor and the oppressed. Education lets us discover ourselves, and be ourselves. It is now the means to solving the practical issues of food, clothing, housing, and social discrimination for the Chamar. The changes modern education brings about are slow but many-sided and sure. They influence both the high and the low to develop social sharing and interdependence."

Some Chamars had pursued modern education in the second and even third generation (and almost all of these were living in Modernganj and Baudhabagh), though most were awakening slowly to the practical value of formal education and technical skills. In Modernganj, a photographer was teaching his trade to Chamar boys as well as to caste Hindus. An employee of a flower shop had learned to decorate cars and front yards of the houses for marriages. He masqueraded as a skilled *mālī* (gardener) from an established flower shop. Missed schooling is increasingly made up by learning a specialized skill like painting houses, repairing sports and musical equipment, mending carpets, or vending seasonal vegetables. The Baudhabagh Chamars, being close to appropriate markets, entered commodity, jute, steel, and utensil shops as semiskilled workers. They learned to solder, mold, and repair steel products.

The preceding discussion of modern education and special skills is symptomatic of the larger and more comprehensive practical ethos that surrounds the Chamars in an urban center like Lucknow. As the Chamars stamp this ethos with their own problems, purposes, and meanings, it begins to express the tensions between tradition and democracy. Though this tension is discussed in terms of specific events, it is a matter of constant social management and interpretation among the Lucknow Chamars, with an accumulating sense of change. Often, the local expression for such a cumulative change is *badaltā samaya* or *zamānā*.

The Chamars' approach to education also exemplifies similar exercises that go on among them with regard to food, clothing, housing, and occupation. Their preferred interpretations also define the social condition. Some Chamars looked only for housing or occupation that was conducive to their changing self-image and expectations. When a flourishing Baudhabagh shoe shop owner refused to change his occupation for a proffered position in government service, he did so to prove that he valued leatherwork, he claimed, the same way as did Saint Ravidas. Like many other Chamars in Lucknow, he insisted on seeing leatherwork as a "respectable occupation," a good business, and "a satisfying self-employment in which nobody could order me around." He argued: "Leaving leatherwork is not necessary for the Chamar's social emancipation; only the demeaning ideas associated with it need to be forgotten. If we flourish in leatherwork, this will be automatically proved. Moreover, why should we leave what we are good at? It is another ploy of the caste Hindus to keep us subjugated." On the other hand, those Chamars who had changed their traditional occupations also claimed increased intrinsic and social worth. Thus, leatherwork or not, the Chamars now often attach more positive significance to their occupation than perhaps ever before. Unless the anthropologist knows about such aspects, the Chamars' occupational changes inform him only incompletely.

Chamar housing is also not simply classifiable as in the columns of a table: houses owned, rented, squatted in, evacuated, abandoned, etc. It is rather what the Chamars convey as they go through the process of acquiring shelter, whether a barely livable shanty or a comfortable house paid for outright in a better neighborhood. A Baudhabagh vegetable seller's residence was a shanty by the flood-prone drain; a politically influential leader, in contrast, had a "rent-controlled house" (i.e., at cheaper monthly rent); a draftsman owned a brick house of five rooms. Thus, as housing reflects socioeconomic position, an obvious point, it also reflects to the Chamar his highly uneven and unsteady social position. Those with a better house may feel prestigious but insecure, and those in huts feel deprived but not without pride. Chamar houses, like their education and occupation, reflect the properties of the practical ethos of a social group that is variously motivating and maneuvering itself to take advantage of the changing climate. Several interpreters and interpretations help them in this exercise.

The Untouchable ascetics participate in the development of practical conduct in a pervasive and critical manner. They observe, interpret, and guide.

Their influence lies in the interpretation of the world, the worldly, and the circumstances of the specific householder. Their interpretation blends empathy and reform and applies to the illiterate and the poor as well as to the educated, the rich, and the powerful. These days as they guide the Chamars to concerted action to improve their self-image and quality of life, the ascetics contribute directly to the pragmatic ethos that democratic changes – political, economic, and legal – have created and strengthened. In addition, the Untouchable ascetics often subtly reinterpret and channel the interpretations of local Chamar leaders and elites. However, as they do so they usually insist on two things: first, rediscovering (and reclaiming) the "true heritage" of the Untouchables as the *ādi*-Hindus, and second, integrating it with worldly gains made under the contemporary circumstance. The two steps usually entail caution against extremism, deliberations before major action, and the investment of self-image in daily events.

Untouchable ascetics, encountered in a Ravidas temple courtyard, an Ambedkar Bhavan meeting room, a party leader's office, a political leader's drawing room, and on a disciple's verandah, readily discussed pragmatic issues. Such discussions revealed the ideals, hopes, and frustrations of the ordinary Chamar. Most ascetics advised practical shrewdness mixed with social optimism and perseverance. Very often, this type of ascetic "affirms individual rational activity within the institutional framework of the world, affirming it to be his responsibility as well as his means for securing certification for his state of grace" (Weber 1963: 173). He represents what Coomaraswamy (1979: 138–43) calls the "comprehensor" (*evamvit*).[1] He sharpens and aids the motivation for seeking and securing improved life conditions; he paradoxically symbolizes both world management and world renunciation. His rituals and words are found to carry the essential germs of political consciousness. (See the case of Achchutananda discussed later.) This ascetic distrusts the Hindu's notions of hierarchy, ritual purity, and sin and interprets them as instruments of social dominance. An ideologist like Jigyasu distinguishes them as products of "the scheming Brahmanic mind," meant mostly for "the easily deluded caste-Hindu followers." He claims the idea of spiritual purity to be inherently equalitarian and holds it to be the crux of all personal and collective notions of purity within the Indic system. All else is held to be ultimately unjust, immoral, and revolting.

Worldly asceticism: a cultural explanation

What triggers such a course of thought is generally the ascetic's ideal of noncontingent love. The Indian system sometimes offers entirely mystical and spiritual answers to such an ideal and sometimes those incorporating moral and social reasons. The latter are emphasized when an ascetic is committed to stopping social injustice and ameliorating human suffering. This "spiritual watchman" cannot remain a bystander to social neglect, and he must pursue a just cause through explicit social action. However, such motivation would be considered "external" (*vāhya*), unless, as is most often true, this "call" is found to come to the ascetic from the divine; it is then "internal" (*āntarika, antarātmā kī pukār*) and truly authentic, making the ascetic a locus of social action to fulfill the divine inspiration.

These calls may come to the ascetic in several different ways, for example, in meditation, during a deity's worship, from his guru, through a sequence of unplanned events, in a dream, or through spiritual disquiet. These spiritual avenues of divine communication, however, apply to the caste-Hindu ascetic as genuinely as they do to the Untouchable ones. For example, Ravidas received such a call from his deity, Rāma, even though he did not (unlike Kabir) want to preach (see *Bhaktamāla* and Jigyasu 1968a). At least eight Chamar ascetics whom I met in the three Lucknow neighborhoods owed their worldly turn to such a spiritual "call." In contrast, fifteen others had embarked on this path primarily after encountering social discrimination and under the influence of such persons as a politicized uncle, a radical elder brother, a reformist neighbor, or a dissatisfied parent.

Personal experiences and decisions, however, played a more direct role in radicalizing the Chamar ascetics. Repeatedly, childhood experiences of social insult, neglect, and discrimination were found to shape such ascetics' commitment to reform. Yet a tendency remained to spiritualize their incentives, for only a few would directly admit that purely social influences were sufficient to them (especially since they had, strictly speaking, already left behind such "worldly" ties and their influences). Normally, the ascetics either minimized the role of such social forces or mixed them with suitable spiritual themes.

When compared to the caste-Hindu ascetic as a social reformer, the Chamar ascetic's idealism and *negative* social experiences clearly stand out. He may become a reformer for either one or both reasons, though idealism alone usually remains insufficient. Villages may now yield protesting ascetics as readily as the cities, I was told, but this simple picture is at present quickly qualified by political complexities. The Lucknow Chamar ascetic also now discovers that he must appropriately politicize himself to become an effective reformer. He must adopt certain "worldly" techniques of leadership and politics if he wants to be effective in his aims. Thus he tends to be more worldly than his predecessors.

This change produces a paradox for him. If he leaves his spiritual world entirely behind, his intrinsic worth diminishes in the society; and if he does not fully pursue what his commitment for social reform demands, he fails himself as well as the expectations of his followers. If politics means engaging oneself in morally questionable ideas and action, he would be considered "corrupt" in one viewpoint and effective in another. However, if these were the two major "pulls" evident among the Lucknow Chamar ascetics, they were also converted into cultural creativity, spontaneity, and tactical leverage by those who could convert the ordinary Chamar's doubt and vacillation (*saṃśaya*) into social activism.

The critical Lucknow Chamar, on the other side, views his contemporary ascetic reformers with increasing skepticism. He finds them morally diminutive and easily corruptible. But the critics assert equally readily that this does not downgrade the intrinsic value of asceticism (which is held to be ageless and absolute). At the same time, not unlike the caste Hindu, the Chamar readily agrees that it is now increasingly hard to distinguish between genuine and spurious ascetics (a fact Ghurye [1964] also records).

An ideologist like Jigyasu saw the problem of spurious ascetics as a serious one and lamented the disappearance of "genuine ascetics" from Lucknow. It forced him, he noted, to withdraw to the company of his books. But at the same time he also decried those who utilized these times to degrade asceticism. He observed during an interview: "The ascetic is a moving synthesis of ideals-under-practice. He enlightens reformers and politicians. He penetrates ritualism, unifies the divided, challenges the unjust, and offers a spiritual connection between what is moral (*naitika*), what is eternal (*nitya*), and what is circumstantial effect (*naimittika*)."

The reforming ascetic was not for Jigyasu merely worldly, but actually a living civilizational treatise on the morally practical and the practicable. The Indic ascetic, in this idealist's view, breaks out of false and unjust hierarchical doxa, oppositions, and history. He corrects the unjust ranking by introducing miracles, mysticism, and moral events. He entertains practical logic and practical action, but, as Jigyasu observed, "it is more to explore rather than to become a prisoner of the practical and its effects." As the "All-Worker," he engages in a dexterous semblance of the practical, inspiring the ordinary person to engage in its successful pursuit. Ideologically, as a model of the Creator, he yields model performance, correcting overdetermination as well as chaos. Jigyasu regarded this world-reforming ascetic as spontaneous and innately powerful; he is never merely a prisoner of institutionalized existence and status-coded power.

This idealist's approach to the world-reforming ascetic offers a closer view of the Indic interrelationships posed between the ascetic and the world. Its first assumption is that the ascetic does not have to become "worldly" (*saṃsārī*) in an ordinary sense to reform the world. Second, his axioms, techniques, actions, and consequences remain different from those of the Brāhman as well as any other type of reformer. He displays a peculiarly open form of moral depth, spontaneity with originality, and variety and eccentricity for offering social alternatives. This freeing profile of the ascetic has been a balm to the Untouchable's civilizational sores, for the Brāhman's rules in contrast always appeared to him parochial, restrained, and custom bound, wielding threats of social censure and imposing the sacred. Third, the ascetic reformer, a godfather to the deprived, can subvert a whole "filiation of ideas" (for a notion, see Himmelfarb's introduction to Mill 1974: 8) for obtaining justice for them.

This world-reforming (not worldly) ascetic is a long-standing Indian exercise in tenacious cultural interpretations, where the ascetic presses into service layer upon layer of symbolic orders to train and channel practical diversities. He draws upon the sacred notion of seamless cosmic unification to understand the "polythesis" and polysemy of the "*universe of practice*" (Pierre Bourdieu 1977: 110ff.). He tries to reduce practical diversities to certain moral prerequisites before handling them. As he applies the logic of spiritual unity to life's diverse practical strains, he introduces a flexible value and perspective in social relationships. He impregnates worldly rationality with an ultimate spiritual significance and makes it a domain open to alternative moral rules and meanings.

In this connection, Jigyasu summarized for me in 1972 a discussion he once had with Bodhananda, a Buddhist monk resident in Lucknow. (Since it was repeatedly difficult for Jigyasu to separate his ideas from those of Bodhananda, we may treat the following as their shared perspective.)

> The world-reforming ascetic's position is always risky. It is like standing on a precipice or trying to balance oneself on a sword's edge. Though the ascetic is motivated by kindness toward all creatures [*saba jīvoñ par dayā*], reform of others involves him in worldly matters. Worldly attachments lurk just nearby. Even a limited success brings praise to him an intoxicant he should stay away from. His followers surround him more and more, reducing the seclusion so necessary for his spiritual equanimity. His personal discipline tends to break down and he spends time evolving moral compromises for his followers. As he spends time on lessening the troubles of worldly men, the worldly comes dangerously close to him. If inattentive, it traps him increasingly in everyday worries of the practical world, wrenching him away from his spiritual "habitus" [*déśa*] and "movement" [*gatī*].
>
> But all such risks usually reflect the inadequacy of a particular ascetic; they are inherent in neither asceticism [*sañta-aur-śramaṇa saṃskṛti*] nor the goal of worldly reform. The genuine ascetic cannot help responding to others' distress; to help and reform the downtrodden is in his nature. His heart melts just at the sight of others' sorrow and pain, and all of his actions, including those seemingly worldly, are a response of his spiritual nature. Thus, for the genuine ascetic world reform is only an extension of his spiritual journey. Sure of himself and assured of his ultimate goals, the worldly aspects can appear before him but cannot trap or bind him. There is no "opposite" [*dwanda*] that can restrain him. His action [*kāma*] is nonbinding and his speech prescient. His presence transcends space and time. In whatever he does he remains a yogi; he remains in communion with the spiritual truth. These are not however only words with us. Many genuine Indic ascetics have exemplified this status in the past and many more will surely do so in the future. They bring about the [unconditional] unification of the head, heart, and hands of the human being.

Overview

The pragmatic ethos of the Lucknow Chamar draws our attention both to a cluster of concrete sociocultural conditions and to the tensions between the

Indian tradition and democracy. The Chamar ascetic plays the comprehensive and critical role of mediator in this picture; he has been performing this role during this century in a distinct manner. He is the bridge between the diverse social forces that postindependent India has introduced in the daily life of the Lucknow Chamar. He has functioned, as the following chapter will show further, to redo popularly shared Hindu cultural ideas and perspectives to make them work for the Untouchable's new aspirations. The Untouchable ascetic, in general, has aided, mostly unintentionally, those appropriate links between the traditional and democratic forces that promote (a) an ideology for radical equality, (b) a political culture for civil rights and organized protests, and (c) a social strategy for doing better in everyday life. These three developments proceed interdependently among the Lucknow Chamars. Each can also transform into the others to create a comprehensive cultural support system for positive social change.

Our discussion of the Chamar's practical affairs will extend the consideration of these three interdependent dimensions as a part of the changing cultural ethos. The Chamar's management of this ethos will be particularly useful to us because it does more than describe a particular case or condition; it also identifies and articulates the Chamar's overall perceptions of the practical world, as well as the meanings and significance he attributes to it. And as he reveals himself this way, he also evaluates the changing society around him.

6. Transition II: The radical and protesting ascetic

The contemporary Untouchable ascetic pursues a varying mixture of Hindu monism (*advaita*), Buddhist "vacuity," the later Hindu notions of "public service" (*jana sévā*, where *janatā* is Janārdana), and the Indian reformist's notions of "humanism" (*mānava dharma*). Such a range of ideas gives the Untouchable and his ascetic a large (and heterogeneous) cultural ground from which not only to maneuver and rebut the resistance of the traditional caste Hindu but also to introduce himself to civil rights and social obligations obtainable under the Indian version of democracy. With independence, the Untouchable ascetic's ideological manipulations have become increasingly receptive to a social radicalism that questions the entire traditional socioeconomic order and its practices.

This radical ascetic usually derives his strength from the close contact he keeps with a scattered but devoted group of followers. He may attract and influence the young and the old, and men as well as women, especially under the conditions of emotional strain and social distress. When a cluster of Chamar ascetics, for example, was systematically investigated for their social influence in the Baudhabagh neighborhood, a whole range of ascetic radicalism, from mild to militant, became evident.

A resident ascetic in the Baudhabagh neighborhood was generally regarded as a veritable social crutch. He served either in the absence of, or to strengthen, a family elder, a locality leader, and a religious inspirer. A childless wife, a long-unemployed man, a troublesome or troubled youth, a maiden awaiting a suitable groom, the chronically sick, quarrelsome neighbors, a devout householder, and a person surrounded by miseries (*gardish mein paṛā ādmī*) – all usually sought, sooner or later, the advice and inspiration of this ascetic. He performed rites like a Brāhman to please gods and to produce charms, amulets, and "blessed fruits" for the distressed. He was the healer of the mental as well as the bodily sores of the deprived. As a soothing and supportive advisor to the distressed, a spiritual staff for the aged and the dying, an astrologer for the one fallen on bad times, a stern master for erring and indolent disciples, and an activist reformer for locality leaders, the ascetic, despite his failure to bring about a total social revolution, served as a wide-ranging social linchpin for the Lucknow Chamar.

The Baudhabagh ascetics had acquired such multiple roles in a socially prominent manner. They had often replaced the Brāhman priest. Usually, each ascetic had also developed at least one specialized role within the community and was known for it. The local Chamars had a clear idea of whom to approach for a specific problem, and what generally to expect from him in response. The ascetics were popularly rated as "effective," "ineffective," or "indifferent" in relation to a specific issue or practical problem. For example, a resident Chamar would know who was best suited for family problems and who for the issues of social and political reform. Mismatching them was usually the sign of a person's social ignorance, and he was quickly offered the required information.

All the resident Baudhabagh ascetics had simultaneous contacts with several households, and all had cultivated a nucleus of specially favored disciples, once these ascetics had performed a mélange of spiritual, religious, and reformist services for them. To a reformist ascetic, for example, a better-employed, activist youth was his spiritual heir. To a staunch Buddhist reformer, his ascetic-guru had taken the place of a Brāhman priest, an astrologer, and a tantrist (i.e., *tāntrika*). In all, there were four such cases in Baudhabagh. To the two local politicians, their spiritual guru was also their reformer-guru. Neither these leaders nor the ascetics found anything anomalous in this because the ascetics were expected to unite the contraries. If anybody, they should be able to do so most genuinely. Two ascetics told me that all of their efforts, whether it was their sudden reproach or praise, or commitment or withdrawal, or traditionalism or radicalism, were designed to reflect and respond to their disciples' conditions within Baudhabagh and outside.

Baudhabagh also had asceticlike householders and householderlike ascetics. Both inspired and advised the common Chamar under social adversity, but in their own way. Anantananda (a pseudonym) had become an asceticlike householder under the influence of his own guru. Though he regularly worked for his living, and worked harder than others in his neighborhood, he practiced renunciation in his daily life. He detached himself from his family, he claimed, though he lived in a small thatched cell outside his main dwelling. He read books in Hindi on yoga, spiritualism, and nondualism (*advaitavāda*). He delivered discourses in the evening at least two times a month blending the concerns of spiritual and social awakening. In his view, if the second was impossible without the first, both were impossible without doing hard, disinterested work for the betterment of others (*niṣkāmakarma*). Like Jigyasu, he tried to eschew Brahmanic ritualism from within Hindu philosophy and spiritualism, and to replace it with Buddhist ideas.

Gyanananda (a pseudonym) was a householderlike ascetic. He realized by his late fifties that, though an ordained ascetic, his mission lay in selfless social service to his own deprived "brethren." He had therefore settled *within* a community. He encouraged people to come to him with their troubles, including when his physical help was required. Though he lived alone and subsisted on alms, he liked social congregations and talked regularly to small groups of men and women within Baudhabagh. He had physically helped Chamars in thatchwork, tending the sick, and cremating the dead. He had looked after the children of a working couple.

In short, the Baudhabagh ascetics demonstrated how they comprised the picture of "All-Workers" for the ordinary Chamar. It was this All-Worker who thought, willed, and acted for the welfare of the Chamar, irrespective of whether he was against the caste Hindu.

Such examples build on the point made earlier that the Indian ascetic acquires a full range of culturally allowed locations within the society. He can also easily radicalize himself for morally appropriate aims. A radical ascetic in modern India usually transforms himself into a political radical – a worldly ascetic who actively tries to convert his ideological rhetoric into political action. A radical ascetic starts this conversion when he encourages a protest, first usually sporadically and later on a sustained basis. Undoubtedly, to do so means to award a distinctly new dimension to the moderate Chamar ascetic we have discussed so far. But this has been indeed so.

A radical ascetic is easily turned into a protesting ascetic once he presses his demands for reform through direct, whether spontaneous or planned, protests. But he represents a milder variety as long as he does *not* resort to organized, representational politics and regards spiritual or personal influence as the backbone of his intended social reform. He is an ascetic first and a social or political radical second. However, a type stronger than the protesting variety appears when the ascetic is a de facto professional politician. He may jump into political frays and arenas with the full resources of a professional politician, even though he is an initiated ascetic. Under the final circumstance, as we will see later, even this ascetic may be found to be deficient, and he has to relinquish this increasingly demanding work to professional politicians and parties.

Although we will discuss other varieties later on, we will consider the ascetic reformer first. He is a critical steppingstone for the Untouchable's entry into the hectic political events of this century. Because Ravidas is so scantily known and lived several centuries ago, and Ambedkar is too late in the century and too remote (in training and education) from the ordinary Lucknow Chamar to demonstrate the *beginning* of *their* demands for moral and social reform, our example should preferably come from the region at the turn of the century. Ideally he should be a radical reform ascetic who turned into a protesting one.

Achchutananda, a regional reformer from Uttar Pradesh working at the turn of this century, best fits our requirements. Not only was he a social reformer, but he also showed all the signs of offering a radical pragmatic ideology to his community. He had a cohesive cultural argument as well as viewpoint (see Jigyasu 1968b). As far as I know, Jigyasu's efforts to restructure the Untouchable ideology are strongly influenced by Achchutananda's insights and cultural enunciations. (Compare chaps. 2 and 3 with the material offered here.) This remains true even though it was Jigyasu who gave to his formulations the needed broad cultural interpretation and justification.

Achchutananda was an initiated ascetic and a social reformer rolled into one. He was neither a politician nor a political reformer. In Jigyasu's account (1968b), he always stood for "just" protests, offering a radical rhetoric to go with them. Actually, he was sometimes so radical that even his community members would back out. His life experiences were the main source of his estrangement from the caste Hindu and a driving force behind the formulation of his protests. When protest was essential to his cause, he did not hesitate to become a protesting ascetic. But he was not merely a protester; most important, he advocated a profound reform of the entire cultural order that bred social discrimination. In this last context, he offered the *ādi*-Hindu ideology to his community, making them residents – autonomous autochthons – of India even before Aryan times. I have labeled this ideology elsewhere "autochthonous radicalism" (Khare 1979). We will present here a short biographical account of Achchutananda, followed by his ideology, and finally its extensive reproduction in an illustrative list of radical cultural theses to which contemporary Chamar reformers increasingly resort. I will depend on Jigyasu (1968b) for Achchutananda's biography and ideology (with some unattributed quotations from the Lucknow Chamar ascetics), and on Sagar (1965) for the illustration of certain derived theses of cultural radicalism.

He was born in 1879 at his mother's home in a village called Umari in Mainpuri district in the state now called Uttar Pradesh, and he was given the name Hiralal. His father was then living in his wife's village "since he and his brothers had quarreled with the Brāhmans and other twice-born castes of their village" (Jigyasu 1968b: 9). After Hiralal's birth, the family moved to a mlitary cantonment, where Hiralal received his initial informal education. By the age of fourteen he was in the company of ascetics and had learned to read and write some Urdu and English in the cantonment. He was inquisitive and precocious, with a flair for religious studies. During his itinerant phase as an ascetic, he learned several more languages (Sanskrit, Bengali, Gujarati, and Marathi), gathered wide-ranging experiences, and acquired a (presumably Hindu) guru called Sachidananda. The reforming Arya Samaja attracted him early and he became Hariharananda from Hiralal. However, since he had soon discovered a wide gap between the Arya Samaja's stated equalitarian ideals and actual social behavior, he left the Arya Samaja (an organization, notes Jigyasu, that continued to hinder his activities long afterward). A long and intensive period of self-education followed, helping him see through the designs of the caste Hindus. This ordinary ascetic and erstwhile swami of Arya Samaja thus became an ardent social reformer who undertook to awaken members of his deprived community.

By 1922, the year of the visit of the Prince of Wales, this ascetic had hit upon "the principle of the *ādi*-Hindu," and had acquired a political name for himself by siding with the British on the controversy of the royal visit. Soon his independent *ādi*-Hindu movement was also started in some parts of northern India, demanding social equality and justice for the Untouchable.[1] However, this movement meant Achchutananda's confrontation with both the Arya Samaja and the caste-Hindu organizations. Internally, the Untouchables were divided between those who wanted to better their lot *within* the Hindu system (Lynch's [1969] account of Jatavs handles this position in Agra), and those, more radical, who attempted to leave the system. Jigyasu (1968b) noted in his biography how this disunity brought lifelong troubles for Achchutananda. (His name itself indicated rebelliousness to the caste Hindu, and it was enigmatic for the ordinary Untouchable, for it meant the one who was blissful in being Untouchable. It was perhaps an attempt to invent that type of symbolic turn that I consider, more generally, an essential feature of Indian reformers.) He was several times so completely forsaken by his friends and community members that he had to go without food and shelter. But he persisted in his goals.

Jigyasu has noted how Hariharananda became "Sri 108 Swami Achchūtānanda." In 1928, during a public meeting of the *ādi*-Hindu Sabha in Lucknow, Dr. Ambedkar had addressed him so in the middle of the meeting, and prolonged applause followed. However, Jigyasu claimed that this history needed to be corrected. He pointed out that this title had, in fact, come to Achchutananda several years before in 1921, when he had "won it from the Hindus themselves by defeating a Brāhman scholar in a debate in Shahdara" (near Delhi). It is symbolically significant that he had become the "world conqueror" as a result (Jigyasu 1968b: 16–17).

It was repeatedly made clear in Jigyasu's account that Achchutananda continued to encounter unrelenting resistance and rejection at the hands of upper-caste Hindus. His term *ādi*-Hindu in particular irritated them: If it deftly linked the Untouchable to the autochthons of India and the caste Hindus to the immigrant, invading Aryans, it also made the former the rightful, peaceful, and original owners of the *Bharat bhūmi* (India). The Hindus were considered "intrigue-filled, ruthless conquerors." This way the caste Hindu's moral right to belong to Bharat was directly questioned. "It reminded the Hindu leader of his ancestors' cruelty and suppression," according to Jigyasu (1968b: 19). To Achchutananda, however, such resistance from the Hindus was all the more reason for not giving up use of the term *ādi*-Hindu.

This leader indulged in similar symbolic contests. When some Chamars and caste Hindus, for example, refused to call him "Swami Achchūtānanda" (implying that he did not deserve the honorific prefix of *swāmi*), he began to call himself "Achchūtānanda Swami" or "Achchūta Swami," incorporating the title in has actual name as a suffix. (Jigyasu argued on this point that his detractors could not have called him merely "Achchūta," since it was not a proper noun.) Achchutananda would himself explain his name by observing that the word *achchūta* meant something entirely opposite to what the conventional usage conveyed. It meant to him *a* (meaning "not") and *chchūta* (meaning "polluted"), yielding "the one who was in a state of purity." The word *sachchūta* for him meant "the impure." So understood, the monthly magazine he brought out was called *Achchuta Prācīna [Ancient] Hindu* (later on simply *ādi-Hindu*), while Achchutananda became (under yet another variation) "Sri Harihar [taken from one of his earlier names] Swami 'Achchūta.' " Here the main name became his nom de plume.

In its final phases Achchutananda's movement began to organize itself in two distinct forums – one predominantly political and the other devoted to spiritual reform. "He participated in both as best he could," according to Jigyasu, but he identified himself more strongly with the latter as independence politics heated up. A consistently ideological recognition of the *ādi*-Hindu, we are told, guided this ascetic leader's movement, and its enunciation was held by his followers to be so original that he was compared to Marx. Jigyasu saw in it a basis for "original socialism," based on Indian ideas and values, run by Indians, and grounded in the spiritualism of Indic ascetics.

Some aspects of Achchutananda's ideology will complete our account (Jigyasu 1968b: 113–14):

1. I believe that God is only one and . . . formless . . . Neither is there any book of His; nor does he incarnate, nor is there any image of His . . .
2. I believe that I am an autochthon of Bharat, hence I am an *ādi*-Hindu . . . .
3. I believe that the religion of saints [*saṅton dā dharma*] is the original religion [*ādi dharma*] of Bharat; being full of humanism, it is beneficial to mankind. Spiritual experiences [*ātam-anubhava* – a favorite popular term of Achchūtānanda] of such ascetics as Sadashiva, Rshabhadeva, Mahavira, Buddha, Kabir, Ravidas, Dadu, Namadeva, and Tulsisaheb can deliver me . . . .
4. I believe that all human beings are equal, and brothers . . .; the feeling of high and low is an illusion. Humans become high and low by their own [individual] virtues and vices. Human heart alone is God's temple, hence to practice equality toward the entire humanity is the "supreme religion" [*paramadharma*].
5. I believe that giving up lust, greed, attachment . . . is one's [true] personal religion . . . .
6. I believe that according to the teachings of Kabir all the Brāhman's scriptures (*dharma gr̥ntha*) are based on selfishness, falsehood, and injustice . . . I will [therefore] never have our rites of birth, tonsure ceremony, marriage, and death performed by a Brāhman [priest].

The cultural import of this autochthonous radicalism, still being discussed in popular publications in Lucknow, can best be reproduced in terms of an illustrative list of the cultural theses that several contemporary Chamar literati and reformers in Lucknow continue to emphasize. Some of the points are straight repetitions of Achchutananda's ideology. I quote directly and in full from the Chamars' statements.

1. The Untouchables, the so-called Harijans, are in fact the "*ādi*-Hindu" (i.e., the original or the autochthonous Nagas or the Dasas of the North and the Dravidas of the South) of the subcontinent, and they are the undisputed, heavenly owners of Bharat.
2. All others are immigrants to the land, including the Aryans, who conquered the original populations not by valor but by deceit and manipulation of the whole society by usurping others' rights, subjugating the peace loving, and rendering the self-sufficient people indigents and slaves. Those who ardently believed in equality were ranked, and ranked lowest.
3. The Hindu and Untouchables have since always remained poles apart. They could never really come together in a major way, despite the best efforts of such reform movements as Bhakti, Arya Samaja, Sikhism, and Brahmo-Samaja. They remained as distinct as oil mixed in water.
4. The cobweb of Hindu scriptures, deities, incarnations, temples, and Brāhman priests is so intricate and pervasive that it has imprisoned the Hindu within his family and *jātis*, and consigned the Untouchable to the bottom. Since there have been no *true* exits in this cobweb – from Manu down to Gandhi, the Untouchable has to take the lead on his own. And this means that he has to examine the Hindu social tactics very closely to get his freedom.
5. The Hindus have suppressed and destroyed all critical literature produced by the Untouchable intellectuals from ancient times until recently. Hence, the Untouchable must start rebuilding his knowledge, moving carefully from the recent to the remote past. At present, one knows little about anything other than the Hindu's side of the story.
6. Marriage, commensality, occupation, *Gītā-Rāmāyaṇa*, and extended family are the five most important sacred domains where the Untouchables encounter maximum discrimination and resistance. The radical solution must therefore reject totally and exactly those reasons the Hindus accept and value.
7. To discriminate against Untouchables on the basis of (beef or) meat eating is an ancient trick of the Hindus for downgrading the *ādi*-Hindu. Such ploys should be clearly recognized and exposed by the available textual and historical evidence.

As a logically related need for the propagation of this knowledge, there also appeared publishing houses devoted to reform literature on the Untouchable's condition, refuting and rejecting the major pillars of traditional Hindu ideas and society (for examples of such publications, see the Bibliography). A book (Sagar 1973) recently involved in a legal case offers a "sociological" study. Written by a trained sociologist, it lists one hundred ancient, preindependence, and modern references to support the argument for the autochthonous status of the Untouchable. This book, incidentally, also contained two tongue-in-cheek testimonials by prominent Hindu functionaries of the Congress party and was dedicated to the renowned Indian Untouchable leader, Jagjivan Ram. In conclusion (pp. 272–6), among other things, Sagar asks his readers not to be taken in by "the Hindu's four Gs" – the *Gangā* (the sacred Ganges), *Gau* (the sacred cow), *Gāyatrī* (the sacred verse), and the *Gītā* (the sacred Hindu song of God). He lists six ideological features of the Hindu religious system (dharma) that should be rejected in order to establish the autochthonous argument: (1) belief in Hindu "theism" (*āstiktā*), and (ranked) hell and heaven; (2) Hindu ideas of (incomplete) renunciation and "spiritualism"; (3) the Hindu orders of *varṇa* and *jāti* (caste) ranking; (4) Hindu philosopohy based on fate and resignation; (5) Hindu practices of violent sacrifices and "rituals" (*karmakāṇḍa*); and (6) Hindu faith in karma orthodoxy and resultant "narrow-minded social views."

The seven cultural theses of the Lucknow Chamar literati and Sagar's six diagnostic cultural features converge but are not the same. Together, however, they offer a picture of what the Untouchable literati culturally plan to do to regain their autochthonous status. It can be shown from the Untouchable's standpoint that this cultural position is not simply an inversion of the Hindu's position but rather offers flexible platforms of political protest that could be used to express opposition or contradistinction or even ambiguity on some occasions.

With the preceding transitional picture of the Untouchable culture and its reforming ascetics, the first part of our discussion, the cultural structure of the Pariah ideology, is brought to a climax. As a radical cultural alternative is offered, an incipient transition is made toward organized protest, competition, and politics on the one hand, and an ideological commitment to individual equality and justice on the other. To disregard any part of this reformulation is to miss the entire significance of the Untouchable ideologist's contemporary exercise. This context of cultural radicalism is not to be dismissed as merely sociologically insignificant and improbable; it is, instead, a gathering and direct culmination of the work of those protest processes that have perhaps repeatedly waxed and waned with the Indian Untouchable over the centuries.

The cultural ideology of Achchutananda, even if it has a cogent social basis, is actually given varied social reception among the Lucknow Chamars. It might still be too radical for some, too mild for others, and even irrelevant for some others. Moderngani generally expressed all three views, while Baudhabagh was ideologically mild. Karampura, on the other hand, found Achchutananda's ideology either too radical or irrelevant. Such varied responses help show why a reformer and a politician need diverse political rhetoric, essentially to convince the majority of continuing social injustice. The reception of this rhetoric is also empirically uneven. If some view it as part of a genuine, all-out effort to blunt the discriminatory caste order, thus also matching and defeating today's Hindu thinker at his own game, others find it a hollow exercise, unless the Chamars really unite and commit themselves to reforming their own community first. Yet to be rhetorical is to be doing something; to publicly protest is to be increasingly serious in practice about one's aims.

Sociologically, the Lucknow Chamars demonstrated a generally patterned response to a radical alternative, depending both on where they stood socially and on their practical experiences, needs, and expectations. For example, those who were repeatedly mistreated at the hands of a caste Hindu and were unable to better their lot through regular networks of personal position, political influence, and social patronage generally became radical in their views. A bitter shoe-shop owner from Baudhabagh, who had lived near a big (25-foot-wide) open drain for years, observed:

> When flooded, this drain sweeps off an entire row of our shacks, killing some. It has repeatedly infected our water supply since a broken waterpipe runs through it. It always remains [for cleaning and repair] at the mercy of indifferent municipal workers on one side, and certain [fractious] local caste-Hindu politicians on the other.
>
> But nobody does anything for us, including even our own political leaders. We increasingly know what Achchutananda, Ambedkar, and Jigyasu talked about, and why. Nothing will change unless the entrenched caste-Hindu interests are uprooted. But this will happen only when we are united.

By comparison, in Modernganj, a better-off locality of the Lucknow Chamar, radicalism is appreciated verbally but with much less emotional edge and social immediacy. A well-paid railway engine driver observed:

> It will be good indeed to have those days come to us when social insult and discrimination will not come our way at all. But all the same we earn most ever and share our joys and sorrows among our own people, expecting little from the caste Hindus or politicians and doing little at their bidding. We know that they are ultimately after their own interests more than anybody else's . . . Despite the *ādi*–Hindu ideology of our reformer Achchutananda, about whom I have heard and read with appreciation, we just cannot change the whole world so quickly. Then, why should we? We are generally much better off than before and do not want to risk the present arrangement for an unknown upheaval. Instead, we want to improve slowly but surely.

Other wage earners in the same locality were passive; one reasoned: "I do not concern myself with these matters; I am busy earning my day-to-day livelihood and raising my family . . . [*apné kāma sé kāma*]." But a draftsman denied promotion at his office felt cheated and helpless. His reasoning was:

> Our own community is so divided that everybody is for his own safety and interests. Whom do I complain to? Who will hear? Rather, I stand the risk of offending my caste-Hindu superiors if I make too much of it with my own political leaders. All powerful people, whether Chamars or caste Hindus, work together among themselves to secure their own interests, and take care of their supporters.

An intellectual, a professor at the local university, who did not reside in any of the three localities but who was in close touch with them, responded, as expected, much more eloquently in a language of social reform. He lamented the ignorance of his community members, the opportunism of his political leaders, and the lack of commitment to social fairness among the educated caste Hindu. He professed Ambedkar's idea of Buddhist identity, confronting, if necessary, the caste Hindu to stop his techniques of "social subversion." He organized a reform society, wrote on social reform, and lectured on these issues as often as he could. "But after all, this is not the work for a lone voice," he reasoned. "Tell me, what more can I do?"

This response, which the radical ideology had begun to receive as I reached the Chamar intellectual, was readily popularized by the glib speeches of a Modernganj politician. He harangued the ethnographer's tape recorder to convince himself (and a few other locality members drawn to his high-pitched soliloquy from his front verandah) of how true and profound his advocacy of the Achchutananda and Ambedkar ideas for uplifting the Chamar community remained. Also, it was done as if to say that this was what he did best as a leader of the neighborhood. One of his sycophants capped it for him: "You have never said it any better."

However, despite the diverse reception given to radical reform, a general point was made: There is no doubt anymore that cultural radicalism is already integral to the self-definition of the contemporary Lucknow Chamar, and that given an appropriate circumstance, it could be translated into prolonged (even militant) protest to respond to any severe social stress or threat. But, over time and space, social radicalism remains variable. What most Chamars considered radical reform at the beginning of this century is today often commonplace and ready to be bypassed.

A relatively varied reception, interpretation, and significance of the radical ideology were also clear within the three Lucknow Chamar settlements. The cases of Modernganj, Baudhabagh, and Karampura were likened to "three glasses, one inside the other," according to the priest at the Ravidas temple (see chap. 7), where Modernganj was the outermost and socially most open neighborhood and Karampura the innermost one. The radicalism of Modernganj had resulted in, among other things, more school education, diverse modern occupations, better brick houses, and an active cluster of local leaders. More residents as a result read newspapers, discussed local, state, and national political affairs, and followed the fluctuating fortunes of the Untouchables in India. Their greater social awareness, in turn, translated into outgoing social expectations and relationships. Their attitude toward "Hindu injustice" showed disgust and impatience. News of violence against the Untouchable in any part of India would make many faces in the neighborhood anxious, tense, and angry. These emotions were repeatedly evident to me during my fieldwork. On such occasions, the Chamars spontaneously talked in groups about the news, especially during evenings. Some were angry, some despondent, and some scheming, but few totally indifferent or passive. The Modernganj resident, having received more from society, readily translated his radicalism into democratic social action – everyday activism at the work place, in the city streets, and in the neighborhood. Their radicalism was less bottled-up, its interpretation was activist, and its overt significance more directly tied to the goals of democratic civil rights.

By comparison, Baudhabagh's radicalism was vocal and involuted; its interpretation was inspired by religious antagonism (including Buddhist reform) but remained mired in social pessimism and political discord. Though its significance was evident for everyday practical issues, it went largely unrealized since the Chamars there bickered among themselves. A Baudhabagh Chamar summed it all up:

> We have a need for major change but feel helpless. We cannot bring it about ourselves because we are too quarrelsome and weak; others do not help us because they know we are weak and disunited. Still since we realize how badly we need the improvement, we feel suffocated and helpless, both at the same time. A reformist ascetic makes the conditions tolerable for many of the Baudhabagh Chamars. He gives them hope, though his opponents think that he only dilutes our resolve to do better.

Karampura, on the other hand, was socially isolated, traditionally passive, and politically neglected. Its radicalism was often limited to occasionally singing old songs in praise of Ambedkar (and even the traditional Hindu gods such as Hanuman and Bhairava). The interpretations of radicalism were, however, diversifying (especially with Karampura youth getting more education) and were being brought closer to the practical problems of Chamar life. Yet its social significance remained sporadic and remote. There was room seen for major improvements here but since the residents themselves did not consciously feel the need as acutely as did the Baudhabagh Chamars, the sharp sense of helplessness and suffocation was largely absent.

More generally, we may observe that the Chamar radical ideology often shows a transition to the mild position upheld by civilizational constraints. The ideology remains shy of radical political options; it also disallows easy ground to any alien political ideology and its values. Actually, a radical foreign ideology has yet to seriously influence the Untouchable movement at an all-Indian level. Ambedkar, no doubt, favored and set this course most recently. He decided to uphold the general civilizational constraints and let the indigenous cultural radicalism develop its way through the secular – economic, legal, and political – arenas of a democratic state. What it has meant is no less significant: The secular achievements of the Indian Untouchable must prove their *real* worth against his needed cultural emancipation from within. Otherwise, he would always feel robbed of the real significance of what he gains in the material world.

The Lucknow Chamars reflected this point in several different ways. An office employee from Moderngan j, for example, complained about the lack of social acceptance among caste Hindus of what the Chamars have achieved, and a hotel bearer criticized the self-deprecating attitude of his community members. The Chamars generally sought approval most from those quarters (and in those terms) where they had lacked it most – from their own (often fractious) peers and from the caste Hindu. A resident ascetic in Karampura exhorted his followers one day:

> Respect yourselves for what you really are and people will respect you. You will thus prove yourself equal to others. If you now have a bicycle while a caste Hindu has a scooter or a motorcycle, you may like to acquire the latter but it will not suffice, for you must also be sure of *your worth to yourself*. Only then will the Hindu change his attitude. But if you imitate him by buying the things he has in order to seek his approval, he will never give it.

Overview

This and the previous chapter trace some of the dimensions of a practical transition that the Lucknow Chamar, with the help of the ascetic reformer, All-Worker, tries to bring about for improving his daily life. There are two views to keep in focus in such an exercise, one external and the other internal. Externally, the democratic provisions of independent India are impinging more and more on the Lucknow Chamar, prompting and challenging him to reformulate his traditional cultural values as effectively as he can. As already indicated here (and to be followed up in later chapters), the Chamar is responding to this challenge in a more comprehensive manner as he "totalizes" himself. Despite all that can be said in favor of the entrenched Hindu caste order (and its ideology), the Chamar is consolidating and connecting himself socially. Variously overlapping and sharing a vastly pliable culture among themselves, the Chamars and the caste Hindus know that they can change now only in relation to each other. Chamars also increasingly realize that all significant change is slow change. But yet the depth and the reach of this slow change in either direction (i.e., toward the Brāhmans as well as the Chamars) may impress an observer; he cannot overlook the radically significant social trends initiated in the previous decades of this century.

Under an objective evaluation, therefore, both the caste Hindu and the Chamar are now involved in changing each other in Lucknow. Both are, it seems, engaged in a significant cognitive remapping and reevaluation in relation to each other and in the way they view Indian society at large. In such an exercise, for example, the ideal ascetic must first get translated into the worldly ascetic, and the latter into the routine, resident ascetic of Baudhabagh (cited earlier). The democratic urban ethos must strengthen the Chamar's equalitarian idealism, and the traditional cognitive processes of self-image and social (i.e., of caste and extracaste) evaluation must redirect themselves. The Lucknow Chamar finds himself in the middle of all these vital exercises, as does the caste Hindu. Both apprehend that this time much more is fundamentally changing than perhaps ever before, and both are displaying an increasing seriousness.

Based on the ethnographic span available to me, therefore, we will consider next how the Lucknow Chamar might be *silently* and *routinely* engaged in a cognitive remapping of himself and his everyday social conditions. To do so, we will elaborate on the practical side of the same exercise we have performed on the cultural reconstruction of the Untouchable's ideology. The same cognitive processes (e.g., articulation, identification, and evaluation and accountability) utilized earlier in structuring his ideology are now directed toward pragmatic and political issues of the Lucknow Chamar. More generally, these same processes may symbolize certain patterns of the Indian Untouchable's current thinking, willing, and action.

The basic inspiration for this quest is found, as some Chamar ideologists also recognize, in the revolutionary Indian cultural formulation *tata tvam asi* (roughly "Thou art that"; Mauss 1979: 76) or in *cogito ergo sum* (cf. Mauss 1979: 87–9), as a modern-educated Ambedkar would claim. The whole – ideal and practical – quest of the Chamar ideologist is finally about that deeply coded, inalienable "thinking" and "willing" that even the "lowest of the low" carry within them. The Chamar may wax and wane in the pursuit of these properties but would never be found without them. When the worldly Chamar ascetic turns toward the society with resolve for enkindling renewed social hope and optimism, he reasons with Schopenhauer, "It is only in reflection that to will and to act are different; in reality they are one" (quoted in Aiken 1956: 109). He seeks to generate within the ordinary Chamar a resolve for his own social welfare and tries to convert this resolve into individual and collective action. We saw both Achchutananda and Jigyasu doing so in their own ways. Both, however, ultimately worked to let the ordinary Chamar develop his *own* thinking and willing.

The thinking and willing we are referring to are not merely the speculative categories of moral philosophy or moral psychology (e.g., see Warnock 1978: 92–106) but are, as we have been showing, a matter of anthropological "description" and verification (in Wittgenstein's sense; see Warnock 1978: 103–6). They represent notions of willed expression, choice, evaluation, decision making, and responsibility. We described aspects of these through the contemporary Chamar's formulations and expressions about self-identity; we will now examine how the same properties might be carried forward, modified, or dropped in everyday social life. The hypothesis, at this point of the inquiry, is indeed simple and direct: If an underprivileged social group thinks and wills itself in the way the preceding ideological discussion shows, it must also correspondingly influence the domains of practical action in some similarly observable manner.

This means that if there are moral strategies representing the Chamar's willing and thinking, we must now find if there are also not parallel practical strategies within the social domain. Fundamentally, it means to discover the translation of the moralists' *ought-to-be* in the context of what socially *is* and what is *feasible*. It means to understand the messages exchanged between the moralist's injunctions "to enkindle" and "to instruct," and the politician's measured efforts to implement the socially possible (Toulmin 1970: 198–9, 223–4). The Chamar must also fare, therefore, through a range of "market" relations (to recall our earlier economic analogue) in order to achieve specific goals that are profitable as well as significant.

7. Articulation of the practical ethos

A striking current issue to which the ordinary Lucknow Chamar repeatedly returns is the diverse "push and pull" he encounters in his everyday life. The society in which he lives is pervaded by what we shall call a "pragmatic ethos" (*kāmbanāu māhaul, upayogī dṛṣṭikoṇa*), which confronts him with some old, but many more new, varieties of social, economic, and political strains.

> Everybody has to run to so many different places, meet so many people, and spend so much time understanding what each wants from the other. If I want something from them, I want to know what they want from me in return. Everybody is after something. But when many people want the same thing, there is bound to be a scramble, a competition [*hoṛa*], even a confrontation [*tū-tū maiñ-maiñ*]. When there are more people and all, whether it is a thing or money, or position, want it more than ever before, life is spent chasing and dreaming and arguing about what I want and what I get. We have to face all of this every day as Chamars. The society has to yield more for me, my family members, and my community. We are weak. But as we get more, we want more.

This was the comment of a shoemaking Ravidas Chamar from Modernganj, an illiterate but a leader and chief of his group (*tāta*), who was remarkably articulate and observant. In testimony, he showed me a letter of commendation from a Lucknow deputy commissioner who had by chance talked with him at some length after buying a pair of new shoes from him in 1964.

This comment provides a good entry into the nature of the pragmatic ethos and its central issues. What this Ravidas Chamar was saying could also be interpreted in more general terms. For example, this ethos essentially highlights practical goals, relations, expressions, and values, and is about how to aspire toward, try for, and achieve a desired social goal. It includes developing or adopting appropriate practical tactics, and an application of one's social experience and priorities in the context of one's specific circumstance. The pragmatic ethos does not deny one's personal or group identity, as this Ravidas Chamar implies, but demands socially flexible, new uses of the Chamar initiative.

Though the idea of the "pragmatic view" may lie in the classical Indic notion of *sakāmakarma* (or *kāmyakarma*, "action with desire"; the opposite category is *niṣkāmakarma*, "action without desire"), the ethos is particularly held to be an intensifying, ever-diversifying "gift of the modern society" (*ādhunika samāja kī déna*). It is seen to be increasingly unmanageable, and hardly simply what the classical idea was. It has now become a dominant social preoccupation, bringing into play the conscious processes of social calculation, tactic, judgment, and management of one's economic and political resources.

What all of this means to the ordinary Chamar is that he must accommodate to more complex and new social forces. The selected illustrations we will consider here will show that the ordinary Chamar's biggest problem (along with the caste Hindu's) is to manage this ethos and to respond to it in a way distinctly advantageous to himself. An old Jaiswar chauffeur from Moderngani observed:

> There is no school for training ourselves to meet the challenges of modern times, only the hard knocks of our own failure. But it is effective; it works. My two sons, one in school and the other in college, are better prepared than I was. I have helped them as best as I could. Yet they must always remain alert to safeguard their own interests, because there are always others also seeking the same goal. Getting any job done, even a simple one, is becoming more and more difficult. There are no simple ways [*sīdhé-sādhé-tarīké*] left to get things done in this society.

Specifically, such comments demonstrate that the pragmatic ethos demands management by the urban Chamar on a daily basis. Like everybody else in the same city, they must understand what is going on, what depends on political influence in different ways, and how to get what they want in *their* social circumstance. They must continuously think, talk, share, and act on whatever they learn from their own and others' daily social experiences. They must become articulate, comprehending and expressing readily their own side of the story. We will refer to this demand of the pragmatic ethos by a cognitive process that many of the Lucknow Chamars displayed, that is, articulateness or (extensionally) *articulation*. Like the Ravidas shoemaker and the Jaiswar chauffeur, who have been relatively successful practitioners of this "art," the deprived distinctly need to connect values, speech, need, action, and impulse to their social condition. Articulation, this way, also symbolizes a comprehensive sociocultural force for encouraging a redefinition of the Chamars' self-identity. They develop this force, as we have indicated, within the larger context of their sociocultural resources, their cultural ideology, and their allies: the Untouchable ascetic on the one hand, and secular Indian democracy, on the other.

This articulate expression has led many Chamars to realize that wealth, position, influence, power, politics, clever speech, and social unity work in the society as always, but are increasingly in short supply and hard to retain. The old system is changing, they find, because the earlier values (e.g., of promise, patronage, and honesty) are neither predictably located in the same quarters of the society, nor do they work with as much certainty as before. This change results because more intricate but fewer commitment-producing motivations enter in one's life. Moreover, there is greater social competition. The Chamars readily recalled experiences, therefore, where they had failed even when they had an influential supporter (just because the other side had a more influential one), or when stronger political strings were pulled, more money spent, and so on.

They also realized that money, social position, political influence, and the reformist inspiration worked only together, not singly, and that this mix should vary according to the social situation. For example, "I have noticed that these [factors] work in a certain mix on one occasion but not on another. This makes things more difficult. The world would have been so simple if the government simply did what it said on paper for our betterment, and if we felt satisfied with what the government did for us." This was the observation of a state government employee, who, as a Chamar, had been appointed to his job under a quota reserved for the "Scheduled Castes" (an Indian government term for "listing" depressed groups to support them in education and employment). He had recently failed, however, despite his political connections, to get a due promotion. A caste Hindu had superseded him.

The "awakened" ascetic

Let us return at this point to the Untouchable ascetic for his role in the coordination and comprehension of the Untouchable's pragmatic ethos. We will consider him as a worldly ascetic to see how he might approach a few pragmatic issues himself, and offer an explanation of the changing society to his followers in some proximate as well as ultimate terms. We recall at this point that the Indian ascetic has played a prominent part in the long spans of Indian social and religious history, as is documented by others (e.g., Ghurye 1964). His diverse sociocultural journey continues to shape those Chamar ascetics found in the three Lucknow settlements. The Chamar ascetics readily subscribe to a number of qualities of the Indic ascetic. For example, that there are "right" and "left" ritual pathways for the ascetic; and that they could also be clothed or naked, active (*vairāgī*) or passive (*udāsī*), Absolutist (*advaitavādina* or *nirguṇī* or *śūnyavādina*) or polytheist (*saguṇī*), and militant (e.g., Niranjanī *akhāṛā*) or nonmilitant. They might also organize openly or secretly, and launch cooperative or confrontational reform movements. They may invert renunciation into indulgence (e.g., the Kapālikas) "to increase their spiritual powers," and fight in and out of the courts to accumulate gold, land, and buildings on behalf of the divine. They also impressively parade, protest, and revolt to make their collective presence felt in the society. In a general view, therefore, the ascetic must impress us with his large role within Indian society. He eminently shows how he has indeed been a boundary-crashing and individuating presence *within* the society, though he stands outside it.

The Lucknow Chamar (or the "low-caste" or the non-*traivarṇa*) ascetic draws on the preceding features as he approaches the contemporary pragmatic ethos. Adapting, frugal, and improvising, this ascetic himself is seldom insulated from the social constraints of the Chamar's pragmatic ethos. Moreover, his clientele has shrunk in some places (e.g., Modernganj) and lapsed into "many stingy and unstable followers" in others (e.g., Karampura). If he stays too long at one place, he faces a cooling hospitality. If he asks often of his followers, he encounters dubious, even suspicious faces. Yet he knows that he actually can impose upon them for his sustenance because he can beg as a moral right. He can receive without giving, and yet maintain or enhance his rank. But he is most often adept and alert in oral reciprocation: He blesses often and tries to help others through his moral and spiritual presence. For example, a reformist (or "awakened") ascetic would readily provide social guidance to the Karampura or Baudhabagh Chamars on how they should meet the challenge of the changing society; the regular ascetic would cater to the devout, perform certain devotional rituals (*bhajan*, *kīrtana*, *pūjā*), and dispense charms and amulets against sickness and disabilities.

The distinction between the "awakened" and regular (*sādhāraṇa*) ascetics is significant for the Chamar. The first stands for radical cultural (*ādi*-Hindu) and political (legal, social, and economic) reform of the Chamar, and of the Indian Untouchable in general. He insists on making the equalitarian individual the basis for all his social reform in India. He generally shares the cultural and political leaders' goals and readily speaks his thoughts on the matter. Unless reticent and secluded by choice, he would most often have a sort of local (*mohallā*) following, would remain in contact with some local political leaders, and would guide them, directly or indirectly, through his discourses (*pravacana*) on major issues. If he is a Ravidasi or Kabirpanthi or Buddhist monist, he is also obviously "opposed" to the caste order, distancing himself from Hindu hierarchical tradition. He is committed to complete emancipation of the Untouchable (*achchūtoddhāra*). Yet if politicians, political favors, greed, and fame or position make him falter, he may fail to realize the spiritual ideal but will still exert a definite moral and political influence.

The proximate and the ultimate in a Ravidas temple

The regular Chamar (or the low-caste) ascetic helps the ordinary Chamar start and direct a form of self-questioning. He also keeps the ordinary Chamar on an even keel. He cannot confront the awakened or reformist ascetic directly any more than he can resist him. And if the regular ascetic finds fault with the radical reformer, it is only to advise his clientele to go slow, lest one lose more than one gains. He often talks about the Chamar's precarious pragmatic ethos.

> Having a place to live, food to feed your children, and clothes to cover all of us with are the things we want foremost. If it is difficult for the caste Hindu, who run the society, to manage these minimum requirements, it is not going to be any easier for us, particularly if we challenge the Hindu outright, just as some others [ascetics] demand. We actually have to encounter, appease, and cajole the caste Hindus in a hundred different ways to secure our share. Kerosene oil today, sugar tomorrow, grain the day after, take up most of your time once you come back from wage work. These things are hard to obtain these days [since they are in short supply and high priced], and I think we should be grateful to Paramātma [God] that we can get some. If we offend the caste-Hindu grain dealer and the ration shopkeeper [i.e., the government-controlled commodity dealers], will the radical reformer or a political leader come and supply us with these daily necessities? Who will lose? I do not deny the need for reform but I advise caution and moderation.

This comment was offered in one of the several informal discussion groups I encountered during my fieldwork. The exchanges in such chance meetings offer us an idea of how different cognitive processes of the contemporary Untouchable work to influence certain immediate as well as ultimate goals. Let us return to the setting and the group's exchange under consideration.

The ascetic making the previous comment was sixty years old. This self-proclaimed devotee of "the incarnate Rama of Ravidas" was sitting on a wooden platform (*takhat*) inside the left verandah of the Lucknow Ravidas temple (located outside the three Chamar settlements) in July of 1978. In his audience were a *khādī*–clad primary school teacher, two young visiting (reformist) ascetics from nearby villages, a Ravidas Chamar priest from the temple, and a shoe-shop owner from Baudhabagh (in addition to the ethnographer). The group had assembled entirely by chance during a long and hot summer afternoon. The primary school teacher was there to inquire about a political function to be held soon in the temple-attached primary school, where Ambedkar and Ravidas were to be eulogized in the presence of a state government minister. An introductory speech was finalized, the temple courtyard was cleaned, and the students had practiced their welcoming song. All was necessary: The minister had been approached for financial help for the temple and its school.

The teacher was practically living there those days, aspiring to become a local political leader; he had "hundreds of things" on his mind. The two younger ascetics were there as passersby to shelter themselves from the heat, and the shoe-shop owner had come to introduce the ethnographer to the temple priest. As part of his job, the priest was there, making sure that all those who entered the temple bowed before the statue of Ravidas, ate the sacred offerings (*prasād*), sprinkled and sipped the consecrated water, and dropped a coin in the collection box. If one wished to approach and touch the feet of Ravidas in the sanctuary of the temple, the priest would stare at the person for a few moments and decide, oftentimes in the affirmative. The older,

Rama-worshiping ascetic (quoted earlier) was there that day from Ayodhya at the behest of his disciple, the temple priest.

The two young ascetic reformers, though actually trying to doze off for a while, had started that afternoon's conversation in response to a laconic social observation that the life of the Untouchable had not improved: It was as hard as ever. The teacher had interjected to object to this flatly pessimistic conclusion, pointing out how much more was now available to the group through education, employment, and government protection. Although he wanted to cite his experiences, the shop owner was trying to cut him short to make his point. However, one of the two reformers had loudly countered: "We need radical reforms, nothing less. A festering abscess needs radical surgery. The caste system and the Hindu rituals are the source of this abscess; they must be removed. If we were not disunited and timid, we would have already found ourselves in earnest just where our seers and thinkers wanted us to be."

The older ascetic had responded to this assertion in his opening statement, addressing himself to "realities of life." But he did not stop before making a few more points.

For example, the true ascetic (*saccā sādhū*) has to be for universal welfare (*viśva kalyāṇa; samasta jana kalyāṇa*), including that of the "misguided Hindu." The ascetic must judge and evaluate himself most, for society deposits its conscience into his, making him the watchpost of both ultimate and proximate human goals. His protest therefore could only be for spiritually and morally sound reasons (including social inequality, suppression, inequity, unfair means, etc.), and moderate, for it cannot be directed to harm anyone. He could not quite see how an ascetic can be a ruthless politician, for one could either uphold (the aim of) universal service or subvert other's interests to one's own advantage through political tricks. He contended: "Achchutananda, as ascetic first and reformer next, was moderate *in action*, though a radical thinker. Jigyasu was an asceticlike householder, but no politician. In comparison, Gandhi was an asceticlike householder and true politician."[1]

The young reformers (one was thirty and the other thirty-five; both were literate and had traveled in northern India) were, however, not persuaded. They saw the increasing necessity of injecting practical radicalism into the pragmatic ethos. The older of the two responded:

> We cannot compromise or acquiesce our main goals for kerosene oil, sugar, and grain. We must assert our rights and viewpoints even if it means confronting the caste Hindu, and some personal hardships. Moderation works only when the other side is not unreasonable. If this aim demands becoming a politician, I shall not shirk it. A long-denied moral order of equality has to establish itself in this land of the ascetics. It is the supreme goal from which even the leaders have gone astray under varied pretexts, giving victory to the opposed group. The significance of asceticism is downgraded by compromising one's spiritual ideals, by timid and half-hearted pronouncements to one's followers, and by ignoring [our responsibility to raise] a whole tough generation [of stout heart and mind] right from the mother's lap. We

can reach where laws and politicians cannot – the families and hearts of our own people.

The school teacher (aged fifty-five) now found the young reformer's position untenable, for he considered it both impractical and simpleminded. Though a radical himself in his early years ("when Ambedkar was charging us up and Jigyasu was locally very prominent"), he had mellowed and sobered with experience.

The hard realities of life appeared before me in the form of raising a family, of finding a job that will give me a secure future. We could not feed ourselves on impractical ideals. This *khādī* [handwoven cloth] became [a symbol of] compromise with practical issues, and a gate pass to connect myself with sympathetic politicians, whether a caste Hindu or a Muslim or an Untouchable. A politician is nobody's friend but his own. I know, in the heat of struggle for power and privilege, he spares nothing, and nobody. You [pointing toward the older reformer ascetic] do not know what it means to be a viable politician these days. If you were to be one, you would have to break every vow of your order. An ordinary politician vouches for the ideals he knows he cannot keep but professes it to barter it for some more immediate goal – often a position of power or authority he does not yet have. He compromises ideals and bends ethics at every turn. He hides most what he is really after. If he carries an image of austerity, it is often to gather wealth . . . [After Gandhi] austerity has become a formula for justifying one's own pursuit of comfort, power, and wealth. He is practical, and listens only to those practical in his terms.

A similar point was also made by the two ascetic reformers, but in a different context: They contended that worldly power did not stay with a real ascetic but *only* with those politicians who feign to be asceticlike. Therefore, those very few real ascetics who aspire to be political reformers fail because they find it tempestuous, devoid of morals, and full of worldly allurements. But these "soiling stretches" had to be waded through, the young ascetics asserted, if radical reform was to be brought about; there was no other effective way at present. They emphasized the ascetic roots (most recently a la Gandhi) of democratic politics in India, and if something was in disrepair, it should be repaired, rather than discarded (or accepted).

The school teacher and the two reforming ascetics had touched at this stage the discontent of the illiterate shoemaker, who found the three of them only a lot of talk. The young reformers had zeal but little more. The school teacher was like any community-failing politician, whereas the older ascetic was realistic but had just about surrendered hope. At this point the temple priest smiled and rose to make offerings of sweets to Ravidas; a devotee had brought them at about half past four that afternoon. The shoemaker conceded he might be rude but asked the two reformers, the older ascetic, and the school teacher to come to his neighborhood (Baudhabagh) to help his neighbors secure better maintenance of their drain-ravaged locality. Could they influence the municipal authorities? Could the ascetics help them secure a cleaner water supply, rather than a "purer soul?" He commented:

I can confront a caste Hindu for his mistreatment and silence him. I do so within my shop. But my community reformers refuse to accept their failures; they cannot be silenced. Their hopes and words for a make-believe reform sustain them; take these away and they must either castigate you or melt into nothing. [This was the same informant who had once rebuked an ascetic reformer in his locality.] I have a big picture of Baba Saheb, and of Buddha. They still do much more for me [than] what you try to do only secondhand.

The temple priest now spoke: "You are at your old game, putting people down. It is not good; do not do it." The older ascetic had found the shoemaker not only harsh but an "unbeliever" (for he guessed that he was a Buddhist, which he actually was). The school master had inquired about the names of the political leaders of the shoemaker's locality in order to influence them (but he had in fact done nothing). The two younger ascetics had promised to come to him and unite the people for their own reform. They had not done so, however, until the middle of 1980. The illiterate shoemaker, the mild Buddhist (as he described himself), was most impressive to the assembly.

The final comment was, however, again from the older ascetic:

Like it or not, we [i.e., the Untouchable ascetics] are all you really have as your own for bringing the worldly and the spiritual together. We are the sentinel of your heritage and hope. The Brāhman can never be yours. We may be neither Ravidas Saheb nor Achchutananda, but we sacrifice our lives to keep their presence alive. We may not be magnetizing leaders like Baba Saheb but still help you remember his banner through the turmoil of the everyday world. We may flounder but are not useless. We are an anchor for your soul and face. We have failings because our ideals are so high, and you always expect so much from us. We will not come and mend your water supply, though this may be uppermost in your mind at present. It will go away. But we offer you the will to overcome the root cause of such troubles – learning to stand up to claim your rightful place within the society. This will keep the essence of what you are secure, and you will do better in getting even kerosene oil, sugar, and grain. Assert yourself. Our presence should assure you that there will appear not only other exemplars like Ravidas, Kabir, and Ambedkar in the future, but we will not let you rest easy without doing better in this as well as the other world.

The shoemaker, rising to leave, quipped to the ethnographer: "I told you I could not silence my own people." Just before leaving, I went to bow before the smiling Ravidas statue. The shoemaker stared but did not ask me if I had found his introduction satisfactory; he simply left agreeing to another appointment with me.

The preceding narrative offers an aspect of the articulation of the pragmatic ethos. It demonstrates how the same informant (e.g., the old ascetic) might formulate his message by raising or lowering, and pushing back and forth, the radical–nonradical, ideal–practical, ascetic–householder, symbolic–concrete, and otherworldly–worldly cultural categories. The ascetic proceeds by articulating them in such a way that difference, diversity, contrariness, and controlled opposition are allowed to weave a host of culturally significant messages. The pragmatic ethos is after all a composition of all such messages and their continual exchange in a contextually meaningful manner. In everyday life, such a process is constantly going on, for although imperfect, incomplete, and indeterminate, it is always indispensable.

Actually, if there were a perfect cultural articulation to which a people could hold, it would still invite imperfect interpretations when it passed into social currency. For example, if nirvana, *śūnya* (vacuity), and self-realization (*átmasākṣātakāra*) were to be the absolute constructs, they still could not be routinely discussed but only their imperfect interpretations. An educated Baudhabagh reformer once remarked:

> It is just the same way as with the *Ātman* [i.e., the uncontaminated Self; the basis of the equalitarian individual]. You cannot directly discuss it but only the interpretation it receives among ourselves. And if these interpretations help make it immanent within the society, as they in fact do, its properties of sameness [*samāntā*], equality [*samatā*], and indivisibility [*akhaṇḍatā*] become our [i.e., the Untouchable thinker's] social goals. If the Brāhman threw over us a caste net [i.e., *jāla* of *varṇa* and *jāti*] by dividing up the *Puruṣa* [the primordial Being], the *Puruṣa*'s indivisibility lets us dissolve the same net at its source.

Such concern with the ideal at this point helps us indicate how it is made a recurrent theme of transition even while articulating everyday pragmatic concerns. Actually, it made a Brāhman informant retort, "The Untouchables discuss *ātman* like carrots and cucumbers of the everyday world and insist on its imperishability and individuality for their vested social interests." A general point was repeatedly evident in such verbal exchanges: The Chamar thinker would usually approach a Brāhmanic principle or position at a commensurate level to criticize it. A spiritual statement would draw out a spiritual argument; an intellectual position, an intellectual reformulation; and a social idiom, a social critique. But equally often, he would also connect his argument to the definite goal of social reform. For example, the Chamar thinker's aim in emphasizing the indivisibility of the "soul" is usually to stake a claim for undivided moral equality first, and social and political equality immediately afterward. In this way, the Untouchable cannot be made the social remainder, "a lesser soul."

As a part of the pragmatic ethos of independent India, quite a few Chamars had also noticed changes in the traditional positions of the Brāhman, the raja, and the ascetic. Concentrating readily on the first rather than the second, ordinary Chamar householders commented at length on the cultural degeneration and dissipation of the orthodox Brāhman. Some of the Chamars' observations were as follows: The Brāhman encounters waves of dispersed but definite social resistance in a democratic society, and thus is forced to examine and modify himself more and more. He now has to openly compete in order to achieve those social privileges and positions that he could traditionally assume. If a politician, he must work with (and capture the votes of) a large number of people, not just castes. An image of the raja, in comparison, appears in more diverse guises, and is actually encountered more often than before. A Brāhman wants to be a powerful politician in order to be a "raja." An erstwhile ruler (i.e., a previous prince), on the other hand, wants to be a saintly politician because that way he could still remain a de facto ruler. To be a public official is also be to a kind of raja. Hence, an Untouchable politician or official also usually wants to prove that he is like a raja. This way he proves to himself and to his people that he now can be socially what he could not be before. The Chamar finds, therefore, small, self-imposing rajas all around. A Chamar teacher observed: "Now nobody wants to be anything else, because being a raja is to be rich and free. It is to feel powerful and superior, with a sense of social approval. Leaders want to be rajalike leaders. But this way the motto of service before self is also conveniently forgotten; self-interest rather than altruism guides these puny rajas. Ironically, such rajas now reside within the Untouchable leaders."

Simultaneously, the ascetic is also found under conditions of decline and neglect. He is declining because, in the Chamar's view, the ascetic neglects his true spiritual pursuit and the society grows increasingly suspicious and doubtful of his moral integrity. The ascetic, not unlike the Brāhman, however, is also trying to assume, as the Chamar noticed, new forms, positions, and functions. A genuine ascetic is still considered the supreme spiritual and moral guide for the majority. He is authentic; the Brāhman is not. He is *more* reliable, even when imperfect, than the Brāhman can ever be. A thirty-five-year-old office clerk from Modernganj observed: "A true ascetic can work with gods, even like one of them, and a Brāhman priest can only appease the divine. Between the two, I could be sure only about the ascetic's intentions." Replacement of Brāhman priests for domestic rituals was repeatedly brought up in such a context. When a Brāhman was not available, a reformist Chamar householder engaged either an appropriate ascetic or performed the rituals himself. I came across a few such cases in Modernganj and Baudhabagh, but these were still infrequent.

As in other matters, Modernganj showed a diverse range of interrelationships with the Brāhman priest. In an extreme case, a whole marriage ceremony was performed without the help of a Brāhman priest. But other residents disputed the claim since a subsequent ceremony was performed in Hardoi district and the claim that the Brāhman priest was absent could not be verified. However, this family of an educated, reformist Chamar was well known in Modernganj for its unconventional ways. On the occasion of his niece's (younger brother's daughter) marriage, the householder had brought an Untouchable "priest" from his native village. The *mohallā* residents repeatedly corroborated the information that he himself performed all small rites and rituals, including the recital of *Satyanārāyaṇa Kathā*, the worship of gods and goddesses during festivals, and the birth rites of his sons and daughters. He sometimes hesitated to do the rituals alone, however, when they concerned a serious illness or death. In the latter context, a Brāhman priest was often considered indispensable because "my old mother insists," as this Chamar reformer conceded. A serious illness also prompted other Moderngani Chamars to explore alternative ritualists, including the Brāhman priests, the tantrics, the exorcists, and the astrologers. However, one almost always approached a Brāhman priest with doubt and a critical eye. Unqualified submission to him was becoming rarer.

Baudhabagh, in comparison, was more clearly polarized. A few (five out of twenty-five) Chamar households had given up on the Brāhman priest. All rites and festivals were performed without him. But they did make exceptions when acute distress, deadly disease, or prolonged misfortune was encountered. The Brāhman priest and his remedies were tried in desperation. A Brāhman priest had proved efficacious with one of these families, however, winning it back into his influence. The rest of the households were divided into two groups: those (twelve) who did get all of their major life-cycle rituals performed by a Brāhman priest, and those (eight) who had either substituted, deleted, or attenuated the Brāhman-supervised rituals, incorporating instead the rites prescribed by resident ascetics. An unqualified and exclusive dependence on the Brāhman priest was absent among all the twenty-five households.

Karampura, located at the urban fringe, and with a significant traditional rural influence, clearly reaffirmed the traditional position of the Brāhman priest, especially among the older Chamars (i.e., forty-five and older). Except when a "learned" pundit was required, the Brāhman priests were invariably drawn from the nearby rural areas for different rites of passage, and for all the routine annual rites and festivals. The younger priests were less satisfactory to the old Chamars, for "they were more and more into money-making schemes, and less into sacred learning and pious living." The younger Karampura Chamars were, at the same time, moving away from the traditional arrangement. They distrusted the urban Brāhman priest as well as the pundit, and criticized all Brāhman priests from the villages. Still, they would let them perform major rituals, with or without a subsidiary role for the local ascetics. Among the households intensively studied in this community, though none had totally barred the Brāhman priest, he was being increasingly substituted for by the ascetics in domestic and festive rituals. Rural priests and calendrical agricultural rituals were deleted as urban employment claimed more time and changed priorities.

In summary, the Untouchable, the ascetic, and the Brāhman are so positioned that no one is a total opposite or a simple complement of the other two, whether it is the Brāhman juxtaposed to the Untouchable, or the Untouchable to the ascetic, or the ascetic to the Brāhman. Controlled cultural antagonism and social dependence characterize the three in relation to each other. This is perhaps a civilizational pattern of articulation that the pragmatic ethos keeps modifying. Only the most radical reformer or politician wants to snap it altogether, whereas the moderate ideologist shows his preference for working within this pattern (see Part I). However, as the ordinary Chamar finds the ascetic's reprieve and repose less comforting, and the Brāhman's social umbrage and antagonism more cynical and less bearable, he strains for faster social change.

Moderation and mediation

The Lucknow Chamar must therefore learn to articulate more diverse social concerns – whether immediate or remote. He must learn to subdue competition and conflict inherent in the practical ethos. We may find that some of these are readily mediated; others are not. Mediation, as a part of the process of social moderation, normally involves both moral and material forces. Mediation could be complete or incomplete, but its general logic remains committed to negotiate wide differences and diversities, and to reconcile, directly or indirectly, various conditions of potential or actual conflict. Moderation does not always result in mediation, however, since moderation is a far more general and pervasive process for self and society in India. It is a part of the Indian's life ethic. Mediation is integral to moderation; it could, by context, remain either superficial or deep, or succeed or fail for a period.

The management of the practical ethos is a multisided activity, bringing into focus household members in different combinations, and moderating and mediating a whole range of conditions, contexts, and cases. The ways to secure food, clothing, housing, education, and employment, and to combat sickness, constitute the nucleus of the Chamar's pragmatic ethos. (Popularly, it is called the *nona-téla-lakṛī-kī-fikar*.) Since any responsible Chamar householder is expected to worry about these matters as a part of his daily life, his concerns with pragmatic ethos persist. The Chamar's successes as well as difficulties in such matters reflect the changing pragmatic ethos. A series of simple-to-complex pictures emerges from the clusters of ethnographic cases encountered here. If we read these side by side (and then in each other's terms), they involve a range of pragmatic forces that the Lucknow Chamars coordinate among themselves.

Case Cluster I

> A sixty-five-year-old widow in Baudhabagh, living alone near the *mohallā*'s large drain, bought fuel and food with the wages she earned from winnowing wheat at a nearby grain shop. Yet she needed help from her daughter and son-in-law for buying rice and kerosene oil from the government-run "control shops." Often she obtained wheat from the grain merchant either as part of her wages or as a gift on certain festivals and ceremonial occasions. The

woman's husband had been a converted Buddhist; he had deleted most of the customary rites in his own house. After his death, however, the widow had revived some of them. She found her husband's conversion inauspicious but instructive. "It made me self-reliant," she observed. "My husband had proved that as poor Chamars we neither had to beg nor borrow if we decided to use our own two hands. We developed a sense of self-respect and I shall retain it as long as I live. He was no less than a guru; others looked up to him." Her husband's social contacts were still helpful: She bought some clothes from a neighborhood cloth shop at low rates because the merchant had sympathized with her husband's views on social reform. She also received some used clothing from a Rastogi family living two furlongs away on a main road. Outside her neighborhood, in her spare time she gathered scraps, cow dung, packing paper, and sawdust from a sawmill to use as cooking fuel. The available kerosene oil was sometimes insufficient for lighting even her two small lamps at night.

But then her practical needs were never only hers. Her daughter's family, being nearby and large, was on her mind in various ways. She would forgo lighting her lamps some nights to let the daughter have two extra bottles of kerosene oil every month. The four schoolchildren (out of seven) needed it for their studies; the daughter's husband, a shoe-shop owner, had recently bought with pride a kerosene stove for cooking, especially when friends or relatives visited. But to conserve kerosene oil, the widow would also gather some cooking fuel for her daughter's family. The Rastogi family, once in a while, also gave her, on its own initiative, used children's clothing. Her daughter reciprocated by getting medicine for the widow's asthma every week from a homeopathic doctor; her son-in-law thatched the roof of her house alternate years and whitewashed it every eighteen months or so.

Case Cluster II

A young couple (man twenty-six, woman nineteen) of Karampura managed their household with difficulty in early 1980, since the man, a seasonal painter and wage laborer, had been unemployed for the past three consecutive months. To support their three small children and the husband's widowed mother, the wife (again pregnant) had begun selling green vegetables at a street corner in the city. She started by taking vegetables on credit in the morning and paying off the debt every evening. Her business brought in two to four rupees in profit every day, sufficient to buy food (essentially wheat flour, some rice – her husband did not eat without rice – and *arhar dāla*) and fuel for the evening meal. But because her earnings did not let her stock any food, the family lived from day to day. On several occasions, they ate only the leftovers of the previous night. Once the vegetable stall failed to realize a profit for two consecutive days, which resulted in skipping main meals at home. Under such circumstances, the household had three alternatives: subsisting on snacks bought from hawkers, going to the husband's elder brother's house (located two lanes away) to eat, or sending the children (alone) to her mother's place in Moderngan j. Several times the two brothers quarreled and the younger brother would miss a meal rather than go to his brother's kitchen to eat. The widow had no problem; she ate wherever there was food. However, she would also often insist that her younger son's family not go without food.

Since she was fonder of her younger daughter-in-law, the older one felt neglected, and yet the mother-in-law imposed on her kitchen as a right.

A point of friction between the two brothers was their different self-images and attainments in life. The elder brother, an employee in a major pharmaceutical firm, considered himself at the opposite pole. He was educated, lived within his means, cultivated friends at prestigious places, and viewed himself as a "reformer" of his community. He claimed his father's mantle and maintained regular contact with his father's reformist guru, who resided in a village three miles away. Though his wife had a bad temper, she managed the family well. Their three children never lacked food, clothing, and schooling. He suspected (and it was true) that his younger brother had lately begun to drink. He complained that his mother had spoiled him and chained him to fate (karma), stars (*graha*), and gods (*devatā*). He regarded his younger brother as a spoiled person who was unable to hold on to his job and who increasingly neglected his family responsibilities.

He had tried to help his brother find suitable employment, especially since his guru had urged him, and he himself had wanted to reform him. But it was to no avail. His brother had run away from work unannounced, which was embarrassing because he then felt he had let his guru as well as some influential friends down. It was ironic, he thought, that a reformer's son could not be reformed, and would remain so poor as to go hungry. The mother had taken her younger son to astrologers and religious shrines of Śiva and Bhairava, but with no improvement. Her son had maximum faith in the stars, however. An astrologer had told him that things would improve only after three years, not earlier. He bided his time, taking all difficulties in stride.

His wife, coming from a better-off family in Moderngamj, had pleaded with him to accept help from her father, but he refused. It was beneath their dignity for both the mother and the son. His brothers-in-law had ridiculed him for his state and had threatened to take their sister back home. His father-in-law had written him off by remarking that he was a disgrace to the name of his father. But his mother-in-law often shielded him from such desperate outbursts.

Case Cluster III

The "photographer's lane" in Modernganj, actually a cluster of five houses in a dead-end lane, offered some further properties of the pragmatic ethos shared across households. The Chamar photographer, fifty-four years old, was one of the most prominent neighbors, with his flourishing training studio. He had trained four lower-caste and six Chamar youths to become roadside photographers. Of the ten, four had done very well; one was living in the same lane. The photographer's other neighbors were an aspiring locality leader, a government-office peon, a clerk in the Food Corporation of India (FCI), and an old shopkeeper living alone. The photographer was popularly known as the "silent reformer." He gave youngsters a prestigious skill that served them for life; he did so unpretentiously and without lectures. He knew some prominent photographers in the city and utilized these contacts well. His two sons were educated and were at present employed in Kanpur; his daughter was married and lived in old Lucknow.

The photographer represented moderation and mediation in the lane, whereas the aspiring leader advocated radicalism. A politically active student in college, this leader had just started as an errand boy in a major hotel. His major expenditures were on clothing and friends, an aspect criticized by his passive father, but encouraged by his politically inclined uncle. The photographer had convinced the youth to have a job before he tested the risky political arena. The clerk at FCI was this leader's closest friend in the lane. This clerk, as an educated youth, had also aspired to become a politician but could not after his father's sudden death. With a large family to feed, he fortunately found a job, married, and had his own two children within two years of the marriage. His mother, a sister of the widowed mother in Baudhabagh (see Case Cluster I), occasionally supplemented the family income with daily wage labor but the family lived in cramped quarters, lacked most winter clothing, and barely had enough food for a whole month. However, no one had to miss meals in his place. The clerk wrote reformist poems and sang them after the tunes of popular film songs. Ambedkar, Achchutananda, and two local saints repeatedly appeared in them. The clerk had a great regard for the photographer, whom he likened to Janaka (a householder who lived like an ascetic).

The photographer took special care of the old shopkeeper who lived alone. Claiming to be ninety, the old man had little to look forward to. His health was failing him and his small shop often remained closed. He had married four times and had eleven children but all had died. His fourth wife had died two years earlier (in 1978) when she was forty-five. He was a staunch fatalist and had given up on ascetics, gods, and astrologers in despair. He awaited death, as he would say, yet he also believed in supernatural cures for himself. Suffering from gout, he went to a special tree near a golf course and sat underneath it for temporary relief. The tree (unspecified) had miraculous powers for him. He claimed it to be a widely known place among those who could not afford doctors and their medicines. The photographer gave him homeopathic medicine, often at no cost, and made sure, when the old man was sick, that he did not go hungry. The others in the lane also cared: It was his custom to open his front door and greet loudly those passing from 7 to 9 A.M.; if he did not do so, the neighbors knew that there was something wrong. Usually, some children would be sent to knock at his door to inquire about his health.

Complementing this picture of amity, interdependence, and moderation were a few long-standing feuds between the photographer's household members and the office peon. The peon's household was spatially and socially most isolated. He and his wife had quarreled, on several occasions, with almost all of his neighbors for one reason or another. He had found the photographer kind but condescending, the aspiring political leader selfish, and the FCI clerk exploitative. In their estimation, the peon not only had a bad temperament and unhappy family life but was also highly insecure. He felt that he had the lowest social prestige and the least income among all of his neighbors, and he assumed that all his neighbors looked down upon him. Social seclusion was therefore the best strategy for him, he thought, though he did not ignore the old shopkeeper.

In the preceding cases the widow, the two brothers (one unsuccessful and the other successful), the photographer, the old shopkeeper, and the insecure peon reflect aspects of the processes of coordination, moderation, and mediation on which the Chamar's pragmatic ethos rests. The social management of daily practical strains, and making sense of what (and where) one is, continue to be the two most important concerns of the Lucknow Chamar. The inspirational role of the ascetic also appears in this context, but indirectly. This is to be expected since the ascetic normally does not live next to a householder. The latter has to go to him (as shown in the narrative set at the Ravidas temple). Consider the widow, the successful brother, the photographer, and old shopkeeper together and they variously reflect on each other, and on the positive identity of the contemporary Chamar.

The Lucknow Chamars exemplify additional aspects of moderation and mediation, offering more information about themselves. For example, a Ravidas shoemaker from Moderngan j observed how he found the Untouchable now facing increasingly pervasive yet diffusing social opposition:

It is now not the Brāhman against the Chamar or any other group of the Untouchable. Instead, it is any Untouchable group against any upper or lower caste or community in whose way the Untouchable might be an obstacle. Since land [*zamīn*], honor [*izzat*], and authority [*kursī*] are the three prerogatives the caste Hindus find hardest to share (and these three remain our most coveted goals), conflicts based on them are most frequently hostile, and volatile. They need the best mediation [*samjhautā*], but either go unmediated or the conciliatory steps tried remain superficial and hence do not work. Achchutananda and Jigyasu used to concentrate on these fundamental conflicts with the Brāhman, but now one approaches this situation with ever-compromising politics.

But this is where real social conflicts arise. As traditional interests confront the democratic forces that protect the "weaker segments of the society" (a government euphemism for the socially deprived), Untouchables must either play the politics of contention or face open social conflicts. The first option is becoming more frequent as the traditional channels (e.g., the *jajmāni* system, and the *dāna-puṇya* rites) of practical cooperation between the urban Untouchable and the caste Hindu are being increasingly eroded, and the sacred devices (e.g., gods and priests) for containing antagonisms between the two groups are also giving way to immediate politicization of economic frustrations and social distrust. This development means that the practical issues increasingly reflect an emotional stress and political design from both sides, and they erode the position of the traditional institutions and their functionaries. Further, as the democratic devices ironically instigate the caste order to pervade the social system (and evidence of this abounds already), it is *not* without cost to the caste ethic and caste cohesion. A definite overuse and overestimation of casteism also occurs. Ironically, caste politics in modern India gathers as well as dissipates traditional caste loyalties and their functions.

The caste Hindu finds us encroaching upon his critical privileges faster than he thinks could be fair, while we find ourselves losing an all-time opportunity because of his continuing resistance. There is a widening gap between our positions. When they find the honor of their caste and lineage [*jāti* and *khāndāna*] at stake (e.g., when we seek to plow a field as its owner), we find our rights denied. Our new social profile is still mostly raised social hopes and expectations. Our officials [i.e., of law and social welfare] and politicians do not understand that we see each other this way. Hence, whatever reconciliation they devise remains superficial. When we are hurt most, they treat us with more promises and little else. They do not treat the cause of increasing discord [*phūta kā kāraṇa*] – our deepening mutual suspicion and distrust [*shaka aur shubaha*]. It is an ailment of mind and heart, not merely of better jobs, more land, and more money. We both know inside that we are not any more what we used to be – the Untouchable, a virtual slave [*gulāma*], and the caste Hindu, a God-fearing, charitable and compassionate master [*dayāvāna, Parmātmā ko ḍarné wālā, mālik*].

This was the assessment of the present caste-Hindu and Untouchable interrelationships of a Chamar mechanic employed by the state bus transport. He also maintained a betel shop (*pān kī dukān*) near a government guesthouse for state councillors, which he opened only in the evenings. Being one of those educated and informed leaders from Modernganj, he claimed to have purposely embarrassed some orthodox Hindu state legislators by offering them betel to chew. However, it was a much more serious and sober affair for him than a mere trick:

Those lawmakers who dare ask my caste (before or after eating my betel leaf) have to engage themselves in a serious argument with me. Is it not appropriate? Actually, I do not enjoy catching them on the wrong foot, but these are sad cases of pretense [*banāvaṭī-panā*] and lip service to democracy. On the other hand, several of these have become my regular customers.

Such examples of practical stratagems for conveying a social message were repeatedly mentioned by the Lucknow Chamars. However, where performance was needed, they knew the empty words of the caste Hindu would go only so far. When loss of their honor and feeling was involved in a conflict, indifference or rhetoric alone would no longer work. The point they thus wanted to make was that if a situation demanded true mediation between conflicting attitudes, it was still the hardest to attain. The Modernganj mechanic also observed:

The goodwill of the government toward us remains feeble and is biased by the officials carrying it to us. They like to fill papers, not fulfill government promises. They are interested in conducting inquiries after the wrong, rather than in prevention of injustice and [bringing about] a true reconciliation. Not surprisingly, therefore, conflicts cannot heal without leaving [emotional] scars.

Overview

Though any basic change in attitudes is far away, the Chamar and the caste Hindu may be found variously positioning themselves, albeit grudgingly and slowly, for a more direct and honest social accounting. They are helped by forces of social circumstance, especially in a crowded city like Lucknow.

Trains, buses, streets, movie theaters, marketplaces, offices, factories, political party rooms, and most restaurants relentlessly shuffle the two traditionally distinct groups throughout the year. If the mediation so brought about is incomplete, as it indeed is, it is still the socially most persistent one, generally with a clear momentum toward greater de facto social sharing. Such tendencies perhaps represent a widening ethos for social mediation.

Just as marketplaces, public transportation, and theaters mix people of different social status in terms of a new criterion of self-participation, democratic politics, whether organized or spontaneous, often looks for new ways to generate and channel social compromise. Though the Chamars complain that there is never enough social privilege coming their way, present political and administrative procedures ensure their widening political involvement, direct training in the practical ethos of modern India, and an insistent quest for greater social justice. Despite all the failures of formal democratic institutions and their reforms, most Lucknow Chamars insist that it is better to have these protections than to risk a reversal to preindependence days. Democratic politics awards a new voice as well as social participation to the Chamars.

As the Chamars now increasingly participate in formal and informal political contests, they must increasingly learn to respond to social influence, calculation, judgment, decision making, and comparative accountability. They know that they must prepare to fend for themselves by developing their own skills in these domains. For example, if politics of culture (i.e., of ideology and norms) can be elating to them, they must also learn to utilize it to their advantage. They must learn to exploit the opponents' social disadvantage, but can do so only if they can also tame popular politics to their goals.

These political skills of the Lucknow Chamar are still being formed, though he is often already coherent, talkative, and expressive. The latter helps him. He must constantly articulate to himself a social commentary on concrete conditions. He must see hope even as he protests deprivation before others, balancing his social despair against recent gains. When nothing else is available, he survives by sheer social persistence. Moreover, he now invests his self-image as much in what he achieves as in what he loses, betraying a new critical frame of mind.

8. Identification of deprivation and its manipulation

As the Lucknow Chamars discuss their social conditions among themselves on a day-to-day basis they survey various aspects of their social advantages and disadvantages. They do so often within their households in the context of the practical problems of obtaining food, clothing, housing, employment, education, and health care. An identification of the nature and forms of social deprivation within and outside the household extends the same cognitive remapping that the previously discussed process of articulation represents. With the process of identification, the social concerns are generally wider, bringing the issues of social deprivation into frequent neighborhood discussion. The ordinary Chamars freely participate in such discussions, though their leaders and reformers initiate major ideas and strategies. They identify uncertainties as well as prospects that democratic politics, law, and economics introduce, and communicate the implications of these to the ordinary Chamars. The range, manipulation, and meaning of such identifications interest the anthropologist, since they help him compare this information to whatever is ordinarily known. The purpose of this chapter will therefore be to identify selected aspects of manipulation and meaning involved in the Chamar's social disability. Set in the context of a sociological discussion of deprivation, we will examine two specific domains: first, the Chamar's social tactics for handling deprivation, and second, his perceptions and indexes of social bias and discrimination.

Because this process of identification focuses directly on a balance sheet that lists the Chamar's current deprivations against his recent social compensations and gains, we will start our discussion in the wider context of the sociology of deprivation, adapting the latter to the requirements of this inquiry. The "Pariah intellectualism" we have encountered among the Chamar reformers is a direct function of their search for an equalitarian, ethical-moral order and a concordantly positive personal and group identity. The more the Chamars encounter obstacles from the caste Hindu as they pursue this quest, the more they rely both on certain Indic cultural schemes to maintain their morale and on their everyday adaptability to social pressures. They must continuously seek the social moderation and mediation that would let them manipulate others' social weaknesses as well as strengths to their own advantage.

Pariah deprivation: a background

When Weber (e.g., 1963: 100–12), for comparative purposes, characterized the social position of the "nonprivileged" in broad sociological strokes, he assumed an absolute exclusivity in their social condition. He attributed to them, among other features, social misplacement, everyday social separation, restricted social interaction, instituted social dependence and isolation, and "exclusion from congregational religion." Whether it was the Indian Untouchable or the depressed European Jew in the early decades of this century, he found them seeking a soteriological religion at one end and an ethics for just social compensation at the other. In this picture, any legalized claim to equality by the deprived must face overwhelming social odds.

To summarize Weber's characterization: He noted the nonprivileged group's need for a "surrogate ideology"; dependence on providence and astrology; need for salvation, functional goals, and saviors; afflatus and charismatic leadership; domesticity of religion; inwardness and edification; and a moral justification for continuous resentment. In addition, he also remarked on the tendency of the nonprivileged to accord equality to women and to avoid militaristic cults.

The Lucknow Chamar, at first glance, seems to conform to almost all of the characteristics Weber assigned to "the Pariahs." He may, in fact, for example, seek a type of "surrogate ideology," and show dependence, one way or another, on providence, salvation, inwardness, functional gods, saviors, and charismatic leaders. We are also sure he shuns militaristic cults (as evidenced by the fact, for example, that one does not readily hear any demand for a Chamar regiment in the Indian army), and suffers a form of "exclusion from congregational [i.e., the caste-Hindu] religion."

However, problems arise when the Weberian characterization is placed against the available ethnography of the Chamars. For example, the Chamars do not accord equality (only perhaps more social room) to women; they have developed dimensions of congregational worship of their own; they increasingly opt for and are satisfied only with "autochthonous" rather than merely a "surrogate" ideology (see Part I); "functional gods" are not exclusive to them, and those they have may not always work because they are also of the upper castes; and they may subscribe to such a form of "inwardness" (i.e., spirituality) that it may alienate them from the "providence" (i.e., karma and *rīti*) of the established caste order. Likewise, saviors and charismatic leaders may either fail to appear when crucial, or succeed only halfway. What is therefore being pointed out by the Chamar's case is generalizable: Though several of Weber's sociological features may appear in any particular case of social deprivation, there can be, on closer inspection, no assurance that they, singly or together, would be both necessary and sufficient to explain fully the Pariah and his social profile. Empirically, it is an important limitation, but yet, as the sociological literature shows, Weber's characterization of the "Pariah" must survive.[1]

This is because social groups must play the game of inclusion and exclusion in some form, and they therefore engage variously in intergroup evaluation, whether institutionalized or spontaneous. This evaluation involves, among other things, observable criteria for identifying "us" versus "them" (and vice versa). Different ideologies are, under the pragmatic view, a result of such intentional differences and of actional patterns of calculations, judgments, and accountabilities.

Relative deprivation

Sociologically, the Lucknow Chamar's traditional social deprivation could be attributed to certain unfavorable exchange patterns with the larger society. He has had to give and take unequally and unfairly (from his standpoint) under imposed social regulations. The Chamars had to give most of those items to the rest of the society that they could seldom receive in return (i.e., physical labor, social services, compensations, advantages, commendations, and immunities). Conversely, they could never distribute those items that they had to receive in abundance (e.g., social blemish, refuse, subjugation, contingency, and cumulative inequality). The Chamar not only collected filth, refuse, remnants, and slurs on behalf of society; he also was made a prime symbolization of social refuse itself.

The Chamar's perception of social deprivation and disability is relative, however. Among the Chamars of all three Lucknow localities, those who faced continuous shortages of food, clothing, and secure employment considered themselves severely deprived. Secure housing was always desirable but obviously could not make up for the lack of the other three essentials. Education was considered increasingly important in urban life but was still held secondary to the necessity of earning a living. Chamar adolescents were therefore readily allowed to leave schools or college on the pretext of shouldering family financial responsibilities. The adolescents themselves also often developed a half-serious approach to education, especially by the time they reached high school. I encountered several youths (boys and girls) in all three localities who had left their education before taking the state-wide high school examination, partly to earn a living and partly from fear of failing the examination. But even a Chamar student who took the exam and failed it was considered better educated, worldly wise, and socially aware. He was privileged in relation to the illiterate or the barely literate. He was expected to understand better the designs of changing times. Thus, although a lack of education was considered in the city to be a definite deprivation, even disability, its relative position among the Chamars was directly related to their domestic circumstances and self-image. One's personal health problems, in comparison, were considered a disability that one's karma (or God) dictated and that usually added to one's state of social deprivation.

Obviously, not all Chamars considered themselves to be equally deprived just because they were Chamars nor were all the incidents of deprivation and social discrimination given a simple and uniform meaning. There was too much contextual variation among the Lucknow Chamars to make such an assertion, though all were of course "significantly deprived" when judged against democratic ideals. As a general rule, one's current economic and domestic conditions were a major factor in perceptions of social deprivation. Even occasional social discrimination was better countered, and was easier to dismiss, if one were satisfied with one's domestic life, had good and stable employment, and had living quarters of one's own (however small). Yet, in a general comparative profile, Baudhabagh stood out as the internally most troubled locality. Its dilapidation, fractious leadership, and cumulative social despair added to the picture of social deprivation. This situation was further verified by the ordinary Chamar's troubled, even confused, sense of self and communal identity.

Tactics of the deprived

When investigated for pursuing social tactics for limiting their deprivation, the Lucknow Chamars display a definite but varying awareness. Though relatively new to democratic politics, all three Lucknow localities I studied demonstrated this new acquisition in different ways. Its practical significance could not be minimized. Basically, to be socially and politically adroit means to be aware of one's advantages as well as disadvantages. The tactful Chamar was an aware, alert, social participant who lived neither in a passive stupor nor in the clouds of ideological claims, but rather was capable of forging different initiatives to meet practical challenges. This Chamar "tactician" learns most, I found, from his personal experience, selecting appropriate social contacts and putting them to work to achieve a definite social goal. He evaluates alternative strategies to reach a manageable goal. If unsuccessful, he is often willing to learn from his failures.

He is often literate but not always schooled. However, his urban surroundings and varied experiences constantly educate him. This tactician actually complements the Untouchable ideologist considered before. He can also be asceticlike, though obviously this is not the only disposition in which he can be found. He could even be the same ascetic who professes a radical Untouchable ideology. A radical ascetic from Baudhabagh explained his idea of social tact as follows:

> To be tactical is to further, slowly but surely, our ultimate goal of achieving social justice. But to do so, one must be able to develop a suitable capacity [*kṣmatā*] for keeping one's eyes and ears open, and for thinking about Chamars' [our] interests [*apnā ūncha-nīcha samajhnā*] in relation to what is going on in the society. We have to accept with a lot of caution now what people say, do, and mean. For they either do not do what they say, or do so, but for their own covert purposes, or say vigorously what they actually never mean. All of this is politics [*rājanīti*]; the society is full of it these days from all directions. Actually, if I were to become a full-time participant in this "game" [*khéla*], I would have to acquire a whole new "viewpoint" [*dṛṣtkoṇa*], equipping myself with new – just like a politician's – tactics and tricks [*hathkandé*]. But this is not *my* preoccupation. I think about it only to guide my followers. The practical world is the real testing ground for what the "Chamar brothers" really dream or want to be. I tell them not only to remember what Ravidas, Achchutananda, and Ambedkar have said, but also [often] advise them on how to tackle today's practical problems of food, clothing, and housing.

Obviously, all ascetics were not tacticians (though a tactical reformer was usually more successful), just as neither all those who were tactical became tacticians nor all tacticians, politicians and leaders of some kind. The ordinary Chamar routinely used some forms of tact as well as tactics, from spontaneous to well planned, to get his work done in the city environs. A painter from Modernganj would hide his true social identity when painting an orthodox Hindu's house. A Chamar working in a florist's shop would deliver flowers at weddings as a gardener (*mālī*), that is, posing as a member of Mālī caste. Hiding one's true identity was relatively less bothersome. It worked in a city like Lucknow, the Chamars contended. However, a different tact was now indispensable in dealing with what some called "the powerful but unpredictable sarkar" (e.g., before the government institutions, the state employment agencies, and the urban politician – a dubious sympathizer). To reveal the true identity was tactful in these quarters; the Chamars expected gains from them as a democratic right.

Has social tactic become so crucial to the Chamar all of a sudden? First of all, two cardinal anthropological propositions need to be mentioned in the context of this question: (a) that all human beings, whether socially deprived or not, always engage in some form of social calculation and cultural judgment as they go through their normal life; (b) that the structures of calculation and judgment are shaped by a people's experiences, values, and changing social conditions. Both of these propositions are found to be critical for the Chamar. They are also equally important for our understanding of the Chamar's changing approach to the larger society and his own placement within it.

The Chamars of the three Lucknow localities had several notions about the place of social tactic in their lives. Most important, it was held to be indispensable in contemporary times, "when one can trust," as a clerk observed, "neither the words nor the deeds of others, sometimes even of those well known." A Chamar mechanic at a bicycle shop in Moderngani had learned to keep his employer happy on festive occasions by cleaning his shop. He thought it much better than being without a regular livelihood. He had taken most of his training in the same shop and had been twice promoted. His tact mostly meant avoiding, as he had put it, "unnecessary talk, unnecessary confrontation and quarrels, and unnecessary criticism of others."

However, social tact in critical matters is seldom a matter for individuals alone. Members of a household are often found to be involved under such conditions, though the actual composition of a consultative group varies with the issue at hand. Just as frequently, the family tactics get discussed among relatives living nearby. Modernganj's lanes repeatedly illustrated this property, especially among the relatives. One lane, popularly named *Netā jī ki galī*, had a cluster of five houses, where two brothers, their father's elder brother, and two of their cousins (i.e., their father's elder brother's sons) lived in three different houses and ate from four different hearths. The leader after whom the lane was named was the older of the two brothers. Gandhian, he was one of the most frequently mentioned politicians and tacticians of the neighborhood; he was a guide to the families and the youth of the lane. He counseled those applying for their first employment, those having trouble with their present employers, and those unemployed. In his own view, social tactics were necessary to minimize the Chamar's social disabilities and to manipulate them to their advantage. Successful social tactics brought about significant practical results, he insisted. As evidence, he repeatedly discussed the economic, social, and political problems of the five-family cluster.

The leader's younger brother, a clerk in the state electricity board, was his first apprentice, but not very successful. His temperament was unsuitable, the older brother had remarked, "just like my father, since both of them cannot hold their temper and mouth." His brother had recently run into serious difficulty because of his criticism of a superior official. He initially kept the problem to himself. One evening, when he visited his elder brother (the leader) to take his advice, his father, uncle, and a cousin were also sitting on two cots, both inside the small courtyard. The clerk had been served that day with a notice of insubordination and he feared dismissal. The discussion first centered around his indiscretions. The father was despondent; he was cursing his son. The cousin, an educated Chamar, was urging a careful review of the whole situation, and the leader was suggesting a dual strategy – to contact some locally influential Untouchable leaders to bring pressure on the official concerned to desist from any drastic action, and to ask his younger brother to repair his relationship with other office members.

The clerk, however, wanted to make the whole issue a glaring case of discrimination against, and harassment of, an Untouchable. He wanted his brother to take the issue before the state politicians and have his supervisor reprimanded for mistreating an Untouchable employee. The leader thought such a course of action largely inadvisable; it was not only unwarranted, he thought (knowing about his brother's culpability), but it might also backfire, hurting the credibility of Untouchable leaders. But everybody, including the leader, insisted that, although the clerk was at fault, he should not apologize to the official in any manner. The official had discriminated against Untouchable employees before, and an apology would only embolden him in the future.

However, this case later became a full-time concern of the leader; it was complicated by the official's insistence on dismissing the clerk. Ultimately, after several appeals to the politicians and to the head of the agency, and after several hours of anxious discussions in the *Netā jī kī galī*, the clerk was spared his employment. He was transferred, however, to another section of the same office.

As this case shows, a social "calculation" must base itself on what is socially feasible. For example, an educated Chamar leader keeps his goals specific and reviews his gains realistically. He calculates his community's social deprivation against the quality and conditions of the gains made, and against the impediments still faced. We do not know the real gain, he asserts, until it is also evaluated against the relative gains made by the caste Hindus during the same period, and the "net gain" is figured. For example:

> If we Chamars now have bicycles and the caste Hindu scooters, ours is a less spectacular gain and our [social] distance from them remains the same. Similarly, if we do better in our occupation and income than did our forefathers in Modernganj but cannot reduce the discrimination, hostility, and suspicion between the surrounding caste Hindus and ourselves, the real meaning [*māné*] of the change is somehow less than our jobs and bicycles suggest.

My informant, a Ravidas shoemaker, who made this comment, was trying to present several interrelated points for measuring significant change. In the first case, he compared values of things to things and figured the "real value" as a difference between "what they [i.e., the caste Hindus] have now [vis-à-vis] what we now have." However, if he had calculated the value in terms of what his forefathers had (or were allowed to have), which included social sanction against owning any form of personal transport, the significance of the real change would have been definitely greater.

In the second case, the informant was weighing the value of the material gains made against the change in deeply entrenched social attitudes, predicating the real change on the latter (see the following section). The third mode of calculation was exemplified when the Chamar must socially compromise to receive compensation. For example, it was when he compromised his "face" (i.e., personal honor, *izzat*) to gain a better house; when he accumulated obligations to a Hindu (*ahesāna*) to gain a regular food supply; or when he received one thing (e.g., a small job) but also lost something more valuable (a chance for a better education). Under such circumstances he found the society putting something in one hand and taking something else (of equal or greater value) from the other. Finally, there were also the strains under which he found social calculation either difficult or impossible. These were usually the situations involving either high emotional tension or social or personal violation (where one's life, family, property, or personal safety was involved).

As the Baudhabagh Chamars in particular had noted, these conditions often involved somebody's carelessness or neglect or outright social hostility, and serious injury, loss of limb, or even loss of life resulted. A Chamar laborer working in a sawmill lost all the fingers of his left hand because, he thought, he was not given proper warning that the machine he was assigned to was old, faulty, and located in a cramped space. He asked for substantial compensation but received the meagre sum of only two hundred rupees (approximately twenty dollars). His observation was that he could have received more compensation if he had had good contacts with government administrators and party politicians. His deepest disappointment was that the owner of the sawmill went completely unpunished. He feared that another worker (perhaps even a Chamar) might get hurt on the same machine. He felt so strongly about this that, with encouragement from his reformist ascetic guru, relatives, and friends, he threatened the mill owner with a public protest if he did not get the machine repaired. In a rare moment of unity, the local Untouchable politicians received support from the city leaders and the mill owner had to remove the machine for repair and relocation. At the same time, however, the efforts to constitute a watchdog committee for Untouchables exposed to occupational risks by careless businessmen were defeated. Beyond the first three weeks, even those who had been injured on the job did not turn up for meetings because, first, they did not want to antagonize their employers, and second, other domestic matters had a greater priority for them.

In summary, although the Chamar's social tactics entailed social calculation, both factors generally shaped the process of identification that the "awakened" Lucknow Chamar now employs to determine the locations and dimensions of his social deprivation. He must constantly differentiate between his genuine "well-wishers" and those who are spurious and unreliable. A popular view of the situation, as a Karampura Chamar put it, is:

> Nowadays every social worker is out to help and reform us, it seems; it is a call of the contemporary times [*ājakal kī pukār*] in which, unless careful, many reformers try to exploit us to serve their own interests [the colloquial phrase often used was *ullū sīdhā karnā*]. Politicians are its oft-cited examples, but they are not alone.

A language of social bias

Analytically, the process of identification (of social deprivation and privilege) is more intricate than the everyday social reading and expression involved in "articulation," a process considered in Chapter 7. But articulation anticipates the social calculation inherent in identification. Both processes together represent the Lucknow Chamar's diverse efforts at "social coping" in contemporary India. The two processes also lead us to a language of social bias that the practical ethos of the Lucknow Chamar routinely recognizes. This bias may be reflected within the "prepolitical" phase as well as the "political."[2]

The Lucknow Chamar identifies social bias by recognizing the language of its expression. It is a subtle language embedded within the ordinary language. This "metalanguage" comprises theme clusters that the Chamars repeatedly encounter and recognize in their everyday life to evaluate (i.e., to ascertain, rank, judge, express, and act out) the social bias directed for or against them. The four category clusters we will discuss empirically illustrate the conditions of the Lucknow Chamar; they show how an expression of bias identification is structured and utilized from his standpoint, and how it is pursued within as well as outside the arenas of organized politics. (My translation of the following terms incorporates the contextual perception and usage of the Lucknow Chamar.)

1. Guilt-raising cluster: *achchūta* ("untouchable"), *atiśūdra* (lowest *śūdra*), *carmakāra* ("leather handler"), *candāla* ("wicked or cruel in deeds"; progeny of *śūdra* father and Brāhman mother), Harijan, etc.
2. Reforming cluster: *ādi*-Hindu (original Hindu), *ātmavādī* (spiritualist, advocate of *ātman*), *mānavadharmī* (follower of "humanist" religion), Harijan (under Gandhian usage), etc.
3. Secularizing cluster: babu, saheb, *baṛé ādmī, mālik* (officers, administrators, rich people, and boss), "weaker segment of society," "Scheduled Castes," *samāna nāgarika* (equal citizens under the Indian constitution), etc.
4. Politicizing cluster: *dalita* (depressed), *śoṣita* (exploited), *alpasaṃkhyaka* or *laghu-varga* ("minority"), etc.

The important aspect of this list is not so much the range of categories cited as the way these units are adroitly woven into a pragmatic, *two-way* language for conveying cultural biases. This language could be directed contextually either in favor of or against the Chamars. The list is offered essentially to demonstrate some tactical uses to which the Chamars put these category clusters. These categories are polysemous; they expand on the cultural bias built into the Chamar's identity. When this language of bias is analyzed, some useful points emerge. For example, one tactic repeatedly used to raise protest before the caste Hindu was to charge that the Hindus openly employed the first cluster to discriminate against and put the Chamar down. In other words, it was used to raise the guilt of those socially "higher." Thus we see, once again, why Achchutananda insisted on calling himself "Untouchable."

"Harijan," in this context, is a clearly double-faced cultural category: Proposed by Gandhi for social "uplifting" of the Untouchable, it has rebounded on the caste Hindu's conscience, argue the Chamar reformers. "Harijan means what we can never be allowed to become by the caste Hindu, and what we may not want to be anyway. It was a superficial way for Gandhi to resolve *his* guilt [*chobha*]." This Buddhist Chamar's opinion was widely shared. Accordingly, though coined to refer to the necessity of forming a new cultural identity for the Indian Untouchable, this construct has largely remained, we may observe, a guilt-ridden Hindu euphemism for the Chamar. However, the government, the educated, and Gandhian Indians continue to call the Untouchable "Harijan," since it appears to them either the "least offending" or the "most illuminating" new name for the Indian Untouchable.

The remaining three theme clusters similarly highlight reformist, secular, and political themes of identification. The problems raised by the reforming cluster now increasingly overflow into the secularizing one, and the latter into the political one. The "scheduling" and "descheduling" provisions of the national government are an example of the mechanisms secular and political reforms employ. These offer the "Scheduled Castes" (which include the Untouchables) certain rights protected by legal, political, and economic measures. This is a clearly different development from that offered by the "autochthonous (*ādi*-Hindu) argument" of Achchutananda, the "nondualist spiritualism" (regarding all "souls" to be morally indivisible and equal) of the ascetic, or the recent variety of "humanism," where, as Jigyasu remarked, "we will regard everybody equal just because all of us are humans."

The secularizing identity cluster also links easily with certain parallel themes pursued among the educated caste Hindus. It is a logical development for Indian democratic secularism, especially when it has to follow certain generally shared sets of values and priorities in different (even antagonistic) segments of the traditional society. This cluster also offers a point of departure for the language of political minority and "class differences." Thus politically sophisticated Chamar leaders insisted on calling themselves outright what they were – a depressed (*dalita*) and exploited (*śoṣita*) group. The other name readily employed was the "distressed [*pīṛita*] minority [*alpasaṃkhyaka*]."

Now we will briefly consider the manipulation of these clusters in relation to each other. For example, the preliminary message-forming tactics included emphasizing one cluster vis-à-vis another, or playing down or deleting one or more clusters in relation to those emphasized. We accordingly found Achchutananda framing his messages predominantly under the first two clusters, whereas Ambedkar (depending upon what he was writing about, and when) increasingly connected the first two clusters with secularizing and politicizing forces. Jigyasu and Sagar, as reformers, employed all four clusters, drawing messages from them according to context. Jigyasu particularly highlighted the deplorable social conditions of the Untouchable by recombining the identifying clusters 1, 2, and 4. He stated in an interview, "The Chamar are *atiśūdra* [“the lowest of the low”] because the caste Hindus have considered us beyond reform and hence also an eternal subject for social exploitation.” In clear distinction, an educated Chamar youth from Moderngani, leaning to the political left, ignored the first two clusters, decried the third one as the vestige of a “decadent bourgeoisie ethos,” and waited for the birth of a “real class conflict” between the exploited workers and the rich to bring about “genuine freedom.” His contempt for a rich Chamar, he had argued, was of the same order as for a rich Brāhman or any other rich caste Hindu. However, such a leftist position was very rarely encountered among the Lucknow Chamars.

We will now briefly consider some uses of these clusters by the Lucknow Chamars themselves. Our cases will be drawn from all three neighborhoods, from men and women, and the young and the old. They will illustrate a series of formulations offered at the beginning of each case.

a. The bias-accentuating categories in one's language generally reflected increased social distance and antagonism between caste Hindus and the Chamars. Modernganj Chamars encountered such situations more on the eastern side of their settlement because a group of Bania houses faced theirs across a narrow lane. Quarrels started across the lane once there was even a hint of the use of derogatory language on the eastern side of the lane. The Chamars often responded by listing past and present instances of exploitation by those higher. Usually, there would be a shouting match. If the conflict became serious, however, the Chamars would threaten to report the case to the proper authorities, invoking their legal rights of nondiscrimination. But to be effective, the Chamar leaders emphasized, this threat should be used sparingly and only under extreme stress. The comment, “They are, after all, Chamars,” was often enough to start a row across the lane, though isolated milder comments (e.g., “The Chamar are people with dirty habits”) were usually overlooked. Some common sources of strain were lighting the smoke-emitting stoves (*koyalé kī aṅgīṭhī*) in the lane, leading to discomfort across the lane; using the lane for sleeping on hot summer nights and thus obstructing passage to the Bania houses; and occasional meat cooking in the two corner houses of the Chamar. The Banias, all strict vegetarians, protested loudest about this problem; they claimed, however, that they had already converted several Chamar houses to vegetarianism. Finally, there were frequent noisy wrangles among the women and children of the two groups.

However, in all such cases the Chamars, rather than the Banias, would employ in their language such terms as Harijan, *achchūta*, and *Śūdra* to characterize the caste-Hindu's attitude toward them. This usually preempted the Bania neighbors and put them on the defensive. They had to say whether they in fact did not think of the Chamars as *achchūta*. From the Banias' side, they often criticized openly the Chamar neighbors for specific social habits or events, rather than for their social status (the latter being an illegal act in a city like Lucknow). The Chamars in the lane complained of continuing social discrimination, whereas the Banias blamed the whole problem on "emboldened Chamars."

b. As a variation of (a), the distance between the Chamars and the caste Hindus increased when the two sides traded insults in public. Though this lane was well known for its social frictions, it had never experienced physical violence (until 1980). Excluding that extreme, however, the two sides of the lane did show strong variations in mood. Usually, sudden silence and stillness (e.g., due to the children's being removed from the street and kept inside their houses) announced either a coming storm or the bitterness of the one just passed. Under extreme tensions, the Chamars described themselves as the "exploited poor" (i.e., *dalita* and *śoṣita*) who had been betrayed by a *sarkār* (government) that made them "equal citizens" (i.e., *samāna nāgarika*). A Chamar political leader living nearby had advised the lane's Chamars to confront the Banias by presenting a petition to the political leaders. But nothing was done until March 1980. In the election campaign, however, the lane's Chamars stoutly opposed the caste-Hindu candidate, announcing themselves as the "exploited minority" (i.e., *śoṣita laghu-varga*) of the lane. They described the Banias of the lane as "the big, rich people [*baṛé*, *amīr ādamī*] of the other side."

c. An increased emphasis on religious and spiritual tolerance usually dissipated the social bias of the caste Hindu to a certain extent and facilitated the pursuit of democratic secularism. The lane's Chamars also illustrated this formulation as they presented the other side of their existence–aspects of social cooperation and convergence. Two Chamar households located at the middle of the lane were educated, devout, and vegetarian. Their ascetic guru came at least four times every year and stayed with them for several weeks. They sang devotional songs every morning and evening, mediated disputes across the lane, and propagated spiritual unity. The Bania households liked devotional songs (in praise of the Hindu gods and goddesses), moderated their own social stance in return, and appreciated the generally improved ethos of the lane. Besides, a few educated Chamar and Bania youths had kept themselves mostly aloof from the tensions of the lane. Their nonparticipation in even heated discussions puzzled the Chamars as well as the Banias of the older generation. Outside the lane and the Modernganj neighborhood, these Chamar and Bania youths remained friendly as city youths, though they still could not honestly say that they regarded each other as equals.

Social bias and the archetypes of privilege

One function of the language of bias identification is to structure contextually sensitive messages on varying daily social issues that the Lucknow Chamars must face. Less frequently, but equally surely, this language must also communicate subtler biases of the officials, administrators, rich people, and bosses toward the Chamar. By becoming a persistent cluster of social authority and influence, the sahibs identify a still different aspect of the Chamar deprivation. The cultural bias found here is usually channeled along three pairs of important cultural archetypes, namely, master (*swāmī*) and servant (*sévaka*), ruler (*rājā*) and the ruled (*prajā*), and leader (*nétā*) and people (*janatā*).

As the Chamar often finds himself at the receiving end in these social relationships, these cultural archetypes help him estimate and rank the significance of his deprivation in different social contexts. For example, a cobbler (thirty years old) from Baudhabagh, sitting under a torn umbrella in the burning midday June sun, related his recent experience:

> Officials [sahibs] are like rulers [rajas], whether they are specially there [i.e., appointed] to help us or exist merely for their salaries. They want us to view them as rulers. If we do not, they place hurdles in our way to convey that we depend on them. They are our *sarkār* [government]. Quarrel with them and your work will never be done. All of this I recently learned the hard way by applying for a [two thousand rupee] grant for establishing my own shoe shop just as my brother-in-law [sister's husband] had done. These officers also want you to realize what you are [i.e., how dependent you are on them], and not only what they are. Their behavior in different ways conveyed to me that I am, after all, a helpless Chamar. If I could have carried to them a recommendation from an influential leader, the grant would have come to me in two or three trips at the most.
>
> Without this support, I have already made seven half-day trips and spent several days' earnings in renting a bicycle to go to this office [three miles away]. Yet there is no end in sight. Next time, I shall offer to mend the clerks' shoes free, and present the section officer (*vibhāga adhikārī*) with a new pair of shoes from my brother-in-law's shop. I am sure I will get the grant from them this way.

(The informant did in fact receive his grant a month after the interview.)

The distinctive function in contemporary India of these three sets of cultural archetypes of social power, position, and authority cannot be dismissed. As the continuing symbols of moral and jural privilege, these archetypes facilitate understanding of an increasingly complex and alienating Indian bureaucracy. Thus, when certain Chamar leaders and politicians hold a durbar ("royal court" in an analogous sense) for hearing grievances, they are readily understood in terms of the customary model (i.e., of *rājā* and *prajā*). But since they mimic the relationships of the traditional caste-Hindu order, the Chamar reformer laments that his people also fall prey to the same wily devices they are expected to uproot, or at least avoid. Yet an ordinary Chamar asserted a vital distinction:

> The Chamars in position [of power and authority] are, after all, the Chamar, and will therefore always remain different from the caste Hindu and other leaders. Even our worst sahib will be ultimately better for us than the best of others [*apnā saheb kharaba ho tabbhī auroñ ké acchoñ sé acchā*].

A local scale of social bias

Actually, the Chamars further identify everyday social bias that they encounter as they measure it against some ready-made yardsticks within their contemporary urban surroundings. These measures sometimes depend on intercaste behavioral norms and sometimes on other cultural criteria, but they are always a part of the Chamars' efforts to identify the varying location and significance of bias against themselves. A repeated discussion with the Lucknow Chamars of such criteria yielded the following five-step scale of cultural bias (with decreasing negative value): (a) whether a Chamar (or a member of his household) was openly (and with impunity) "insulted or mistreated within (or at) his own house"; (b) whether he and his relatives were "insulted or mistreated or misused, in word *and* deed, outside his house but within his own locality or community"; (c) whether he indirectly encountered discrimination "through word *or* deed outside his own locality and community members"; (d) whether his close relatives and friends (but not he himself) had encountered insulting behavior that they had seen "with their own eyes"; (e) whether some other Chamars he knew (but neither he nor his relatives and friends from the *mohallā*) had encountered mistreatment, "though I [i.e., my informant] have neither seen it nor can I get it corroborated by those whom I trust."

This scale of negative cultural bias is based on the social experiences of Baudhabagh Chamars. The phrases or clauses reproduced within quotation marks in the five formulations come from informants. They are culturally coded messages. A Baudhabagh Chamar, a literate, small shop-owner, illustrated how he, a newcomer to the city twenty-five years ago, had experienced almost all the five steps of discrimination. Dilapidated and unoccupied for over two years, the shack he had moved into was near the big *mohallā* drain. He at least had a roof over his head. But within three months the owner of the place appeared and he insulted and evicted the Chamar "at my own doorstep" (as my informant put it). He said he would never forget that day. The next day he had seriously thought of committing suicide, he recalled, because for months he had lacked adequate food, clothing, and housing. But his better times started soon after, when in the winter he decided to sell roasted peanuts on a roadside spot two miles away from his own locality. Though still largely considered a failure, he had built a hut of his own. He was beginning to get attention from some other Chamars. Within two years he had opened a small shop, become literate by borrowing four Hindi books from a grain dealer's fourteen-year-old son, and found a guru, a Chamar ascetic at the Ravidas temple in Lucknow. He became a locality leader, married, and had two children within nine years from the time of his eviction. Though he thought that he would never be above social insult and discrimination, he had not personally encountered verbal or implied insult for the last several years. Nor were other Chamars insulted before his own eyes, especially because he was a political activist and an outspoken critic of the discrimination-practicing caste Hindu. Personally, however, he did not think that discrimination against the Untouchables would really end soon.

This success story was exceptional. Even his own relatives in Baudhabagh had related how hard it was to move away from the negative cultural bias of the caste Hindu. His cousin (i.e., his mother's sister's son) had gone in the opposite direction – from a secure social and economic position to insecurity and despondency, after he had begun drinking at the expense of his job and domestic responsibility. His "fall" had started, he recalled, four years earlier, when his employer, a caste-Hindu grain merchant, not only suddenly dismissed him from the job but also verbally abused him. As the informant himself put it, "I could never be a better worker because I was a Chamar." With no income and a wife pregnant with their sixth child, he first became desperate, then despondent, and finally withdrew. He became increasingly convinced of his worthlessness as he tried to, but could not, give up drinking. Beginning with the behavior of the caste-Hindu grain merchant, his identity crisis – his nemesis – traveled homeward until it reached his parents, wife, and children. By 1980, he had become so different, he acknowledged, that he did not recognize himself. Yet he did not want to give up. He had found a sympathetic friend in an ascetic in Karampura and had given up drinking for the past several months. He had returned home to his wife and children in Baudhabagh, though he still remained confined to his house. He refused to see his close relatives, for they had abandoned rather than helped him in his hour of need.

In these cases of bias, we may note, locality, social distance, direct and indirect experience, word, and deed (along with the biased assumptions of the Chamar himself) variously illustrate the five-step scale. Normally, word, action, food, and women become successively more important symbols of one's social approval or disapproval. The Chamars, like Hindus, measure social insult and mistreatment against one or more of these four indicators, offering us a graduated scale for bias measurement. Invariably, insulting and mistreating one's female family members are held to be the most serious acts of social disapproval and defiance.

Identifying and measuring the deprivation thus usually demand from the Chamars social awareness as well as assertion. This they gradually acquire, as shown, by redefining and rearticulating their cognitive categories, especially with a helping hand from postindependence democratic forces. Actually, these forces invade and strategically fraternize with those who are congenial in the contemporary Chamar's customary life. However, each tends to redefine, translate, or reposition in relation to the other, depending on contextual need. Both could also variously equivocate either to deepen or attenuate the social bias. Thus, democracy has so far been a helpful but ambiguous social development for the Chamar.

For limiting unfavorable bias, however, the Chamars from Modernganj usually displaced, repositioned, or rejected the Hindu sacred. Whether it was a railway engine driver or a vegetable seller or a cartographer or a primary school peon, everyone had skillfully handled negative social bias to manage his practical affairs. The driver encountered bias often from a superior railway employee; the vegetable seller from the members of a vegetable-selling caste (Khatika); the cartographer from his boss at the municipal board office; and the school peon from the Brahman headmaster. Yet the fact that they all persisted in their work evidenced their skill in transferring, deflecting, diffusing, or confronting the bias. This was variously underscored in interviews:

> We will not allow ourselves to be passively exploited and discriminated against any more. When we become somebody, it is only by our pure toil and sweat. I therefore confront those who try to put us down. To give up easily in society now is to humiliate not only ourselves but also our spiritual and cultural heritage. If we do so, then what is the use of going to Ravidas temple next day and making an offering there? This way we let down Ravidas sahib the most. He is my guru, though I do not denigrate Hindu gods and goddesses. I actually worship the [Hindu] goddess; she gives me strength. She has actually worked for me on previous occasions.

This was the comment of a railway engine driver (fifty years old), who was an avid collector of the Untouchable's reform literature and of multicolored pictures of the Hindu deities in his spacious drawing room. He would reassess the role of the sacred and confront the bias afresh.

The vegetable seller (illiterate and thirty years old), in contrast, had gone to his guru, an ascetic resident in the Ravidas temple, to seek his "magical" intervention "because a Khatika was giving me trouble." His life was easier after several months, however, when three other Chamar hawkers joined him and occupied a corner in the vegetable market. But because the market was adjacent to the Chamar locality, the Khatika could not press the matter. (The Chamar's guru had also worked, in his view: His guru was his deliverer.) The cartographer (forty years old), on the other hand, had rediscovered a Hindu deity "after ten years, during which I had totally given up worshipping and praying to Hindu gods. I had gone to Buddha, but did not become a Buddhist. It was a trial that taught me much, including that I could not reject all that is good in the Hindu gods." He went to the Hanuman temple for several months to seek relief from a caste Hindu working against his promotion in the office, and was finally promoted. His observation: "I let Hanuman turn aside this caste Hindu's opposition. Hanuman works for us as well." He would thus reposition the Hindu sacred and deflect bias through it.

The school peon (literate and fifty years old) was a converted Buddhist, yet a victim of upper-caste bias. As he vehemently denied that he was either a Chamar or a low person, he observed:

> When the headmaster discriminates against me, I just see it as an odor coming from his decaying society. I only pity his ignorance. He cannot remove me [since his position was permanent] just as I cannot do anything to him. We will both go our ways when we retire, not before. But now the younger caste-Hindu teachers criticize him, not me. They often share my agony [*piṛā*] and are ashamed of him. This new attitude speaks of a change.

Rejecting the Hindu sacred, he would diffuse the bias with help from liberalizing social attitudes.

Overview

More than the specific cases and relations considered here, this discussion illustrates additional procedures the Chamars apply to find out who they are and what to do to disperse social bias. The Chamar thus uses his approach to serve as an example to the wider Indian society: He demonstrates his market-relations approach toward others. If the Chamar's identification of his social condition is marked by social calculation, there is a corresponding effort to determine and confront the odds still posed by social deprivations. The Chamar shows how he utilizes his social resources and expectations to politicize and challenge the given biases and deprivations. He also injects a certain idealism into pragmatic interests, opening up new options from within old restrictions.

Our exercise shows the range of social skill he has acquired thus far in these actions under differing circumstances. He now makes more social decisions and accepts more responsibilities. He classifies his deprivation and social biases to encounter them better. We might thus also be seeing how the Pariah is turning into *Homo politicus* in full view of the caste Hindu. And this change (not unlike the caste Hindu's) is being brought about, as we have seen, through a conscious willing and thinking, a restructuring of cultural categories and their meanings, a production of metalanguage, and a slow but definite subversion of the traditional social inequality and dominance. It is thus also that the Chamars enter the domains of newer social and political accountability. Their practical issues and interests offer the contexts for testing and developing this accountability. Whether emerging from the sacred or the secular domains, the accountability acquires significance for them only when it is a part of their composite system of meanings and meaningful "things" (see Sahlins 1976: 206–7). This system may neither totally annihilate nor substitute for the caste Hindu's order of values and claims, but it certainly manipulates them in new ways to acquire a distinct social presence.

9. Evaluation and accountability

The Lucknow Chamars thus engaged in identifying their position in postindependent India lead us to a discussion of how they accommodate secular forces of contemporary Indian society.[1] These secular forces are strategically significant to the Indian Untouchable. The traditional disabilities are reevaluated as new dimensions of reformed self-identity and awareness are introduced, and as democratic economic, legal, and political measures are pressed into service. These forces can make a vital difference to "the ageless Untouchable," although they can be effective only in ways (and degrees) in which he can make them meaningful to himself and his own conditions. Both the pursuit of new social opportunities and an evaluation of specific hurdles are vital to the Untouchable. We will consider here how the Lucknow Chamars might proceed in such a direction under certain contexts and how new social forces encourage them to acquire a new social accountability.

The secular culture, for our purpose, is best translated as resulting in *additional* orders of social relevance, perspective, estimation, and accountability. Indian democracy is an important, but not the only, source of these orders. Given Indian conditions to date, these orders must compete in a politically "open" (but not socially nondiscriminatory) arena. Caste idioms, weak and strong, pervade this arena although it remains accessible to different social approaches and perspectives. The secular culture of India (as perhaps anywhere else) can therefore be assumed to be neither homogeneous in content nor uniform in strength and expression. It is expressed through multiple views and values, and comes from within and without the Indian order. The Indian secular domain hosts wide-ranging internal and external forces, whether cooperating or competing or conflicting or neutral.

Contemporary Chamars face the task of rehabilitating themselves within such secular contexts. From one perspective it is now that "given" of the social condition that offers them "escape routes" from the traditional order and its values. It brings them a new "mentality" with which to approach themselves, their caste behavior, and wider social surroundings. In the last thirty years or so, the secular culture has acquired a distinct significance for the Chamars, allowing some of the educated ones to argue that democratic values have given a new direction to their reformist thought. This secular culture and its newly acquired democratic values have already caused the sacred to yield a new social space to the Indian Untouchable.

One impact of the secular culture shows up when the Untouchable, who customarily has a "noncompetitive" and subjugated social status, discovers through experience that competition is one of the major mechanisms for his social recuperation and that he can make tactical tradeoffs between his options of "exit," "voice," and "loyalty" (e.g., see Hirschman 1970, taking this scheme to stand for a much wider tactic for politico-economic action).[2]

To do so is to claim a new social right and responsibility. The Lucknow Chamar finds the incentive for this claim in his reformist ideology. If the social reality still places numerous impediments in the way of such a development, his efforts to seek social justice and fairness continue to grow. His claims for positive social accountability demand a basic change in the alignment of power relations within Indian society. The Untouchable's view of the caste systemic justice is essentially Thrasymachean – offering "enforced obedience" – whereas the democratic alternative brings to him the Socratic version, in which power and sanction express a "general will that represents the consensus of the society's members" (see Dahrendorf 1968: 129–50).[3]

As a result of the democratic ethos, Lucknow Chamar thinkers now increasingly engage in a focused discussion of *comparative* social responsibility – of their own toward themselves and to the society, and of the caste Hindu toward them and Indian democracy at large. Obviously, their discussions relate most often to the events and conditions of their daily life. As we will see, the Chamars are now developing a sense for comprehensive social accountability, an accountability that will award them equality in the eyes of the rest of society, and let them be responsible for themselves. Such an accountability is innately positive and it includes varied forms of individual and social responsibilities. Chamar thinkers make a clear distinction between positive and negative social accountability, since the Chamars have been the victim of negative accountability, they argue, all through Indian history. Chamar thinkers also emphasize, however, that they must constantly claim, compete, and contest in modern India to acquire the desired positive accountability. Society will not present it to them without dissent, remonstrance, and contestation.

Evaluators and evaluation

The Lucknow Chamars demonstrate a logical connection between social accountability and evaluation when they repeatedly identify why they are what they are under a certain circumstance, and how they might be accorded some *positive*, *undisputed* social accountability. They evaluate what others do to them vis-à-vis what they themselves actually do (or can do) to others under normal circumstances. Any social evaluation cognitively involves ascertainment (*jānanā* and *patā lagānā* in Hindi) and estimation (*taulanā*), usually in quick succession. Knowing what others (e.g., the caste Hindus) might be doing toward them is insufficient unless it is also accompanied by an idea of what it means to them, and their own social contribution to a particular event or situation.

When the three Lucknow Chamar localities were examined for such distinctions, some of their resident ascetics and reformers translated these processes into their concerns. Ordinary Chamar ascetics crowd to do such translation now, since the genuine ascetic *hero*, the root of all charismatic reform, is extremely rare. One Baudhabagh ascetic observed:

> There are now no genuine Ravidasas, only Ravidas temples. But this should be no cause for despair. Instead, there should be a renewed dedication to our ideals. My concern is that the low-caste ascetic is increasingly timid; his protest is not selfless and therefore neither genuine nor influential. This is perhaps a part of the divine plan. Yet we [i.e., the routine ascetics] must make our best efforts for the betterment of our people. I am not a leader and do not want to be one, but I have ideas about what my followers tell me, what I have experienced and observed, and what the Untouchables' previous experiences have been. The Chamar has been too simplehearted [*sīdhā-sādhā*] and too gullible for too long. We believe too quickly whatever we are not. Our recent social experience [*sāmājika anubhava*] demands that we change; we need to discriminate [i.e., exercise *vivéka*] between our positive role and responsibility, those of others, and the importance of what we do [as against that left undone]. We should no longer be the duped buyers [*ṭhagé kharīdadār*] either of the caste Hindu's platitudes or of the politician's flattery. We are now learning to test [*parakhanā*] others' intentions and actions toward us, and weigh and measure [*nāpanā aur taulanā*] our response toward them. We must also tactfully disguise and hide [i.e., keep *gupta*], as necessary, our true aims and intentions from our social adversaries. To recommend it is not to encourage falsehood but only to be tactical [*paitaṛébāza*] in order to survive.

Such an evaluation is encountered in the same type of ascetic who would position himself in the previous chapters (e.g., 4, 6, and 7) sometimes as an ideologist and at others as a pragmatist. He is seldom a tactical leader himself but a promoter of social and political tactics. He is one of several nodes through which politicization of the local Chamar goes on, since he sows the seeds of social evaluation and accountability among his faithful followers and listeners in a surprisingly effective manner. Such an ascetic is a social guide as well as a guru, casually telling his followers ways to survive in a world of hard knocks (*ṭhokar mārnéwālī duniyā*). Such an ascetic usually helps the Chamar formulate a positive social accountability for himself through practical and political initiatives.

Although this type of ascetic remains a crucial link, he is by no means alone in this task. He is joined by an increasing (and restive) group of educated youth, office workers, the work-seeking unemployed, and new leaders. The last is a heterogeneous group, ranging from a leaderlike householder in, say,

Karampura, Baudhabagh, and Modernganj to a professional party politician. Unlike the protesting ascetic (e.g., Achchutananda) who is a "brink man," and unlike the syncretizing leader (e.g., Ambedkar) who would be a "bridge" devoted to attaining politico-economic rights in terms of a new cultural or political ideology, the new leader is essentially a manager of immediate pragmatic interests. He is still being formed and hence shows signs of being fickle, impatient, and inconsistent. Yet he presents a distinctly multifunctional leadership that must be reckoned with (see Khare 1979).

At a later point we will discuss the variety of protests raised by the new leader. We must note here his counterpart, the new professional and administrative elite, a group that is still very small but quite aware of its prestigious social placement. It is this group nevertheless that significantly contributes to strengthening the processes of social evaluation and accountability. A product of modern education and secular provisions of independent India, this Chamar elite is shaped by an all-Indian Westernized "rational" ethos. On close inspection, however, such an ethos quickly begins to dissipate into uneven regional cultural and pragmatic strains. The Westernized rational ethos is thus encountered most often only under formal organizational rules. But since it also quickly adapts to indigenous social forces, it helps open the traditional sectors of social life to external forces.

What it means sociologically is that traditional social loyalties pervade this Western, rational ethos from the front as well as the back door. The Lucknow Chamar elites begin by pursuing this ethos as something new, genuine, and liberating. However, the more they do so, the more they learn what it actually is and how it really works. Though the Untouchable elites are a desirable subject and statistic for the annual Reports of the Commissioner for Scheduled Castes and Scheduled Tribes (e.g., see Part I of the report for 1975–7), they are of much greater practical and tactical significance to the ordinary Chamar. They are the cream of the community, looked to for help in personal and social matters. They evaluate social conditions for themselves and for their relatives, friends, and emulators. The ordinary Chamar places much hope in them for "getting the work done in a city."

But even so the Chamar elite also goes through a phase of estrangement from its own people. This is so because a Chamar official usually finds his role models on the "other" – the caste Hindu – side. If he therefore neglects or forgets or offends his own people, he disappoints them and feels guilty. He is charged with becoming a cultural amnesiac. As he acquires greater social experience and perspective, however, he finds himself alienated from the larger caste-Hindu counterpart and its "secular society" and from his own "less educated people." He discovers that whatever he is in the office is only an incomplete achievement, for it can lighten but not remove the Chamars' social burdens. He also finds that his own people isolate him in subtle ways. These strains thus demand that he be tactful toward the caste Hindu as well as the Chamar; that he control and manipulate his power and influence; and that he constantly evaluate his competing social responsibilities.

The new leader, the new elite, and the reformist ascetic are therefore some of the major social agents who discuss the significant questions of Chamar social evaluation and accountability. Let us briefly consider these evaluators in an ethnographic context.

A prominent new leader in Moderngani was a *khādī*–clad employee of the general post office. He lived on the outskirts of the neighborhood with his educated wife and their daughter, and he was readily conspicuous to the ordinary Chamar. Actually, he was an exception in that as a prominent person he lived so close to an ordinary Chamar locality. He himself had remarked on it. Though a Gandhian Congress party member devoted to helping his community members, he admitted to neighbors that he favored some Chamars over others. Several Modernganj Chamars recalled situations in which he had been critically helpful, especially those concerning government offices and hospitals. He had helped a Chamar get a government permit for buying cement from a controlled shop. The Chamar needed it urgently since the rains were imminent and the roof of his house had cracked. A gravely sick Chamar woman was neglected in the public hospital and the leader had to exert indirect political influence over the hospital administrator to get her proper attention. The same leader one day remarked before six Chamar youths, his followers, on the necessity to press for attention and to engage in self-evaluation:

> If we want the caste Hindus to stop criticizing us for our inappropriate social habits and attitudes, we should be fully prepared to make self-evaluations and self-criticisms. If we become aware of the problems we have, and if we have the resolve and the initiative to correct them, others in the society will have to recognize our worth. If they still do not, the law of the land is on our side. Today, we try to improve ourselves but only half-heartedly, because we still doubt our strength and the goodwill of the society at large. We explore the opportunities half way, and remove the impediments half-heartedly. This is because we are as unsure about the democratic changes in the society as we are about ourselves. But we are not alone: The caste Hindus also suffer from the same malaise. The old ways do not work with them as surely as they want them to, and the new puzzles and unsettles them. Thus while we wonder what they are up to, they fear what we want to grab next. Because both are insecure and both a little confused, the situation is so complicated that everybody has to look out for his own interests. And we, the Chamars, can secure our interests only if we learn to evaluate and assert in our lives. The passive Chamar, who only waits to be judged by others, is a loser in today's India.

Such a leader was absent form both Baudhabagh and Karampura, though both localities depended on several new leaders resident outside. Locally, there were either some relatives in touch with such leaders or those who had political ambitions of their own. These local contacts are critical for social evaluation, for they introduce the ordinary Chamar to assessing changing social pressures and illustrate the role of democratic politics in daily life. A Karampura Chamar, a night watchman at a government building, collaborated with an employee in a pharmaceutical firm to form an ad hoc team for advising the local youths on their problems in getting education and employment. An intransigent caste-Hindu employer, an evasive officer, an unsympathetic moneylender, and a Bania grocer (i.e., a stingy *paṅsārī*) who refused to sell any more food on credit all created immediate problems for the ordinary Chamars, and the two-person team helped them.

Whether the ordinary Chamar assigns him similar roles or not, the local ascetic often assumes the role of an evaluator on their behalf. He may take it to be his right, considering the moral and spiritual guide (i.e., a type of evaluator) he must always be to his disciples. Practical and political tactics are the natural next step for this type of ascetic. A young, literate ascetic from Baudhabagh observed:

> I decided to enter the fray of everyday life for bringing about social reform. What cannot be cured from a distance and needs urgent reform must merit this type of involvement, provided first that I am sure the aim is clearly to enhance the [Untouchable] community's welfare [*samāja kalyāṇa*], and second, that I know how to limit my involvement in it. If I were not already an ordained ascetic I would have been a political leader. My father enjoyed respect as well as social following in my own and neighboring villages.

His face would light up when talking about such subjects before an ethnographer with a tape recorder, especially when also surrounded by a few younger community leaders. He would freely indulge in prescriptions, recommendations, suggestions, and his own evaluations, making his enthusiasm evident to the Chamars in the audience.

Much harder, however, was to come across the situation in which an administrative Chamar elite also simultaneously participated in the lives of his community members on an everyday basis. The higher his position, the busier, more socially aloof, and less personally open he was likely to be. He was seldom found to live in the same locality as the ordinary Chamar; the latter had to go to him at the official's convenience, and to communicate with him within the situational limits he set. Much less accessible than the routine ascetic, but commanding far more worldly prestige and influence, the Chamar administrator, albeit rare, was a bright spot for those ordinary Chamars who cultivated his contact and friendship. (Being a relative of such a person was helpful but not always sufficient.)

But, as the Chamars repeatedly remarked, the administrative elite were often more principled than the elected leaders, who were harder to influence (given their own long-standing sycophants), and usually expected cultivated political loyalty. When an ordinary Chamar was a relative of such an administrator, he saw him on certain ceremonial occasions but did not automatically receive more favors. He had to cultivate the contact carefully in order to be in a favorable position. Only a selected few, I discovered, could cultivate such prestigious contacts on a sustained basis within the three localities.

More generally, the majority of the Lucknow Chamars entered into exercises of self- and social evaluation *after* a significant social action, event, or initiative. Loss of a job, a family quarrel, sickness, and an incident of discrimination invited such an exercise. The only exception was found among professional politicians, who must continuously engage in such evaluation. Some new leaders, however, engaged in them both at the beginning and conclusion of a particular endeavor, carrying "lessons" (*sabaka*) from one experience to the next. Generally, *failures* intensified these experiences, enabling the new leaders to apportion blame, responsibility, difficulty, and helplessness (*bébasī*) among themselves and the Chamars. The issue of who, or what, was most accountable for a particular failure was integral to such discussions. On the other hand, happier but less penetrating evaluations tended to follow success.

Events resulting in loss of honor, livelihood, daily food supply, and physical safety led to serious stock taking of self and society. As these events carried social lessons from one experience to the next, they also exposed one's helplessness. Spontaneous gatherings appeared repeatedly for sizing up a critical event like an accident or injury. The leaders and elite sympathetic to the aggrieved were immediately consulted and their advice was taken for an appropriate response. "Learning done on such occasions is permanent; it etches the mind of all, whether an ordinary Chamar or not" (the comment of a Baudhabagh Chamar leader).

In contrast was that evaluation conducted on a daily basis, as a normal cognitive activity. Its impact was "temporary" and was usually lost in the fare of daily life, with now pleasing and then sad memories left behind. The local evaluators – new locality leaders, ascetics, elders, relatives, and friends – randomly participated in this process in Modernganj as they handled, for example, the following situations: a small boy beaten up by a few caste-Hindu boys, a woman deprived of collecting cow dung from a particular street, a Chamar customer rebuked and rebuffed by a local shopkeeper, and a misbehaving upper-caste office colleague. Evenings and holidays were the normal occasions for working men to discuss and evaluate such incidents. In general, of the three localities studied, Baudhabagh seemed the most riddled by everyday social stresses, spending also commensurately much more time and effort in soothing itself with aid from those who were experienced, influential, and wise. The routine ascetic demonstrated his healing function best under such circumstances, variously placing ultimate values over proximate ones (and vice versa). Such an ascetic made the ordinary Chamars' living conditions endurable; he stressed hope and persistence to despondent Chamars.

Generally, we may observe that the greater the *everyday* accumulation of personal stress around the issues of self-image, food, housing, and livelihood, the more restive and resentful the Chamars' social evaluations become and the more intensive the yearning for radical change.

Some general tendencies stand out as the Chamars evaluate their social conditions. They are (a) holding *others* primarily responsible for their social stresses and deprivations; (b) criticizing their own low social estimates of themselves; (c) translating social subordination (and their "innate inferiority") into a confrontation of cultural ideologies, and the latter into a contest of pragmatic and political tactics; (d) raising a positive accountability for themselves under a secular democratic ethos; (e) multiplying practical and political arenas in which to test new provisions of their rights against traditional responsibilities; (f) campaigning for stronger government support and protection to quickly right accumulated deprivations; and (g) seeking to reconstitute their identity and individuation so totally that they become culturally genuine and unconditional recipients of social equality and justice.

Protest becomes a social technique and resentment a catalyst for such a comprehensive view of Chamar social evaluations. The efficacy of protest becomes apparent when we consider how its different versions (from mild to militant) are employed, and how its social consequences (whether positive or negative) are followed up by context. The ultimate goal of protest is to reduce the institutionalized disabilities of the Chamar. An appropriate political rhetoric usually remains a significant ally of the Chamar, though it usually presents a picture that is several steps removed from actual social conditions.

The new leaders and elite Chamars, who use the most rhetoric, illustrate a proposition: The less explicit the acceptance of responsibility for the Chamar's social position, the greater the maneuvering room available for holding the opposite camp accountable for the Chamars' own social disadvantage. Protests are evaluated for their impact both during and after their expression, according to these leaders. The leaders thus tend to inculcate an ethos of protest in all three Lucknow localities. According to a new leader from Modernganj:

> We do so to keep our community members awake to the exploitation by the Hindus. We try to make noise even at the slightest provocation; it deters those who may have taken us for granted. All of this now works because there is always some politician out in this city ready to hear our protest [and identify himself with it] for his own political credit. This politician does not have to be a Chamar.

Analytically, what the new leader and the reforming ascetic are doing is to refine social uses of protest until it becomes a fine-tuned instrument for the desired social change. If their protest has become a tactical weapon for them, the quest for a new societal accountability becomes its directing force.

The new leaders among the Lucknow Chamars were socially and politically sensitive but often neither professional reformers nor politicians. Most were moderates (*naram*), and only a few were radicals and militants (*garam*). Often educated and stably employed, they handled their leadership role as anything from a social service to a serious vocation. Although not a politician himself, a new leader from Baudhabagh would routinely approach a politician he knew well to manage issues of immediate interest (e.g., getting a government grant, acceptance at a school, a scholarship, a bank loan, a hospital admission, or employment) to himself and to his relatives, friends, and followers.

This new leader varied, according to the situation, his political tactics, protest, reform rhetoric, and social stance. He would, for example, make the caste Hindu his "brethren" on one occasion and his opponents on another. From his point of view, this got the maximum mileage out of the condition at hand. He increasingly considered the most effective way to protest on a particular occasion – when, how much, and in what social language. He would tend as well as contend protest. He suppressed it to convey one message and indulged in sloganeering to produce another.

As a cultural type, such a new leader is essentially a loose assembly of the babu-ascetic-politician roles and values. He aspires to be a babu of the "middle class" in modern India by garnering personal position, influence, and wealth; he wants to practice self-control to remain true to his ascetic heritage; and he becomes a power broker to improve his own lot and that of his "brothers." In practice, these three elements are never free from an internal strain. When strong on the first and third roles, for example, he is rated a Hindu-like leader who is more a babu and a politician than the Chamar's well-wisher. One who is strong on the first and the second is considered a "guide."

Readily accessible, these leaders were informally doing more for themselves and their community members than the formal elites and professional politicians. They represented the awakened eyes, ears, and hands of the Chamar community on an everyday basis. This point was illustrated during a meeting of five locality members – a Baudhabagh ascetic, two new leaders (one, my host, was mild and the other radical), a school teacher, and a shoe-shop owner (quoted also in the context of discussions at the Lucknow Ravidas temple in chap. 7). Sitting under a large (5 foot by 4 foot) painting of the beckoning Baba Saheb (Dr. Ambedkar) in my host's drawing room on a cloudy and cold Sunday afternoon, they themselves composed for us a portrait of the instrumental strivings of the contemporary Chamar.[4]

After introducing me to the group, the ascetic observed as follows:

> We have discussed here over the years many problems of our locality, some urgent and some concerning who we are and what we are becoming. I check, criticize, and differ from these four on many occasions but they return to meet me because they know I mean well toward all. Narayan *bhāī* [i.e., the shoe-shop owner] is illiterate but experienced [*paṛhé nahiñ par kaṛhé adhika*]. His acid tongue does not spare anybody, not even Baba Saheb [Ambedkar], when necessary. But listen carefully to what he has to say. Master saheb [i.e., the school teacher] is just like me, though a householder. He has a son in college, earns a regular salary, keeps helping as best he can the locality youngsters inside the school and outside, studies often what our reformers have written, and remains unruffled under difficult circumstances. But do not mistake him for a bookworm [*kitābī kīṛā*], for he is at once very practical and knows about political strategies [*rājnītika hathakandé*]. He must have been a "real"

brother [*sagé bhāī*] in his previous birth to our host [i.e., the father of the medical graduate]. A quick-witted person [*hāzirajawāba*] and now retired from a long-held office job in the city, he is our "eyes" as he tracks down what goes on within our locality [actually he meant keeping a watch on the two lanes of the neighborhood], and "hands," because he also keeps contact with several officers and politicians. When *he* asks them, they take care of us.

That the other four only nodded to (but did not dispute) what the ascetic had to say not only showed the way this type of ascetic maintains *his* position and influence within a group of effective evaluators, but also illustrated the social composition, coherence, and resources of such groups to manage the rights and responsibilities of the ordinary Chamar. We will reenter this ethnographic context a little later.

Accountability

The Lucknow Chamar, most simply, orders his accountability under the immediate–ultimate value axis and the "we"–"they" axis. He simultaneously handles the strains of his practical-social responsibility along these two axes, contextually raising or lowering the significance of each. Thus, for example, if an ordinary Chamar considers himself primarily responsible for securing food, clothing, and housing (*rotī, Kapṛā, aur makān*; also incidentally the title of a recent Hindi movie popular with my younger informants) for himself and his family, he must do so by means that will maintain his personal honor and dignity. To do so is to be accountable to himself and to the Chamar community. Further, because he is often these days also something more – either a local politician or a faction leader or a competitor or a claimant (for employment and democratic rights) or a complainer or a recipient (of social welfare services) – his responsibility before himself and the larger society is perhaps more complex, prominent, and persistent than ever before. Not only does he want to be counted, but contemporary Indian society cannot discount him.

Overall, and as expected, Modernganj Chamars gave greater attention to pragmatic aims than did those in Baudhabagh and Karampura, although one could also argue that this might, in part, have been due to a relatively weaker role of ascetics in Modernganj. One encountered significant differences within Modernganj as well, however. There were, for example, locally prominent political leaders adept at practical solutions, and those who had sacrificed their jobs in order to maintain their honor.

The case of a Modernganj mechanic illustrated several sides of the Chamar's social accountability. Though skilled in his work, he had recently resigned from an automobile repair shop because he was paid less than some others for doing the same work. His grievance was overlooked despite his polite representations and protests. Though he felt he was working hard (actually harder than others), the owner was not paying him appropriately. After repeated protests, he felt isolated in the shop. Since his pressing concern was feeding his family, he did not leave the job at once despite provocations. His attitude toward the owner (and of the owner toward him) had changed, however. He felt that others in the shop kept their distance from him. One day the owner criticized him for repairing a car that broke down several times in quick succession, and a heated exchange ensued. The owner could not condone harsh words from a Chamar, according to the mechanic, and he was suspended. The mechanic resigned on the spot, as he later said, "to save the honor and dignity of my forefathers and myself."

He and his family faced very difficult conditions for the next six months as a consequence. He took to gambling in a small lane half a mile from his house. His wife had to take up daily wage labor, although their three children (ages one to four) needed her care; she was able to buy barely enough food for the family. But the mechanic did not stray far because his self-pride (the same factor that had made him resign his job), his sense of duty toward the family, and his guru (who offered him constant moral support to try again) had stood by him. Meanwhile, he met a dealer in automobile spare parts (new and used) and worked for him for six weeks. The owner (another Hindu) liked his skills and hired him for good pay. The mechanic soon became the manager of a section. He felt that he had vindicated himself as well as the Chamar pride. He commented on this dimension of accountability his way:

> By my guru's and God's grace I am flourishing. I did not forget my duties, though I was just about to do so. Living in the same society, the Hindus are answerable to us and we are to them. They will have to be held accountable, sooner or later, for their unfulfilled obligations and violated promises; we will be held accountable for our deficiencies. Our lives will be less tense only if they fulfill their reponsibilities and we ours. However, even if they do not, our rights and responsibilities [*adhikār aur kartavya*] in independent India are increasing and the Chamars should do their share. The Hindus will have to follow us.

Accountability, thus, is given added prominence and interpretation among the Lucknow Chamars. If they can now manipulate somewhat the contexts and relations of their own positive accountability, thanks to the postindependent ethos, they must still be prepared to handle themselves under social stress and disability. To consolidate their positive accountability, therefore, they find that they have to make a two-pronged movement: tactfully exploiting the caste-Hindu given institutions, rituals, and ethos (*māhaul*) among themselves, and consolidating their economic and political position to nudge the educated caste-Hindu's ambivalent conscience. Through experience, they find even this caste Hindu evasive, doubting, and wavering. But to a new leader from Baudhabagh social accommodation is inevitable for both:

> Neither we nor they [urban caste Hindus] are going to disappear. Their self-interest is best served now by recognizing the changing times. Our hope lies in the fact that

they will finally realize that this society can now work only by cooperation and sharing, not dominance and exclusion. Obviously, we also will gain little by making them our all-out opponents, although a few militants among us do think this way.

Further, several Chamar political leaders commented that their "minority status" brought them ambiguous recognition. They argued that their "community" was neither a truly religious minority nor yet a sufficiently cohesive political or ethnic group. Since they were also unsure whether they really wanted to be counted *only* as a political minority, their ambivalence toward minority status was clear. Actually, they wanted to secure the legal, political, and economic privileges guaranteed to a minority under the democratic system, but they refused to identify themselves as a minority group only. As an educated leader in Karampura noted:

The Untouchable is not a minority like the Muslim and the Christian, because we are neither immigrants into India nor aliens to the formation of this culture and civilization. Our number is much larger than the census indicates. Our stakes in this civilization are much higher and we are prepared to wage a long struggle to secure our rightful place within it. If minority politics can be helpful in this aim, we will make its full use but we will not settle for anything less than what is really our place.

We may remark that a Chamar political leader, though not a political analyst, also understands certain basic limits of Indian minority politics. He most often learns its efficacy by seeing the Muslim in political action. But he concedes equally readily that he cannot practice this politics, either the same way or with the same results. He cannot acquire the position of another religious community fully without losing his civilizational position. The force of Indian cultural ethnicity thus becomes obvious in a new way under democracy: Even the most deprived people discover reasons to forge a positive cultural identity and dignity for themselves. The Chamars do so in terms of the larger Indic culture. Without it, they lose their self, their credibility in their own eyes. For the same reason, the primary cultural cleavages between the Chamar and the Muslim are normally considered too unpredictable and risky. The Chamar may politically court the Muslim, and vice versa, but it is mostly for limited tactical reasons. Their interrelationships underline the point that if both seek protection – legal, economic, and political – from the majority, they want it on their *own* separate terms, and for two very different cultural reasons.

At this point let us reenter the ethnographic encounter portrayed earlier. As the context brings together an ascetic reformer, two new leaders (one mild and the other militant), a school teacher, and a shoe-shop owner, it advances our discussion by itself. It informs as well as articulates first hand a perspective on composite social accountability.

A discussion led by the new leader (the mild one, who was forty-five years old) brought out some salient features of *their* comprehension and evaluation of minority politics. The leader initiated his comment on the intense political ethos thus:

Politicians have made us a minority [*alpasaṃkhyaka*] in the first place, adding a new weapon to their armory. They call us whatever suits their purpose best. Sometimes they say that we are a larger group of the small group [i.e., a majority within a minority], sometimes merely a smaller group of a small group [i.e., a minority within a minority], and sometimes a small group of the larger group [i.e., a minority within a majority]. It is really a puzzle hard to figure out in any other way than as a politician's miracle [*karishmā* or *camatkāra*]. But my politician friends tell me that this is not so; it is instead a part of the complex society in which we live, and that we should leave all of this for the politicians to handle. But how can we? Actually, it makes me doubly suspicious of the politician. There might be hidden somewhere in it a new trick of the caste Hindus.

At this point the militant new leader (twenty-five years old) interjected:

I have been telling you that all of this is a fabrication of both [i.e., the Untouchable leaders as well as caste politicians]. We are duped and kept dependent through these talks. I know this is a noose that will only tighten to exploit us until we rise in unity to combat those who are the perpetrators of injustice. We must seek a confrontation [*samanā*] and a battlefield [*morcā*] of our own choice. [This excerpt is the abbreviated version of the original comment.]

The last comment prompted an irritated glance from the ascetic, whereas the shoe-shop owner encouraged the militant to go on. The school teacher, however, joined the discussion on his own at this point:

What good is this talk when you and I know that we lack unity among ourselves? You refuse to see it, hoping your talk [i.e., rhetoric] will bring it about. But it will not because all is not that bleak. As with the keys of a harmonium, politicians work on us to select their tunes to sell what will keep them in power. They will, of course, make us look big or small, strong or weak, and good or bad through such tunes. If we still fall for the politicians' ploys and quarrel among ourselves to gain their small favors, who is to blame? Our problem is that we can neither totally break away from nor embrace those who oppress [*satāté*] us. I hold this state to be due to that root of casteism [*jātiyatā kī jaṛa*] that we still do not know how to remove and destroy. But we are loosening this big tree and the soil around it. He [pointing toward Ambedkar's portrait] started it. We must carry it on with patience. Once we have our roots, however, this hesitation to break off will go away. You [i.e., the militant leader] must join all of us in establishing our own root, for who can survive without it?

Pleased and nodding his head in approval, the ascetic added:

The basis for a genuine alternative root lies within us – the Untouchable. The only real seed [*bīja*] is our *ātman* [soul], and the ascetic [*yatī aur yogī*] tells you how to nurture [*poṣaṇa*] it to let a sapling develop on its own root. Do not [pointing toward the militant leader] become so impatient that you sell your soul for false hopes. But at the same time do not let up and do not forget what you really are. Genuine change [*saccā parivartana*] can come only this way. Once you remember this caution, pull and tug at the caste Hindu (or other social opponents) as often as situations permit. Now politics is a part of life, so why not play it to your best advantage? Most of all, if this is inevitable for the removal of injustice [*atyācāra*], it becomes a part of our dharma. It gives us added responsibility [*uttardāittava*].

The school teacher and the ascetic, in general, advocated gradual but irreversible change, building on slackening institutional restrictions and gathering secular gains. They thought that the future would be built exactly on such opportunities, bringing about "a genuine revolution (*krānti*) from *within* us."[5]

Overview

The preceding discussion demonstrates how the Lucknow Chamars account for themselves and the society in which they live. It reveals a range of cognitive platforms for mediation between thought and action. These platforms, in turn, indicate some general characteristics of the Chamars' approach to contemporary secular and political forces. One characteristic is repeatedly evident: The Chamars gravitate most often toward a middle course, one that moved away from militant radicalism as well as social passivity. We have seen how (and why) the Chamars must prevent militant radicalism from gathering force. But simultaneously we also show how their thoughts, language, and social actions are undergoing a pervasive cognitive reorganization. There is an edge and urgency in their social evaluations. The depth and sweep of their cognitive remapping spell out the seriousness of their social condition.

A fuller sociological significance of the pragmatic strategy of the Chamars emerges when juxtaposed with the Hindu caste system and its praxis. I shall make some general observations on the issue (see also n. 5, this chapter) now that the evidence has been presented. An important point in this regard is that whatever the Chamar ideology and pragmatism do occurs every day in the face of the caste order and its institutions. Our evidence supports the view that the contemporary Indian social order as a whole carries *several* culturally significant evaluative and decision-making structures and that the caste order, with its emphasis on the rules of prescribed ritual coherence, is only *one* of these. We must recognize that caste-generated values and social perspectives yield primarily caste-bound views of Indian society. Only the study of a whole range of evaluative orders (including those anticaste or noncaste) can help us reach a view of Indian civilization and social reality that is neither incomplete nor distorted.

This way certain false theoretical battles will also be removed from center stage. The anthropology of an entire civilization will not be reduced to the sociology of the Hindu caste system. Alternative schemes of cultural ideas and actions will not be judged for authenticity simply by their cogency to caste ideas and relations. The dualist, dichotomous explanation of the Untouchable (see Moffatt 1979) will not have to stretch to do what it evidently cannot, that is, explain a system that rests on more than dualism (for certain formulations in this direction, see Marriott 1976; Khare 1976, 1978). A point of larger theoretical strategy will also remain clear: Though considering caste principles, functions, and purposes against a much larger canvas of Indian civilization is neither to belittle nor bypass the continuing significance of the Indian caste system, it is to deny the caste order the final and complete explanatory significance when other indigenous moral orders may explain more, and explain it better.

Some precautionary distinctions may therefore be necessary for a sociological analysis of contemporary Indian society. For example, it is one thing to argue that the Indian caste order bases itself on a cluster of critical civilizational constructs (for nobody can deny it), but quite another to argue that this cluster is the one and *the only one* that is morally (i.e., by dharma) most authentic, sociologically real, and practically pervasive within the Indian society. Even within caste studies, it is one point that the caste order is hierarchical but quite another that it is *only* so and nothing else. It is one argument that the caste order is socially tenacious, massive, and enduring but it is quite another that this is the only social terra firma available to the Indian. The general point these distinctions make should not be misunderstood: Although a careful sociology of caste has offered invaluable learning, its formulations (and their explicit assumptions) need careful and objective examination from several different directions, lest they assume, conflate, appropriate, conceal, and discard whatever is found to be different from or contradictory to caste logic. Indian civilization, besides caste, also includes the noncaste, the extracaste, and the "uncaste" domains, and all could be regarded as equally authentic under alternative forms of cultural reasoning.

Placed in this larger analytic perspective, the Lucknow Chamar data show how their conflict *and* consensus must move in relation to the local caste Hindu. We learn how these two groups must adapt and evaluate in terms of each other; and how, in the face of the caste collective, the Chamars must contextually *individuate* as they think, express, evaluate, decide, and act under a strong pragmatic ethos.

Because (a) "social actions are comments on more than themselves," (b) "where an interpretation comes from does not determine where it can be impelled to go," and (c) "small facts speak to larger issues . . . because they are made to" (Geertz 1973: 23), the pictures of the Lucknow Chamars that we have pieced together and interpreted draw attention to a whole chain of deeper civilizational issues and social processes.[6] The ideal (equalitarian) constructs are translated into a pragmatic grammar of willing, thinking, "voice," and instrumental action. The instrumental social action necessitates social calculation, market relations, identification of odds, decision making, and practical action. Finally, as the practical action becomes competitive, it demands evolution of pragmatic strategies, social responsibilities and participation in organized political confrontations. Such a chain of developments lets us see how the Untouchables' traditional social disadvantage must now respond to a wavering pragmatism from within the Indian cultural system. However, the middling measures of compensation and compromise mute any premature hope for social equality and justice.

Conclusion: Aspects of significance

Rather than following a rising curve of cumulative findings, cultural analysis breaks up into a disconnected yet coherent sequence of bolder and bolder sorties . . . Every serious cultural analysis starts from a sheer beginning and ends where it manages to get before exhausting its intellectual impulse. [Geertz 1973: 25]

A recapitulation: the four strands

Miniaturized and simplified, the following will be a dominant and four-stranded profile of the discussions this study has produced. The first strand, as ideologically explicated, rests on a transcendent, ultimate order of Indic equality and justice. It aims at absolute spiritual equality and gathers support from spiritual ascetics and heroes to reform the social. The underlying principle is to demonstrate the superiority of spiritual over worldly morality. The second strand reflects the first's difficulty in the actual world and is marked by the ascetic's and the hero's efforts to reform. It presents the prospect of social reform, often slow and sporadically inspired. We may recall the regional ascetic (the Untouchable as well as the low-caste) reformers in this context (e.g. Achchutananda, 1879–1933, from the then United Provinces and Jotibe Fule, 1827–90, from Maharashtra, to whom, incidentally, Ambedkar dedicated his first book, *Who Were the Shudras?*).

The third strand is concerned with organized political protests and their culmination in a pragmatic pursuit of legal and economic claims (and its contests). Though a logical extension of the first two, this strand has, of course, been distinctly shaped by the changing politico-economic character of Indian society during this century. Ambedkar (1892–1956) is obviously the fountainhead. A dynamic and charismatic (but fettered) leader in life, he posthumously became a cultural hero and demigod for the Untouchables. He led them through the processes of countercaste demarcation, competition, confrontation, and routinization of politics. The Lucknow Chamars followed him with awe and inspiration. Still his political achievements had to be remarkable for their ambiguity: When he drove a hard political bargain (as with Gandhi, leading to the Poona Pact; see Ambedkar 1948; Keer 1962) he had only mixed results. (See also Shastri 1977, for a popular account of this pact written in Hindi for the ordinary Chamar reader.) When he "exited" from the Hindu order, he landed in the related alternative (Buddhism) that was both weak and defunct on the subcontinent. This strand of religious, legal, and political claims confronted, therefore, Hindu moral structures the length and breadth of a whole new nation. But again it yielded further tensions. If the earlier moral issue was thus made thoroughly political, linking to the affairs of a secular state, a politicized democratic morality also captured the Untouchable. A wider social strife engulfed him.

The fourth strand is a stagnation of the third. It concerns a decline in cultural innovation and a rise in the free play of pragmatic evaluations and accountabilities. The claims for moral, legal, and economic equality start a pervasive politics for equal social rights. The democratic inspiration of Ambedkar translates into the routine rhetoric and politics of the regional and local leaders. The changing group dynamics of local leaders and their immediate interests further parochialize the original inspiration. The fourth strand represents a step toward the routinization of politics for social equality. A national leader-hero like Ambedkar is best recalled as a past thaumaturge, remembered more and more only by erecting his statues and icons (with appropriate ceremonial panegyric). The national dimensions of his plan are continuously dissembled under parochial practical pressures, until brought together once again perhaps by another avatar of the hero.

Consider these four strands weaving together, in different patterns and under different regional lights, and we may have a thumbnail sketch of what engages the Untouchable's mind.

More generally, he is found to be partly resigned, partly protesting, partly rhetorical, but largely politicized. His thinkers insist on treating segments of the Indic *Philosophia Perennis* not unlike St. Augustine's "wisdom uncreate, the same now that it ever was, and the same to be forevermore." They interpret and modify the Indic principles to derive a congenial moral and philosophical ethics. But as they raise *their* cultural model and reconstruct its "history" (actually little known so far), they demonstrate their deep-seated intellectual *différance*, a strain that allows conditional overlap but no agreement with Hindu thought. This intellectual stance fosters an alternative thesis and dissenting epistemology (*pramāṇa*). The Untouchable, as a true civilizational member, continuously totalizes the ideal and the practical to conform to a nondichotomous view of knowledge and reality.

Had this not been so, our approach to and evaluation of their ideological schemes would have been significantly different. We could, then, have considered their ideal formulations simply as Hindu implanted, and decaying and sophistic. There would have been little merit in examining the internal logical and cultural structure of their ideology (see chaps. 1–4). We could have easily dismissed the Untouchable reformers on the basis of their wavering argumentation, slim scholarly evidence, and gnawing ambivalence. But this was not to be. Their careful explication of nondualism, asceticism, yoga, and recent Buddhist ideals showed a seriousness that derived from their social condition.

Simultaneously, the Lucknow Chamars also comprehend, assess, decide, and act in order to explain their social reality to themselves as best as they can. They must make sense of why it encourages as well as disappoints them. An anthropologist cannot afford to disregard this indigenous "feet-finding" procedure because it is likely to disclose a group's particular social proclivities and evasions, and thus alerts the anthropologist to review (and modify) some of his analytic assumptions. This procedure demonstrates why a single-theory explanation, whether it is based on caste consensus, dialectical materialism, or democratic ideology, cannot fully explain the position of the Indian Untouchable. Our ethnographic evidence on the Chamars supports this conceptual position.

As we handle a whole range of the Chamar's social concerns under his own impetus, we discover how he engenders competition as well as cooperation, sharing as well as exclusion, conflict as well as consensus, and change as well as nonchange. He is not only excluded, but for different reasons he excludes those who exclude him. His moods, motivation, and emotion are as genuine a part of his treatment of social reality as are his politics of protest and hope.

Empirically seen, however, the Lucknow Chamars' ideological and intellectual devices succeed in minimizing their cultural disabilities only in a certain way and to a certain extent. Still, such devices produce a critical assessment of the caste-biased ideas, representations, and meanings, and offer culturally "good" reasons to improve their own self-image. As they gain self-assurance, they posit their own ideas, politics, and strategies. As recent democratic forces buttress the Lucknow Chamars' social boldness, the caste ethic accommodates it under some circumstances and confronts it in others. A widening range of social responses is emerging between the Chamar and the caste Hindu to suit the changing social pressures, but the basic confrontation is far from resolving itself. Since the final results are not in, we can draw no conclusion on the general issue of the Chamar's social prospects. We can only identify the dimensions of new arenas of social conflict and compromise. Both a daily evaluation of social odds and a tactful response to the caste Hindu's resistance are essential parts of the Chamar's life. Yet an overall ambiguity surrounds the Lucknow Chamar; we will comment on its nature and extent at this point.

Ambiguity

The Untouchable thinker starts, as he must, with a priori assumptions about cosmological equality and justice, and locates them in the ultimate Indic constructs. He is free of ambiguities here, awarding these ideological assumptions their inviolable "own-nature" (*svabhāva*) within the Indic cosmology. He rates this ultimate morality as superior to that of the caste (which is held to be merely "conventional" – *vyavahārika*; *saṃvṛtti*), merging finally and totally into those *amoral* mystic and spiritual goals that Vedantic nondualism and Buddhist vacuity bring to him. He thus pursues a specific form of spiritualism and mysticism to transcend those moral and social gradations of the caste order that bedevil his quest for equality and justice. He is not detained by philosophical critics who claim that Indic monism and mysticism are either only amoral (for a clear discussion of this issue, see Matilal 1977) or merely a matter of social morality (i.e., when the societal would become only a matter of *vyavahāra* with no ultimate spiritual basis).

The ordinary Chamar facing the everyday world translates this heritage under the prevailing conceptions of the morally permanent versus the evanescent. He views his body as ephemeral and his soul as permanent. But his social experiences bring him only paradox and ambivalence. This obtains because the society often remains disadvantageous to him; social traditions are disparaging to him and the alternatives are risky. The Chamar genuinely experiences a "double bind," perhaps a sociologically expected condition among the deprived. Hence, whatever he thinks, constructs, and does, a "deconstruction" (elucidated later) immediately takes over. As he assembles his new identity, he also feels that a dispersal and blurring take place. As he decides on a new plan, a dissipation begins to occur. This recalls Derrida's subtler conjugations of "structure" and "deconstruction" (e.g., see Derrida 1976; Culler 1979: 154–80).

At this point we will employ two Derridan concepts to interpret the overall condition of the Indian Untouchable. These concepts prove to be congenial vehicles for reflecting on a deep civilizational paradox and ambiguity that neither the caste order nor the Untouchable can get away from.[1] Generally, as we have seen, when the Indian Untouchable comments on his civilizational condition, he forces the observer to think about the caste order as a paradoxical segment of the much larger Indic cultural system.[2] We will bring in Derrida here essentially for a "rectified" structuralism that, I think, refines certain concepts and procedures in exactly those ways that would render them more sensitive to the Untouchable's condition as well as the Indic hermeneutics. However, there is neither any need nor suggestion to transport his particularized Western philosophical contexts and assumptions. (For a summary of the highlights of Derrida's thought, see Gayatri Spivak's preface to *Of Grammatology*; also Culler 1979.)

Let us remember that Derrida "argues within a particular philosophical system but at the same time attempts through the productivity of language to breach or exceed that system" (Culler 1979: 178–9). He tests the limits of logocentrism, engaging in "deconstructive reversals." If "deconstruction" means that "we *must* do a thing *and* its opposite, and indeed we desire to do both, and so on indefinitely," the Derridan "double [read abyssal] bind" helps us characterize the civilizational bind in which the Untouchable in fact exists. He continuously constructs and deconstructs himself in relation to the caste Hindu (and vice versa), without knowing whether this "perpetually self-deconstructing movement" could ever be total and complete (quoted, with emphases, from Spivak 1976: lxxviii).[3]

This brings us to another Derridan term–that is, *différance* (a French term meaning "difference" as well as "'a differing or a deferring'"). It "thus designates both a passive difference already in existence as the condition of signification and an act of differing or deferring which produces differences" (Culler 1979: 165). Again, the Untouchable, unlike the caste Hindus, traditionally symbolizes passive social differences, but now tactfully engages in "differing" *and* "deferring" devices through his speech, writing, and political action. The contemporary reformist Untouchable wants to represent himself in terms of a "suspended status," not unlike that represented by *différance* (see Spivak 1976: xliii). As democratic India attenuates his social disability, deferment of resentment permits accommodation between him and the caste Hindu. As both sides betray their double bind (as our ethnography has shown), they discover themselves beyond a simple opposition. *Différance* also questions the general structure of binary oppositions, a genre of question congenial to the Untouchable's ideological position and experience.

Our short interpretive journey with Derrida's ideas finds another concept meaningful – "dissemination." Spivak (1976: lxv) offers us its characterization in a language relevant to our context: It represents "a sowing that does not produce plants, but is simply infinitely repeated. A semination that is not *in*semination but *dis*semination, seed spilled in vain, an emission that cannot return to its origin in the father. Not an exact and controlled polysemy, but a proliferation of always different, always postponed meanings." The Untouchable is caught in a similar semantic and symbolic condition, and faces its bind. He finds that his seminal ideas do not always germinate. His texts, speeches, and actions usually *disseminate* his cultural argument, sometimes along and sometimes across the caste Hindu's furrows and their "cobweb" (a favorite expression with the Lucknow Chamar). Since he cannot avoid doing so within the Indian condition his ideas must also keep falling into infertile tracts. But if he has to face such odds, he knows from experience that he must not become a mere prisoner of circumstance. He must let his ideals and words multiply, and construct his ethic with the ultimate goal of lifting caste morality above social injustice. This effort represents the Hegelian *aufhebung* relationship, "where the second [e.g., the ascetic's spiritual morality] at once annuls the first [the caste systematic morality] and lifts it up into a higher sphere of [moral and spiritual] existence" (Spivak 1976: xi). To do so within the Indic system is to grasp the ultimate reality, according to the Untouchable ideologist.

The preceding Derridan formulations help us interpret certain subtleties of the Untouchable's argument: (a) There is a genuine civilizational bind characterizing the Indian Untouchable and his sociocultural deprivation. (b) This bind is actually double-faced, partially "deconstructing" the caste Hindu as well as the Untouchable. Indic spiritual values provide hope to the Untouchable as they rein in the Brāhman's impulse to hierarchize and dominate. (c) The bind produces an endemic cultural ambivalence, since the dichotomous Hindu categories (e.g., pure and impure) exclude but do not disown the Untouchable (and vice versa). Such a lopsided relationship does not yield a "balanced" (complementary), complete, and total opposition. Instead, equivocating interpretations abound. Recall the Ravidas case study in Chapter 3 and compare it with the discussion of social deprivation in the Ravidas temple in Chapter 7. These interpretations despairingly complicate the arguments and meanings as they proceed; the paradoxes, inconsistencies, ironies, and anachronisms persist between the caste Hindu and the Untouchable.

We can, thus, oppose the Brāhman to the Untouchable, but neither totally nor fully. For there remains that "spiritual" idea that cannot let either the Untouchable or the Brāhman monopolize all the sources of cultural authenticity, authority, and verity. The Indic ascetic significantly contributes to this "off-balance" (i.e., a necessarily deconstructing) structure by being a deft practitioner of *différance*. His spiritual powers and his worldly mimesis variously combine to make him, apropos of Coomaraswamy, the "All-Worker."

The ideology and ideologist

Despite these ambiguities, however, the Untouchable now attempts to establish himself sui juris by his politics of culture. His thinkers and reformers, despite their uneven scholarship and polemical diversions, try to congeal a genuine cultural locus. The ideologists reflect a wide array of intellectual positions, from fertile to redundant, raising voices from the antagonistic fringe and from the ordinary core. They draw upon their ascetics, new leaders, and elites to claim equal social rights. This democratic goal now usually diverts them from completing their exercise on the Indic moral order. It usually starts with a partly spiritual and partly resentful didacticism (a procedure reminiscent of the traditional Indian scholastics; see Prasad 1958: 201, for a general purpose of the latter), and culminates in a commitment and perspicacity in written form. The ideologists make use of suitable Hindu philosophical traditions and concepts but often come out launching their own cultural reformulations and insights. If the latter reflect the ideologists' intellectual "independence" (or "arrogance" in the Hindu's eyes), they also cast them outside Hindu traditions of scholarship.

Given the absence (as far as I know) of any systematic, objective study of the analytic genres of the Untouchable's ideologies, this attempt has analyzed selected properties of only one ideological genre and its internal structure.[4] Although alternative formulations exist, with their distinctly different emphases, we have discussed the one considered fundamental by the Lucknow Untouchable thinker. Like other Indian schemes, this Untouchable's scheme also carries multiple avenues of interpretation, which allow us to allude to wider interpretations of social deprivation, anomaly, and ambiguity. Such an ideological scheme demonstrates a whole range of concerns, for example, from a spiritual and moral anxiety to a shared *Weltanschauung*, to a populist scheme of reform, to political and economic competition.

The Untouchable ideologist now powers himself through a Schopenhauer-style nexus created among "free will," "ideas," and "reality." Emboldened by democratic provisions, he disdains those less risky institutional relations that have continued to deny him (and his kind) social justice and fairness in the past. His "caste acts" often symbolize a disenchantment or protest now, reinforcing his more explicit political resentment. He finds that he can afford to express himself socially even when anticaste and antitradition. This protesting intellect often works to translate social resentment into strategic practical action.

But this protesting intellect is still not free from a deep social anxiety; it waxes and wanes, becoming vigorously emotive now and rational and calculating later on. It is also often ambivalent and indecisive. Yet its overall achievements are more significant than its failures, given the Untouchable's persistence and increasing assertiveness within Indian social circumstances. Actually, this same intellect shows the ability to selectively imbibe, probe, and reformulate ideological platforms and perspectives. It does not merely genuflect. In language often direct, didactic, and aphoristic, the protesting intellect shows a Nietzschean aversion to the (caste) "established" Hindu ideas and institutions. As it rhetorically proclaims "freedom from" the Hindu gods and castes (*dévīdévatā aur jātapāñta*) and "freedom to" acquire moral and social equalitarianism, it actually makes known its deep opposition to social injustice and exploitation. This way the protesting mind ultimately does what it has wanted to do most – challenge and rectify age-old injustices within the Hindu order.

Simultaneously, some Untouchable thinkers are disposed, as we have seen, *against* a collectivism that usurps others' social rights. They would rather work actively for the realization of a new kind of person, that is, one that represents immutable equality, akin to the Nietzschean notion of "self-fulfillment and self-transcendence." Jigyasu and Achchutananda illustrate the protesting intellect from one part of India. Actually, it seems to have had all-India resonance, especially during this century (e.g., the *ādi-dharmī* in Punjab [see Census 1931]; the *ādi-Dravidas* in the South [Kumaraswami 1923]; the *ādivāsī* in Bihar [Thakkar 1945?]).

Chamar thinkers freely reflect religious sharing with Hindu, Buddhist, and Jain thinkers, but retain substantive distinctness and distance from such specific reform movements as Virashaiva, Brahmo, Arya Samaja, and Swaminarayan. This is an expected cultural property; it underscores the uniqueness the Chamars assign to themselves as the prototypic Indian Untouchable. Thus, although one Untouchable reform movement, in sociological profile, may look like any other one, it is, from a cultural point of view, a special configuration of conduct and meaning.

The Untouchable thinker, from his standpoint (as we have discussed in chap. 4), extends this movement to the culturally most profound level as he constructs a process for equalitarian individuation (and individual) from within the Indic civilization. We could summarize his larger Indic scheme with help from a famous verse from the *Pañcatañtra*:

> For the sake of family one man should be sacrificed, for the sake of the village the family should be sacrificed, for the sake of the bigger territorial unit [*janapada*] the village should be sacrificed, but for the self [*ātman*] the earth should be sacrificed.

This verse could have been congruent with Western sociological assumptions if the last clause, the controlling one, were not thrown in. However, this is exactly the paramount civilizational axiom that supplies the correct frame of significance for the rest. It resolves the important issue of egoism and altruism under an Indian assumption.

> That good of all is served by the enlargement of a person's moral and spiritual concern for himself, for his self eventually encompasses all selves. The importation of the egoism–altruism distinction seems to be foreign to the spirit of Indian philosophers of life. [Potter 1965: 259]

Informing our sociological endeavor, therefore, the Indic scheme of the Untouchable ideologist posits as follows:

a. that there is a cognizing individual (self or *jīva*);
b. but that it can only be a reflection of, and is ultimately guided by, a spiritual construct, the unconditional Self (*Ātman*) at all levels, and always; and
c. that (a) and (b) variously represent the Indian conception of the Whole and its parts, as one would distinguish between "a pot and the pot halves which 'compose' it." (See also Potter 1980: 241–67; Larson 1980: 303–16.)

However, as social conditions award more than one value to the Whole, ranging from the transactional to the transcendental, the equanimity of "self" (conditional and unconditional) offers social hope to the Untouchable. The spiritual properties of irreducible equality, freedom, perfection, and utopia rush to characterize this "self," one of the most fundamental and versatile constructions of the civilization. This pervasive (and popular) construct is considered to be *more than* any or all social attributes put together. Fundamentally, in this scheme the Whole is assumed to inhere in its parts, and vice versa (see Khare 1978; we also recall *samaveta-samavāyin* relations in Indian philosophy, see Potter 1963: 118–29). The "Self" (i.e., an image of the Whole) is found resident in each and every member (self) of all caste groups – the highest as well as the exteriormost. All practical and ideal domains are seen as creations around this individuating "self."[5] The winning rule of this scheme is Do not lose your individuality (i.e., the *ātman*) along the caste-engendered differences, lest you mistake "chaff for grain."[6]

As the Untouchable has been returning with several social movements from different parts of India (e.g., see helpful recent studies and bibliographies in Rao 1978), and as his quest for equity and justice intensifies, his intellectual and ideological need for individual rights also increases. A basic hypothesis is thus corroborated: The deeper the change within Indian society, the more fundamental will be the reformulation of individuation. It means renegotiations between the master constructs of self and society, both Indic and Western.

The Lucknow Chamars illustrate this negotiation at two – "inner" and "outer" – levels. They do so as they develop a culture of regeneration within and among themselves, and as they wage a politics of rights and resources with the society at large. In both ways they negotiate reidentification for themselves, trying to extract a new and positive social accountability for themselves. The more serious they are about this acquisition, however, the greater the social adjustment demanded from the caste Hindus, and the greater the caste Hindu's resistance to it in practice. Such a resistance today means more politics and more volatile political arenas, guided by contextual strains between the Chamars and the caste Hindus. Politics in India thus becomes a language of intensifying conflicts and conditional compromises.

Toward *Homo justus*

In summary, the Untouchables produce what we may call a containment theory of the caste order, and a correctional strategy for its "moral maladies." The containment theory reduces the caste Hindu to the twice-born, and the latter to the Brāhman, bringing him face to face with the Indic ascetic. Like this ascetic, the Untouchable does not tolerate caste hierarchy and its inherent disposition toward inequality. Exploitation based on status privilege is considered a degradation of the Indic (*and* Hindu) cosmic order, and of its ultimate values of spiritual individuation, equality, morality, and justice. In the Untouchable's view, the Indic civilization houses and controls the expression of *varṇa* and *jāti*, not vice versa.[7] (See also chap. 9 and its n. 5.)

The Untouchable's correctional strategy starts with a confrontation between the privilege-securing Brāhman and the genuinely reforming ascetic, who, with time, becomes a locus for nurturing political activism to establish a just moral and social order. To do so is to force the caste order to transform its ethic from within, even if grudgingly. Thus the Untouchable becomes an "altar of conscience" for the just caste Hindu, urging him to sacrifice his unjust privileges. Because this mild nudge is often found to be insufficient, the correctional strategy also calls for debating the cerebral Hindu, opposing the orthodox caste ritualist, cajoling (yet resenting) the privileged, and challenging the Westernized Indian, especially in the name of Indian democracy. With these multiple fronts, the Untouchable wants to secure a comprehensive and enduring social justice, and not merely the removal of this social deprivation or that.

Our study of the Untouchable thus offers us a glimpse of the issues *Homo justus* faces within India. Immediately many questions take over that this inquiry finds challenging but beyond its scope. For example, how does *Homo justus* manifest himself in India, both within as well as outside the caste ethic, and how are Indic notions of justice related to Western notions? This study has brought up one configuration of values facilitating such an inquiry. It has underscored the importance of such notions as moral individuation, social adaptability, self-correcting social justice, and a positive pursuit of social accountability. It takes anthropology and sociology in a direction where they would neither condone hyperorganicism nor ignore the full cultural import of the different forms of individuation and the individual (see Burridge 1979, for a reasonable argument).

Homo justus, which is philosophically and practically irreducible to certain objective formulas (e.g., see Ryan 1935; Rawls 1971; Galston 1980; and Walzer 1983), exists and works within a rich and fragile terrain of cultural mediations of fact and law (see Geertz 1983). As the deprived seek social justice, they take us into these terrains of claims, negotiations, and protests. Even if justice, in practice, always remains ambiguous and imperfect for those who are deprived, its pursuit encourages the people to depend on their morality, reasoning, and experience, and to negotiate by circumstance and for the common good. The nature of this dialogue and negotiation, as this study shows, draws on a whole matrix of such interwoven distinctions as dualism and nondualism, the individual and the collective, moral merit and worth, hierarchy and amity, rule and spontaneity, form and meaning, and social classification and cultural transformation.

Seeking justice from the surrounding system, the Indian Untouchables still labor under a whole series of paradoxes, ironies, and double binds produced by the fickle nature of a changing system of social justice. However, as we are brought to this threshold, the Untouchable's progress as well as problems confront us at once within a new frame of reference. And the subject matter of another inquiry, perhaps of the anthropology of *Homo justus*, takes over.

The following two paradigms of justice, disparate yet vigorously symbolizing the indispensability of social justice within any society, might best represent the Untouchable's claims and dilemmas. One became the basis for Western democratic justice and the other brought forward the Indian caste version. Both showed that justice must ultimately prevail according to a shared sense of fair play and equity among all members of a society.

"Justice is the virtue because of which all have their own"; "Justice is the constant and unremitting will to render to everyone his own right." [Aristotle and Ulpian quoted in Galston 1980: 102]

Justice, being violated, destroys; justice, being preserved, preserves: therefore justice must not be violated, lest violated justice destroy us.
The only friend who follows men even after death is justice; for everything else is lost at the same time when the body (perishes). [Laws of Manu translated by Bühler 1964: viii, 15, 17]

Notes

Introduction: The inquiry and its context

1. What should those people be called who, under the laws of independent India, do not remain what they have been, but who reject newer euphemisms as "insulting"? From the Untouchable's standpoint, their name has great significance. It matters to them because, as the Lucknow Chamars observed, whatever they are called affects their self-identity and social image. This problem of nomenclature stares the investigator in the face, limiting his alternatives. For example, if called "ex-Untouchable," the Chamars object because it does not reflect the social truth. "Harijan" has proved to be an empty hope for them. If it suits the educated, urban caste Hindu best, and the Indian bureaucracy backs it up, it is still empty, they argue, because although it might lighten the caste Hindu's guilt in some ways, it does not ultimately achieve the intended transmutation. It is even parochial to some and patronizing (i.e., Hinduizing) to others.

   Lastly, "Pariah," though acceptable in sociological jargon, has its own problems. Most of all, it was originally regional (i.e., South Indian) in cultural denotation and usage (though regarded as comparative and analytic in connotation for sociologists; e.g., Weber 1963: 108–9; De Vos and Wagatsuma 1967). The Lucknow Chamars rejected it for the first reason, and I abstain from using it within the main contextual discussions in deference to regional ethnographic differences. (However, I retain it as a sociological term of analysis in a context-free manner.) To call them what they insist they factually are, was therefore the only viable option left. However, if the task was to call a spade a spade, it was not necessarily to claim a better legal or social definition of the "Untouchable" or "Untouchability" (see Galanter 1972: 243–6, 303), but it was to approach what the people themselves conveyed.

   It was also to approach a definite reformist conception the Chamars had about themselves. The cultural category of *achchūta* was seldom merely a word to them, though its gloss, "Untouchable," was first employed in print in 1909 (see Sayaji Rao 1928). If *achchūta* represented their social degradation, it also recalled a whole cultural reality that was truly theirs. As we will see in Part I, the term is integral to the Chamars' ideological struggle. It helped them evaluate what the present and future could or should mean to them in terms of their past. Finally, this century added political meanings to the word *achchūta*.

   Such multiple properties render the gloss "Untouchable" (or any of its Indian variants such as "unapproachables"; e.g., see Rao 1979: 5) an analytic term for us. I will so use it throughout this study; there will be no place for it as a pejorative term. Simultaneously, we recognize, however, that this term is neither sociologically problem free, nor in common English usage (as a common noun and adjective) uncolored.

2. Though rarely systematically studied in their own right, the thinkers of Indian radical culture seem to have had a genuine but uneven and indirect intellectual impact. Remembering that "radical culture" is a relative category, where what might have been radical in the past could be commonplace today, these thinkers are neither always of low caste nor the non-Hindus nor the (ritually) left-handed. Actually, the early Indian textual (*śrūti* and *smṛti*) commentators offer a vigorous line of "radical" idealism (e.g., Prasad 1958). If we juxtapose as diverse epistemologist-commentators as Gautama, Nagarjuna, Caraka, and Carvaka, we may get an idea of the place of countervailing cultural radicalism in India. Though we cannot investigate this issue here, these figures might be taken as early representatives of indigenous intellectual radicalism in India and could be juxtaposed to some of those drawn from the West. For example, Kant, Bentham, Schopenhauer, and Nietzsche may be particularly useful to interpret the Untouchable's condition.
3. Max Weber (see selections in 1963; 1958; and Sigrist 1971) will often be explicitly or implicitly discussed (or alluded to) during the course of this study. Sometimes oversimplified, sometimes conditionally relevant, and sometimes disputable and outdated, Weber will seldom be totally irrelevant. His logical characterization of social deprivation will be of clear value to us. His approach is comprehensive because it combines social "interest" and "strain" theories in accounting for the nonprivileged groups (e.g., Weber, 1963: chap. 7; Gerth and Mills 1958: 61–5; Geertz 1973: 201–7).
4. Systematic historical research is required on the eighteenth- and nineteenth-century Untouchables in different parts of India in order to study the intellectual and reformist work they might have produced in the prenationalist phases of social history. Obviously, although this task was beyond my purview and expertise, some useful clues were made available to me for the Avadh region during my fieldwork.

   The oldest contemporary Chamars could take me back to the last three decades of the previous century, claiming that some members in their group were always literate, though fewer wrote on a sustained basis, and fewer still cared to (or could) preserve these writings. "One used to receive education by charity or chance. If several persons were literate in one generation within a distance of twenty or thirty miles, there were usually fewer in the next. But most important, the Hindu detractor was always there who would degrade, ridicule, misuse, and, if permitted, destroy our writings." This was the observation of a ninety-year-old Lucknow Chamar, who had shown me three handwritten historical accounts (in Persian and Urdu), allegedly by his "ancestors" of the last century. But he would not part with them even to let them be copied, for he "utterly distrusted everybody." Since he and his descendants were literate (but at present neither in Persian nor in written Urdu), these documents were treated as a family relic. They were held for a reliable Chamar scholar. Thus though the difficulties encountered in the field in gathering such evidence could be considerable, the intellectual payoff will not be insignificant.
5. The first category of references will be offered by the Untouchable (most often the Chamar) writers and reformers themselves. They will provide us with chief documentary evidence for examining the constitution and direction of their cultural ideology, showing how they may perpetuate their cultural ambivalence on the one hand, and create radical cultural constructions on the other. The

second category of references will be concerned with selected sociological studies of the socially deprived, of the Indian Untouchable, and of social change (see also Khare 1979). I include such a combined list of cited and relevant references at the end of this study. The third category of "references" utilized in this study is rather unconventional: It will comprise a series of tape-recorded interpretations, discussions, and cognitive profiles that my Chamar or other Untouchable informants, whether thinkers, reformers, leaders, or ordinary people, repeatedly provided during the fieldwork and in correspondence. Though hard to list, these "references" are of direct significance to this study and will be cited in the text with due consideration for anonymity. Many Lucknow Chamars worked as more than informants for this study; they undertook to discuss themselves with sensitivity and candor. It was a sharing an anthropologist seeks, and wants to be faithful to.

6. Although the following references are of variable significance to a cultural analysis, all inform, directly or indirectly, about the Indian historical and regional variation integral to a study of Untouchables. I have found some studies empirically more useful than others, but *all* have contributed toward the conduct of my inquiry–ideas, language, and analytic schemes–on the Indian Untouchable.

Though sparse and mixed in quality, a group of preindependence references gives us an idea of this century's earlier cultural ethos on which perhaps the present studies of Untouchables have variously drawn (e.g., see Sayaji Rao 1928; Gokhale 1903; McGavran 1939; Rajah 1925; Farquhar 1917, 1967; Ouwerk 1945; and Agarwal 1934). There are some group or regional studies of the same period that have been more directly helpful to my attempt (e.g., Briggs 1920; Wadia 1932; Bhagat 1935; Aiyappan 1944, 1965; Crooke 1903; Rose 1919; Kumaraswami 1923; and Stevenson 1930). This period is generally characterized by the Christian missionary accounts, British reports, social-reform proposals and pronouncements, and a few secondary-data accounts. In contrast, the postindependence period is marked by a preponderance of empirical field research and documentary studies, usually based on a specific locality or group.

Among the recent ethnographic and analytic studies from which this attempt takes off to formulate its own analysis are Bouglé (1971); Kane (1941); Srinivas (1962); Marriott (1968, 1976); Dumont (1980); Srinivas and Béteille (1965); Cohn (1955, 1959); Béteille (1965); Rudolph and Rudolph (1967); Brass (1965); Hardgrave (1965, 1969); Moffatt (1979); Harper (1968); Lynch (1969); Bailey (1957, 1960); Mencher (1974); and Galanter (1972). These studies give us several baseline as well as change-sensitive formulations from different directions–caste, kinship, politics, economics, hierarchical ideology, law, inequality, and social change. They give this study the conceptual background to explore, critique, and improve. This study may illustrate not merely a variant but different route, where cultural categories and principles of the Untouchable, as offered by the Untouchables, are examined on their own grounds, and pursued back and forth through the ideal, symbolic, and practical contexts.

The preceding references also help piece together an "all-Indian" social picture of the Indian Untouchable, whether normative, politically moderate, or radical. Important historical and regional information is added to it by such attempts as Zelliott's (1966, 1969, 1970a, b, and 1972) on Maharashtra's Mahar movement, and on the cultural style of Ambedkar. Lynch (1969) undertook a perceptive social analysis of the Jatavs from Agra in Uttar Pradesh, whereas Aiyappan (1965) and Rao (1979) did so on the Iravas of Kerala, Babb (1972) on the Satnamis of eastern Madhya Pradesh, Ramaswamy (1974a, b) on social change and identity of the "Scheduled Castes" in Andhra Pradesh, Parry (1979) on the "degrees" of Untouchability in the Kangra Hills of Northwest India, and Mencher (1972) on limited change in the Paraiyans of Tamil Nadu.

7. Since an important aspect for this study is to be accurate in designating Indian cultural ideas, categories, and relations, the indigenous terms and phrases will occur frequently. They will be most often produced with a gloss. However, since all glosses are imperfect, they should *always* be considered within quotations and always be accompanied by an appropriate indigenous term. Moreover, since the same terms alter their signification with issues, contexts, and vantage points, they will demand careful translation from one contextual usage to the next. Such a procedure therefore becomes so complex that a few decisions are inevitable from the start.

The first stipulation is that all glosses throughout this study will be assumed to stand within quotations (showing altered signification by context), and that they should be so read, especially by Indianists. Second, all indigenous terms and expressions will be introduced with a gloss at the first instance, often allowing the gloss to stand for them later on. However, several exceptions will be allowed by context. Third, since the contemporary Indianist is served best when the indigenous expressions are introduced with a definite analytic purpose (assuming that he himself will supply those that have become a routine part of the craft), I shall exercise selection in supplying the terms. Generally, we will include terms or phrases for little-known idioms, altered usages of well-known cultural concepts, and new cognitive-thought categories embedded in ethnographic contexts. As I do so, however, I will expect the expert to follow my caution on glosses and to supply himself with appropriate connotations of such terms as dharma, karma, *jāti*, *santa*, and *achchūta*. The last step will help control the textual complexity for wider reading.

Yet the issue of indigenous concepts remains difficult, particularly when (e.g., see chaps. 2–4) classical textual and/or contextual categories (e.g., karma or *jivātman*) undergo either ideological refashioning or popular reinterpretation. Further, as I supply the Untouchable-offered meanings (e.g., in chap. 4, notice "irreducible presence" for *nityatā*, "consciousness" for *caitanyatā* and not merely *Cittavṛtti*, "free will" for *svātantrya*, etc.) to some critical constructs for developing the central argument, the demands on my expert colleagues are bound to increase.

In general, the ethnographic interpretations of the terms will prevail in this study, modifying, as necessary, even the established meanings of classical concepts. This problem will tend to reach a climax in chap. 4, where "body," "person," "individual," and "collective" must become what the Untouchable ideologist does to the classical categories to handle his goals. Classical, contextual, and (Western) sociological meanings will continuously negotiate in such an exercise. Similar complications have appeared recently in the discussion of even a single category like karma; see O'Flaherty (1980). The papers relevant for this study are by Potter and Larson, where they recognize postulations of individuation.

8. The Chamars, noted the Census of India of 1931, were found all over the then United Provinces (now called Uttar Pradesh). The British Territory had some 6,197,113 Chamars, 5,534 Mochis, and 476,634 Bhangis (Part I; Report: 637). The population in Lucknow district in 1931 was 251,097 against 217,569 in 1921. The Gazetteer of the Province of Oudh (1877: 337) found Chamars to be 11.24 percent of the total Hindu population in the Lucknow district. In comparison, the Brahmans were 8.41 percent and Kori, a caste the contemporary Chamars look down upon, were 2.19 percent. Like the Thakur, the Ahir, and the Pasi, the Chamars were in more than average numbers in the district. The District Gazetteers of United Provinces, Lucknow (1904: 70–1), noted that the proportionate representation of the Chamars was the same as before (i.e., "less than 12% of the total"), with the remark that they were most concentrated in the *tehsīls* of Lucknow and Malihabad.

Unfortunately, these earlier accounts do not mention the social profile of low communities within the city of Lucknow, though the three localities (*mohallās*), or neighborhoods, studied here are mentioned by names essentially similar to those of today. However, as I note later, I will use pseudonyms for them to uphold the wishes of my important informants and to protect their political sensitivities.

9. This two-tier internal social classification of the Lucknow Chamar is primarily along the subcaste–e.g., Jaiswar, Ravidasi, and Balmiki–groups, helping them to carry out the selected functions of their traditional *panchāyat* (jural council). The Ravidasi, in particular, emphasized the role of *ṭāṭs*, which literally denotes the coarse jute mat (called *ṭāṭ* in Hindi) that they spread on the floor to receive their guests. A subcaste is divided along several *ṭāṭs*, and the local Chamars as a whole are classified into several *thoks* (i.e., "whole clusters"). The *thok* lines therefore run among subcaste groups, and *ṭāṭ* lines run within *thoks*.

10. Empirically, this study is based on the following clusters of households by *jāti* (or religious grouping) and by *mohallā*:

	Modernganj		Baudhabagh		Karampura	
	No.	%	No.	%	No.	%
Jaiswar	11	40.74	5	20.00	4	23.53
Ravidasi	7	25.93	6	24.00	4	23.53
Balmiki	7	25.93	2	8.00	6	35.29
Neo-Buddhist	2	7.40	12	48.00	3	17.65
Total	27	100.00	25	100.00	17	100.00

Obviously, these households were consciously selected from different lanes of the three localities, and on the criteria most useful to the aims of this inquiry. Initially, a regular ethnographic study of the *mohallās* was done, followed by that of the clusters of households lane by lane. Not all the members of the households were equally studied, though special emphasis was placed on husband-wife, men-women, educated-uneducated, leader-follower, and household-ascetic interrelationships. Occupational diversity was sought out within as well as outside these clusters of households.

11. This range (and emphasis) may be itself a sign of the change in perspective that the Untouchables at present demand of an investigator. Looking back over this century for the study of Chamars, if Briggs started an initial (if a flawed) genre of studies, and if Cohn on Senapur offered a more perceptive next genre, this study might represent yet another one. Each successive genre of study had to become increasingly responsive to the Chamar's shaping of his own cognition, proclivities, and values. This direction of sociological reappraisal must go on to keep up with changing social reality. Recent Untouchable thinkers, radical reformers, and political activists present the complementary half of this picture from "within," fertilizing the studies done from the "outside."

12. As Coomaraswamy (1979: 102) pithily observed about an anthropological point: "General considerations are also of highest importance if anthropology is to amount to anything more than another satisfaction of our curiosity; if, that is to say, it is to subserve the good of mankind by enabling men to understand one another, even to think *with* one another, rather than merely *of* one another as strangers" (Coomaraswamy's italics).

The last point is crucial to this study, for if anything this study is conducted *with* the Untouchables rather than being only *of* them. As the Untouchable now expresses in various ways what he thinks most about himself, we will place him in wider social surroundings to look "inward" (i.e., for the larger indigenous schemes) as well as, when meaningful, "outward" (i.e., for the analogical ideas and relations from Western thinkers). The Untouchable's–and the Lucknow Chamar's–perspectives will thus inform us appropriately about comparative civilizational issues. In this view the Untouchable is necessarily civilizational in propria persona.

1. The moral basis

1. A scrutiny of the literature directly bearing on Indian asceticism reveals a sparse and varying quality of analytic discussion. Essentially, three types of studies are available: First are those that assemble and collate authentic examples, normative rules, and general features of Indian asceticism (e.g., Bhagat 1976; Ghurye 1964), but these offer little critical analysis. Second, there are a few analytically rewarding studies but they tend to be selective in evidence and restricted in perspective (e.g., Dumont 1960: 33–62; for later improvements, see Das 1977: 18–56; and Uberoi 1967: 87–100). Indological attempts are the third type; they are usually so specialized (and philologically fine tuned) that they generally do not yield much room for comparative observations. But for a useful series of Indological exercises, see Heesterman (1964: 1–31; 1971: 43–7) for a summary characterization of "renunciation" (i.e., of ascetic *tapas*, *tyāga*, and *saṃnyāsa*) within Indian civilization; and Heesterman (1981), for perceptive and clear interrelationships between the householder, the wanderer, and the renouncer. (See also Thapar 1981 for a historical-cultural assessment.) Indic renunciation brings forth, he remarks, "separation and independence," the themes so clearly manifest in the Untouchable's quest for his unblemished spiritual "self." Also notes Heesterman (1971, pp. 46–7): "In the Indian case the transcendent point of reference lies with renunciation. The ultimate values are renunciatory ones. The contradictory consequence is that society has to understand and legitimize itself in terms of a renunciatory idiom that negates society's very basis."

2. In comparison, the normative Hindu culture may accord asceticism an ambivalent reception. For example, as Bhagat (1976) noted with respect to different Hindu legal codes (e.g., consider Arthaśāstra and the Gita), control in the pursuit of asceticism was considered necessary for various reasons. Two major reasons that readily appeared behind such attempts were (a) to prohibit the practice of asceticism to the Śūdra (e.g., Bhagat 1976: 12, 26, 298ff), and (b) to discourage its uncontrolled prevalence within caste and community. Renunciation practiced outside of the four-phase (*āśrama dharma*) householder's order was considered "anti-Vedic" and abnormal (pp. 47, 310). Undoubtedly, though such rules seem to help the supremacy of the Brāhman and the caste order, the real controls on asceticism have varied with historical circumstance.

The fundamental cultural significance of asceticism remains, however, undisputed within the society as long as such cultural concepts as *tapas* (i.e., austerity ranging from severe self-mortification to self-training and discipline), *tyāga* (renunciation or detachment), *ojas* ("spiritual power"; see Bhagat 1976: 74–5), and yoga (coordinated physical and contemplative exercises) pervade and attract the ordinary. These concepts produce the fibers out of which the Brāhman is himself made. Whether a Manu, a Śiva, or a Vishnu, Jigyasu observed in an interview, "all are found dependent upon asceticism for performing their functions, and for being what they are. Different Hindu mythologies show how dependent they are on asceticism to guide the cosmos as well as the depths of one's soul." (For example, see also Bhagat 1976, chap. 8; Holck 1969; and Das 1977: 18–56.)

Buddhism and Jainism, in comparison, are popularly regarded as traditions that are the direct products of asceticism. Jains develop it perhaps in the most consistent and extreme manner. The Untouchable thinker, as we shall see, wants to build upon such a "non-Hindu" basis to consolidate his own ideal scheme.

3. In a normative, classical model of the Hindu society, however, a pious Brāhman's image also resides within every heart; he represents a commanding principle of learning and ritual position and thus also inspires the rest to achieve them by imitation. In a sociological overview, the ascetic represents the "horizontal integrator" (woof or weft) and the Brāhman a "vertical integrator" (warp) of the Hindu social fabric. Both together, and only together, in this view, would be considered necessary and sufficient for just social order.

But obviously this view will be rejected by the Untouchable thinker. A Karampura ascetic remarked: "Precisely because the Brāhman has failed as a Brāhman, he has become a fountain of social division and selfishness."

4. For example, Coomaraswamy's (1978) discussion of the Indian principles of Sacerdotium (*Brahman*) and Regnum (*kṣhātra*) amply show the force of the underlying *spiritual* premise in Hindu formulations, forms, and functions. It led him to observe, "The essence of the traditional politics amounts to this, that Self-Government [*svarāja*] depends upon self-control [*ātmasaṃyama*], Rule on ruliness" (p. 85). Following Indian cultural thought, Coomaraswamy (1978: 50ff) placed Sacerdotium and Regnum within a larger picture, and in the metaphors that Indian thought sustains: "The people are 'food' for the King, but the King is 'food' for the Brāhman . . .; while there is another for whom the Regnum and the Sacerdotium both are 'food.'" This is "the Eternal Law, the Truth [dharma; *satyam*], the 'Kingship of the Kingship.'" The ascetic roots himself within the last principle to pursue it through his techniques of self-control. Sacerdotium and Regnum must also follow the same principle to be what they are. The first is located *within* the second by the virtue of the "self-possession" that asceticism offers (see Coomaraswamy 1978: 77ff). Thus, "only a ruler who rules himself can long rule others" (Coomaraswamy 1978: 86).

To the Indianist, the preceding offers a culturally comprehensive (and perhaps a more complete) conjugation of the Indic notions of "spiritual authority and temporal power." It should convey to the reader that larger cultural raison d'être of the Indic asceticism on which the Untouchable thinker rests the authenticity of his ideological argument.

5. We cannot go here into the cultural richness of this tension within the Hindu tradition. Although a finely tuned hermeneutics is employed to control the spiritual antagonism between the Brāhman and the ascetic, an irrepressible ideological contention grows between them, often in a culturally creative manner. However, the Brāhman's ritual rules on the one hand, and the ascetic's attempt to bend, bypass, and flout them on the other, produce a seesaw tussle. It is amply recorded for the regular Hindu in such a vernacular writing in North India as

Bhaktamāla. If the Brāhman ritualist is repeatedly found losing face in this literature before the devout (*bhakta*) saint, whether a Brāhman or not, the Brāhman is not dislodged or permanently humiliated, but only subtly cultivated by the deity or devotee himself. In addition to the other things in his favor, the Brāhman attempts to turn the devotional movement to his advantage by tactfully submitting himself to it, and subtly bending its rules in his favor.

6. We shall exclusively concern ourselves here with the cultural constructs of the ideology, making observations on the practical tactics in Part II. My sources of information on the Untouchable's ideology will be the Lucknow Chamar thinkers and reformers, and a whole set of popular Hindi publications on the "ascetic tradition" issued by a publishing house in Lucknow (which must remain pseudonymous). See a list of citations in the Bibliography. I specifically depend upon Jigyasu's *Santpravara Ravidās Sāhéb* (1968a, 2 vols.) alongside Kabirpanthi's *Viśvagurū Sadgurū Kabīr Sāhéb kā Mānava-Saṃdeśa* (1972, original 1954), *Nirvāṇaprāpta Bhadanta Bodhānanda Mahāsthvira* (1965), *Bābāsahéb kā Upadeśa-Adeśa* (1965), and *Swāmi Achchūtānanda* (1968b, 2 vols.). When I employ the generalizing phrase "the Untouchable" in the following discussion, it will be either to echo the generalizing stance of the Chamar ideologist or to refer to a widely shared structural or symbolic property.

7. To establish historical, mythological, and even archeological antiquity of the ascetic tradition (e.g., in terms of the Indus Valley civilization since it is older than the "Vedic-Aryan" religion) is important for the Chamar ideologist. The greater the unbroken antiquity of a living tradition (*paramparā*), the greater is the authenticity accrued. Jigyasu thus repeatedly invoked lists (and qualities) of the earliest ascetics agreeable to the Untouchable's ideology and identity. The popular published accounts in Hindi also repeatedly offer it (e.g., see Sagar 1973; Jigyasu 1965, on Bodhānanda; 1968b on Achchutananda; and others like Rāhul Sankṛtyāyana and Ambedkar, often summarized or quoted in such accounts).

2. Formulations, categories, and procedures

1. Jigyasu's procedure to uncover the roots of the medieval ascetic in the ancient principles is, thus, already evident. It is initiated by producing a clear dichotomy between the indigenous and the external (i.e., the Brahmanic) ascetic traditions. Extending it back to the Indus Valley civilization and to Pasupati (probably a prototype of the later god Śiva), he roots the ascetic order in pre-Aryan times, and awards it a distinctive, if not an exclusive, cultural style and content up to the medieval times of Kabir, Ravidas, and Dadu. An important point for Jigyasu, like other Untouchable thinkers, is that he should draw only upon the non-Brahman, the *Śūdra* (i.e., artisan caste and lower), and the *atiśūdra* (or the Untouchable) ascetics. Though the third category proves his point best, he feels secure as long as the ascetics are drawn from the non-Brahmanic groups.

2. See also Farquhar (1920: 193–4) for a list of the related twenty-eight "manuals" of this literature and its place in the Śaiva system. The Āgamas are also supplemented by Upāgamas, making the total 198.

3. Since I am not in a position to adduce the needed historical evidence (supposing it is available on certain points) to prove or disprove the veracity of this information, I must leave this matter to those more qualified. I will be content to handle it as a datum of the cultural system.

4. This function is indirectly supported by another indigenous use of the genealogical structure. For example, the Kanya-Kubjas employed genealogies as a template to organize the continuity or discontinuity of their occupational ethos (see Khare 1973).

5. I allude here to a Nietzsche-style "undoing of opposites" or a Derrida-style *différance*. This mode of thought becomes evident with the Untouchable thinker. Quite centrally (and subtly) the reformist ascetic employs all the three senses of Derrida's master concept – differing, deferring, and detour (see Spivak 1976: xliii). The Untouchable ascetic and the thinker practice cultural evasion as a social necessity. Such an evasion dwells on "the difference of the other [i.e., of the caste Hindu], the other as 'differed' within the systematic ordering" (Spivak's quote from Derrida; 1976: xxix). See also Conclusion.

   Such a dimension of the Untouchable's argument, I suggest, will be significant throughout this study. It might help us approach the Untouchable's cultural formulations for their promise as well as ambiguity.

6. It would be another matter, however, if we were to compare Jigyasu and Bouglé as social observers. Obviously, then, a partisan ideology must remain a prime concern with Jigyasu and a detached analysis with Bouglé. If the two were compared for their substantive diagnosis of the Buddhist alternative in the Indian context (cf. Jigyasu 1968a: 1–45 and Bouglé 1971: 63–79), the striking point is not that Jigyasu is as distinct from Bouglé on the subject as he is (for he is expected to be) but rather that Jigyasu's insights are as analytic and piercing as they are. This feature should be sufficient reason to accord him serious attention.

7. Although this ideological stance is well articulated with a few, and known to the majority, of the Lucknow Chamars, it is not the only ideological formulation. Three other ideological positions were encountered in the field, all comparatively minor. Logically, they appeared (a) when the aforementioned traditional position was either rejected as unsatisfactory and unworkable, (b) when it was entirely recast in favor of a secular democratic position, or (c) when it was replaced by a strong leftist ideology of foreign origin. But unfortunately these alternative formulations are still not anywhere equally worked out and are difficult to ascertain and evaluate.

8. Although the evidence readily available to me is from a set of Ambedkar volumes and the Untouchable's reform and protest literature published in Hindi from Lucknow, I would expect a similar literature to exist in other parts of India (e.g., Zelliott 1970a, b; R. J. Miller 1967).

   In order to maintain uniformity in the treatment of popular textual data on which this and other discussions (chaps. 1–4) are based, I have depended on local Hindu translations of Ambedkar's major books. For example, see Zelliott's (1972: 466) bibliographic entries on Ambedkar as 1945, 1946, and 1948, which, when republished several times in Lucknow, are Ambedkar 1972a, 1972b, and 1973. These writings provided me with a background against which to examine the structure of ideas presented in Jigyasu (1968a, b, 1973a, b); Sagar (1965); Jadava (1971); Bansudas Kabirpanthi (1977); and Mani (1975). Though by no means exhaustive, these popular books or booklets gave me access to a large segment of shared ideas, whether original, imitative, or repetitive. In distinct contrast were Achchutananda's (see chap. 6) significant aphorisms, poems, and lectures, carrying the imprint of the pre-Ambedkar phase (see Jigyasu 1968b).

   Another small segment of writings that has been indirectly useful to this study concerns inventing, collecting, adapting, and explaining Buddhist rituals intended to substitute for those of the Hindu (e.g., see Jigyasu 1968c, n.d.; and Lal 1973, 1975). However, because they are marginal to the aims of this study, we will be unable to discuss these writings in detail.

9. I have gained from Macpherson (1964) in formulating these points in a language *symbolically* implicating individualism from Western political theory. Macpherson analyzes what he calls "possessive individualism" in English political thought from the seventeenth to the nineteenth century. His discussion progresses by treating the problems of social cohesion and equality in the West. Some of the issues of Indian political thought have already been alluded to (see n. 4, chap. 1), and will be handled again in Chapters 4 and 5. The point at this stage is to recognize that "self-possession" or "self-rule" is an essential *analogue* indigenously present in India, and that it is now communicating with the Western paradigm of "proprietorship" of one's "own person and capacities." Thus, though it would be obviously hasty and unwarranted to equate "self-control" (*ātmasaṃyama*) with a specific Western political category, one cannot deny the affinities recently developed between "self-control" (*saṁyama*) and "self-rule" (*svarāja*) within the nationalist political movement in India. We must recognize, therefore, that an ideal Indic construct, like any cultural model, remains amenable to several different translations over time.

3. Evaluating an ideal ascetic

1. Jigyasu (1968a: 92–3) briefly narrates how he had initially thought of Ravidas as an idolator–"a routine Hinduized saint"–until the late thirties (this date was given in an interview) when his fellow student and friend Swami Anantananda (who founded and led a monist congregation) showed him an old manuscript, *Nirguṇa Sāgar*, by Adiguru Ramtārāma Chaturbhuji, "who," according to Jigyasu, "was a contemporary of Ravidas." It contained purely nondualist poems and spiritual aphorisms by Ravidas and helped change Jigyasu's view. It convinced him because it was written, as he remarked, "by one who was contemporary of Ravidas and Kabir, and had lived for a full one hundred and twenty years himself."

2. In the earlier accounts (e.g., Bhandarkar 1965 and Farquhar 1967), Kabir usually preempts Ravidas for innovative inspiration and relegates him to a more Hinduized stance. Any resurgence of scholarly interest in Ravidas remains feeble in this century. It appeared in a limited way in Briggs (1920) in the context of the northern Chamars. In Westcott (1953) on Kabir, Ravidas is mentioned only once (p. 11) in a footnote.

Unfortunately, Briggs's pitying approach to Chamars left little room for considering the early twentieth century reforms among them. This was, indeed, the period when reformers like Achchutananda and Jigyasu were active in the Lucknow-Kanpur region, and others in Meerut, Shahjahanpur, Saharanpur, and towns nearer Delhi.

3. This is despite information (e.g., see Westcott 1953: 11) that Nabhadas was a *dom* (sweeper) by caste. The original version of *Bhaktamāla*, the Chamars argue, is now impossible to obtain. "The Brāhmans," a Chamar *bhajan*–singer from Karampura remarked, "have gradually but surely reworked this book to reflect only their point of view."

4. It does so, however, as we have noted before, by less rigorous procedures than those required for an empirical study. Whenever, for example, historical certainty is absent, orally available information, whether mythical or legendary, is accorded equal reliability. Kabir and Ravidas are thus made contemporary at Banaras, one Kori by caste and the other Chamar (Jigyasu 1968a: 6–7). There are limited reliable ways to test Jigyasu's exaggeration of the historical data on asceticism, and only ambiguous standards and signals from Ravidas's own writings. The same problem persists in assessing the historical validity of Jigyasu's unequivocal classification of Ravidas as being "outside" the Hindu order. However, Jigyasu is careful in disallowing an ambiguous interpretation of his own writing. Yet he is not entirely free from occasional slackening. For example, Ravidas is shown to have moved unsurely, rather than unequivocally, away from the Hindu, idol-worshipping position (pp. 142–3).

5. The ascetic is distinct for his pursuit of the Supreme Spirit. But how? It is by following the well-developed path of yoga (Jigyasu 1968a: chap. 15). Yoga is not the property of the Hindu alone, Jigyasu remarked, "because the non-Brāhman and Brāhman ascetics have *jointly* evolved and perfected this path." Ravidas had reached an advanced stage of yogic attainments, for we find him saying that he "has crossed [the phases of] ant and fish, and wishes to attain [the yogic phase of] the bird" (pp. 134–6). "Ant," "fish," and "bird" symbolize three modes of spiritual progress, where an ant walking on the ground is slower than a fish (which is dependent on water), and a fish is slower than a bird (which is independent of any support). To reach the third phase is to be spiritually free, achieving deliverance (nirvana for Jigyasu). Ravidas achieved the highest state, since he, like Kabir, "did not leave behind his body" after death (p. 137). Note how Jigyasu here accepts the same miracle that *bhaktamāla* reports, but to illustrate his viewpoint: It represents to him the highest yogic state by being in communion with Rama, the Supreme Spirit (*śabda Brahman*), not the Hindu incarnation Rama or Krishna.

6. The limitations of the argument, however, arise from expected quarters. Foremost among them is the overlap between the cultural categories of the Brāhmanic and ascetic orders, despite the ideologist's attempts to separate and contrast the two in contending terms. The argument, therefore, must suffer from an ambiguity, dispersal, and weakening even if the basic characterization of the ascetic–Brāhman axis is insightful. The pursuit of this axis shows a philosophical and cultural discernment that is serious and engaging, but it does not allow the ideologist to enunciate a totally unambiguous scheme. This ideological argument will reach its climax in the following chapter, where it formulates a notion of "equalitarian individual."

7. Illustrating a similar refutation, a low-caste reformer from a village in Kanpur district dedicated his reform pamphlet (1961) to his mother's father (*nānā*), who had opposed the reformer's education, and to his father, who had insisted on educating the reformer in the twenties to give him "true freedom." This dedication takes us back to the second decade of this century when his grandfather had remarked to his father, "Why are you forcing this little boy [the reformer] to study; after all, he will have to depend only on an oxen plow?" This remark is significant for its early date and location, though it could still be heard among some older Chamars of Karampura and Baudhabagh.

4. Moral individuation: A climax

1. In simple and popular terms, the human individuality that the ascetic carries is based on (1) ideas about indestructible self; (2) practice of some form of self-control, involving spiritual, mental, and bodily austerities; (3) pervasion of spiritual principles in the moral cosmogony and cosmology; and (4) recognition of a full, autonomous, and indivisible "unit of being," which in the Indic scheme is not a true monad (Greek, *monas*) until it is also a true *Homo asketicos*. The content, boundaries, and course of this unit are kept as spiritual as its genesis.

2. Unfortunately, Ghurye (1964) offers no such list for comparison, nor does a more recent attempt (Sinha and Saraswati 1978). Such qualities are, in fact, not exclusive to the Untouchable ascetics by any means. However, N. K. Bose's provocative paragraph quoted in their preface by Sinha and Saraswati offers a cultural observation sympathetic to our goal.
3. Jigyasu (1968a: 114–16) also offers a highly abstract and terse version of spiritual individuation under the nondualist (*advaita*) cosmology. It is esoteric and quite technical, but could be symbolically instructive to our discussion if alluded to briefly for its general cultural logic. Although the specialist might like to go to Jigyasu's original version to see how deeply he encodes his message, hybridizing Hindu nondualism with Buddhist idealism, I will bring forward only a few crucial constituent categories and their relations to give an idea of this scheme. First, there is a recognition of the precreation void (Jigyasu employs here, as elsewhere, a number of technical adjectival terms of diverse – Hindu and Buddhist – backgrounds, for example, *mahāśūnya*, *anāma*, *parāvāka*, and *paraṃsvida*). Second, there is a primal motion (or energy) postulated to give rise to "I" (or Ego or *ahaṁa*) complemented by "am" (or *asmi*), where the former is held synonymous with "pure inactivity" (*śuddha niṣkrīyatā*) and the latter with "all the transactions of creation" (*sṛṣṭi kā vyāpāra*). Third, when "I" and "am" come together, they give rise to "sound" (*nādā*), the synonym for "Word" (*Śabda*), the latter a synonym for Universal Spirit (*Brahman*). Compare Deussen's discussion (1966: 39–40) of this basic Upanishadic idea.

   The structure these three steps illustrate is clear: Starting from an absolute nonrelational phase, it first goes through a stage of complementary opposition and then of transformative conjugations. This basic structural paradigm is recombined only to derive further constituent distinctions (e.g., as between nondualism and dualism, *nirguṇa* and *saguṇa*, and such subsidiary fivefold distinctions as *pañcabhūta*, *pañcaprāṇa*, *pañcajñānindriya*; see Nikhilananda 1963: 361–88, for a reliable explanation of these categories in English). Essentially, these signify constituent relations of the cosmos at creation, and then of dispersal at destruction (*pralaya*). In the former context, Jigyasu's derivation proceeds as follows (arrows represent transformation):

   Attributeless Brahman (i.e., Universal Spirit) → Brahman (or B) with attributes → B with fivefold material elements (*pañcabhūtātmaka* – space, air, fire, water, and earth) → B with fivefold organs of perception (*pañcaviṣayātmaka* – eyes, ears, nose, tongue, and skin) → B with fivefold breath *pañcaprāṇamaya* – vital energy for breathing, bowel movement, body movement, body nourishment, and "ejection" of "soul" at death) → B with *manas* (or the "mind" or the "inner organ" consisting of "desire, deliberation, doubt, faith . . . intelligence, and fear"). The last one, with "name and form" (*nāmarūpātmaka*), completes the formation of human *individuality*. Nikhilananda (1963: 109–11) also makes this connection in a footnote as he translates a cosmological scheme from *Mundaka Upanishad*: "Brahman expands by means of austerity, and from it the primal matter is produced; from matter, Prana, mind; from mind, the elements; from the elements, the worlds; thence works [karma]; from the works, their immortal fruits. From him who knows all and understands everything, whose austerity consists of knowledge – from Him, the Imperishable Brahman, are born Brahma, name, form, and food."

   The purpose of this quote is twofold: First, it gives a textual scheme for comparison with Jigyasu's. Second, it helps us interrelate Brahman, austerity (*tapas*), creation, and individuation within the Hindu conceptual scheme that may still influence Untouchable ideas. But we should not hastily equate the two, for the Chamar ideologist is not only altering nuances of the Hindu scheme (e.g., see the absence of karma in Jigyasu's scheme, and its inverse sequence – from matter to mind). He is also rearranging, deleting, replacing, and adding some significant building blocks and their relations to each other. This becomes clearer when Jigyasu is read as a whole and in the historical context in which he develops his formulations (e.g., see chap. 15 in 1968a).

4. Like individualism in the West (e.g., Dumont 1965, Lukes 1973), the Indic development carries its own strong assumptions. In cultural conception and expression, these are very distinct but not unique. One critical feature that could not find place with Dumont is what we have approached as everyday, ordinary representations of "spiritual" (*ātamika*) individuality. I do so in front of the "Durkheimian social" without embarrassment, for this construct represents not merely a mystical or esoteric ideal, but also a massive moral presence that is recurrently translated throughout the society. The translation occurs through sectarian and ritual institutions (e.g., as under sacrifice, gift giving, hospitality, and worship) of the Indian society.

The ascetic is a prominent example if this individuation. He is variously transsocial, linking the ritual, personal, and spiritual domains with one another for meaningful transformations. As shown, a nonsocial placement of the ascetic generally enhances his influence within the society. The more mysterious the individuality, the greater its cultural symbolization and interpretation, and the more consequential it is found to be by the society at large. Such an inosculation of self and society seems to be fundamental to the Indic scheme.

5. A generalizing study of individuality is feasible under such a structural formulation. Whether the formulation of individuality is history bound or mythical or a combination of the two, this subject might be best studied when freed from its West-centered historical specificity and treated as *a* logical relation characteristic of universal human cognition and ordering. If societies demand morally responsible personhood in order to cohere, they must also treat the questions of its divisibility and indivisibility in cultural terms. (For a *Sāṅkhya* scheme not handled in the text, see Larson 1980: 303–16.)

6. The accountability we have considered here (and elsewhere in this study; see chap. 9), it must be evident, is moral. It needs to be conceptually distinguished in idea and inspiration from the purely economic model and its extended implications. Our emphasis here is on cultural judgments and socially tactful activities. In the popular context, Hindu moral accountability is fundamentally underwritten by the principles of karma and dharma, and *pravṛtti* and *nivṛtti*, especially as they operate in terms of the individual (Potter 1980: 241–67). The divine accountants must therefore appear within this cosmology (Chitragupta, Yama's functionaries, Vidhi, etc.).

Since the spiritual accountability the Indic ascetic illustrates is not merely karma bound, and since it is of both ultimate and proximate human significance, it carries greater explanatory power essentially by becoming a several-lane bridge to connect the widely different spheres of self and society. Compare Douglas (1980) for her use of this concept detected in Evans-Pritchard's work. The inspiration, context, conception, passage, and consequence of my use remain different but not unrelated, however.

7. Our usage of this idiom is symbolic rather than economic. "Market" represents for us an arena where a view as well as a course of practical action develops to yield a cognitive remapping of the participants. The Untouchables may there "shop" for values, whether the old ones are refurbished or the new ones framed in a familiar cultural language. But as they do so they must exit the ideologist's mentality and enter the market one. Selection, prioritization, and relative evaluations mark this domain, since costs and benefits must be assessed in advance from the "buyer's" as well as the "seller's" point of view. The participants must plan, evaluate, decide, and act to minimize risk and maximize satisfaction.

However, as we pose a distinction between the two (i.e., ideal and practical) mentalities, we must also be prepared to see how, as this study has posited, the two contextually are transformed into each other, and how, at a still deeper level of abstraction, the two might be derived from the *ātamika* principle of freeing the moral will from captivity. But to propose this is also to remember the following remark of Nietzsche's (quoted in Aiken 1956: 219): "It is certainly not the least charm of a theory that it is refutable; it is precisely thereby that it attracts the more subtle minds. It seems the hundred-times-refuted theory of the 'free will' owes its persistence to this charm alone; someone is always appearing who feels himself strong enough to refute it."

The Untouchable ideologist, likewise, finds the caste Hindu refuting his quest for free will. The caste Hindu ridicules the Untouchable on this issue because, as Jigyasu once remarked, "it will wreck the caste Hindu's social dominance."

8. Victor Turner (1980: 18) also observed: "It is perhaps not surprising that the concept of the individual in general in the West arose most explicitly in the Judeo-Christian tradition among people belonging to minority cultures whose strongly held world views were under constant direct and indirect assault from a vast range of powerful environing politics and belief systems."

5. Transition I: The worldly ascetic

1. Recalling Coomaraswamy at this point is not inappropriate, provided the context of use is clearly defined and his scholarly observations are carefully qualified. Though he (1979: 135) tries to distinguish between an apology for and an explanation of the caste system, and associated himself with the latter in a clearly perceptive manner, he will still be unacceptable to the Untouchable thinker or reformer for interpreting the caste order. But because Coomaraswamy is often concerned with ideal categories of the caste order, and discusses their deeper cultural significance, which the Untouchable thinker is also working toward, his relevance to our discussion becomes cogent.

Essentially, he should be cited in the present context for two reasons. First, he offers a singularly insightful, erudite, and comparative explanation of certain vital cultural Hindu and Buddhist categories. For example, consider "Progenitor *in divinis*" (pp. 133–4) – the Brahman; *varṇa* (p. 134), meaning "to 'cover' or 'conceal' "; and karma (pp. 138–40), meaning not only work or action but also "sacred operation," "justice," "natural law," and a form of "equality of opportunity." His interpretation is still fresh in some ways for the contemporary sociology of caste (e.g., see his use of Hocart). Second, his comparison with the West remains sensitive, deep (forgetting his polemical and derisive asides on the contemporary West), and useful to us, though unfortunately he does not engage himself in a systematic study of such interesting concepts as the "All-Worker" (cf. Lévi-Straussian "bricoleur"), equality of "all inner *men*" (p. 143), absolute and contingent liberties, and "perfected workmanship" (p. 142).

6. Transition II: The radical and protesting ascetic

1. Since the *ādi*-Hindu movement is not under study, we will exclude its chronological and substantive details, attending to only those aspects that would tell us something about style of leadership. We may note, however, that this movement, originally socioreligious, became increasingly political, but it lost its momentum in the face of the more comprehensive social movement for Indian independence. However, claims Jigyasu, the *ādi*-Hindu movement offered a cultural parallel to the *ādi*-Dravida movement of South India, and to those of the *ādi*-Dharmis of Punjab, and the Ādivāsis of Bihar and Bengal. In a final tribute, Jigyasu makes Achchutananda a Marx and Ambedkar a Lenin of the "original socialism" of India (1968b: 27).

7. Articulation of the practical ethos

1. Gandhi is a celebrated, but difficult, case in this category, for if he most of all – and perhaps best of all – married politics to asceticism in this century, he himself eluded any easy classification by extending asceticism and politics, in manner and content, into each other in a characteristically paradoxical way. The more intense the political situation, the more directly would he also be found relying on the ascetic, personally austere, principles and approaches (see Iyer 1973). Ambedkar was different, however. If he was an "ascetic" at all, it could be only in the last phase when, by converting to Buddhism, he began to be increasingly seen as a "Buddhist monk" by the Untouchables themselves.

8. Identification of deprivation and its manipulation

1. There are two levels at which this question, as already suggested, can be approached, that is, empirical and structural. Empirically, Weber can be easily improved upon by later research, but he cannot be logically rejected. This is so, especially because Weber, even if neither always explicit nor uniformly abstract, incorporates several *logical* relations (i.e., the structural), which Pariahs, as an excluded minority, must follow, irrespective of their contextual variations. For example, if the Pariah is, by definition, a severely low and weak social group, an emphasis on different forms of exclusion by the strong must logically follow. This exclusion need not only be from the congregational religion of the majority, but could also be expressed through a dependence on fate, inwardness, salvation, and saviors (i.e., mechanisms besides and beyond the normal ones). For all such factors can be shown to represent varieties of exclusion (from the dominant group's position) and circumscription (from the Pariah's standpoint).

Because Weber's logical reasoning centers around inclusion and exclusion, he bases himself on such a fundamental structural feature that, despite historical changes in deprivation, the logical dimensions of his model must continue to be significant as long as there is *any* perceptible social exclusion. Thus, if Weber's model needs to be properly evaluated, its domains of both strength (logical) and weakness (empirical) must be clearly recognized for India, not only in terms of each other, but also as its logic of exclusion brings into play the processes of sociocultural calculation, judgment, and decision making between the "sated" and nonprivileged groups.

2. I am using party-based democratic politics, not just any politics, as a divider of the two phases. The point is important because we obviously cannot maintain that the Indian social circumstance always precluded, until very recently, all political relations – competition, confrontation, and tactically planned exercise of power or influence to achieve (personal or collective) practical goals. Whether connected to the structure of a political state or not, political relations can be recognized in all kinds of activities and conditions – among families, sects, saints, mythological characters, and even contending sacred principles. Since anthropologists (see Bailey 1969: 12) now make use of this most generalized notion of "political relations," the foregoing stipulation is made to draw on the full significance of the distinction this analytic division is capable of yielding for us.

Here we may also note that the two senses – specialized (i.e., connected to state, democracy, voting, etc.) and generalized (as in "political relations") – for us interweave a language of political idea and action that the Chamars illustrate. They profusely employ this language to identify themselves across the traditional and nontraditional domains. Their pursuit may all along be to juxtapose the politics of morality and the politics of practical needs, treating one in terms of the other until the social antagonism really begins to erode or diffuse.

9. Evaluation and accountability

1. I admit to several reservations in using "secular" as a label for all of the cultural context in which the discussions of this segment will develop. It is obviously insufficient and trite in one way and inaccurate in another. Since the sacred also evokes a complementary and simplified opposition with the secular, it further complicates our task, unless we use it merely as a convenient label for only one domain of that total pattern that this inquiry has been pointing toward–namely, the "pragmatic ethos" of the socially deprived (see also chaps. 7 and 8). Thus a general point should be obvious: Although the Indian Untouchable is at present going through a heterogeneous range of pragmatic ethos, our inquiry has considered only three aspects most significant to him (and to the aims of this inquiry), that is, cultural idealism, social deprivation, and everyday practicality.
2. Consider, for example, how close the relevance of the following questions to the contemporary Indian Untouchable could be. (They were in fact found to be highly relevant to the selected contexts of the Lucknow Chamar.) "Under what conditions will the exit option prevail over the voice option and vice versa? What is the comparative efficiency of the two options as mechanisms of recuperation? In what situations do both options come into play jointly? What [ideas and] institutions could serve to perfect each of the two options as mechanisms of recuperation? Are institutions [and radical organizations] perfecting the exit option compatible with those designed to improve the working of the voice again?" (Hirschman 1970: 5; words in square brackets are introduced to contextualize the questions.)

   Since we notice that options of "exit" and "voice," like "loyalty," attract specific cultural meanings in India, our use of Hirschman's discussion will be analogical. Though the context of Hirschman's discussion is not anthropological, its orientation remains suggestive for our purposes.
3. Dahrendorf's conclusion that justice is "the permanently changing outcome of the dialectic of power and resistance" (1968: 150) cannot be accepted without reservations if we wish to remain genuinely sensitive to the Untouchable's cultural *ideology* (and its core symbolizations). The Untouchable wants to protest to achieve the needed *corrective* justice and then be, as it were, in harmony (i.e.,in moral consonance) with the cosmic system, ideally forever. For if we do not so postulate we will miss his entire cultural reason for going to Upanishadic nondualist spiritualism, Buddhist nihilism, and Indic asceticism.
4. This painting was done in 1975 by a young Chamar, a fully trained physician. His father had proudly hung his rosary on one side and his son's stethoscope on the other (but both unfortunately were removed when the photograph shown in the Frontispiece was taken). The painting depicted Ambedkar, with large, bespectacled eyes and an oval face, holding a copy of the Indian constitution in his left

hand. His fully raised right hand beckoned to the masses. Set against the round, whitish contours of the Indian parliament building, the leader projected a massive ground-to-sky physical presence and was dressed in a dark Western business suit and tie. The local Chamars considered this painting as much a tribute to the painter's father's reformed outlook as to the talent of the painter himself. The portrait was draped in a large marigold garland and included all the major degrees and titles of both Ambedkar and his painter.

5. So we have come full circle. The practical, the pragmatic, and the ideal are trained to serve, not exclude, each other. The ascetic represented in the image of the archetypal *Puruṣa* (or Buddha), the school teacher-reformer in the image of Ambedkar, and the new leader in the image of an Indian official and politician – the three provided a whole range of practical guidance to the Lucknow Chamar. They also represented a general Indian paradigm for bringing about social reform.

If Chamar social deprivation must result in social differences and conflicts, and if the practical experience must distinguish between the feasible and the infeasible, then both of these constraints must inform and influence the Indian pragmatic ethos as a whole. This ethos generally discourages extreme options to serve immediate interests. Ideologically, category opposition and its transcendence are endogenous to the Indian system. The Untouchable, as we have shown, is as much subject to it as is the caste Hindu. Both groups oppose each other at one level and transcend opposition at the other. Considered as parts of the larger whole, both represent dissimilarity (nonreduction) at one level and similarity (reduction) at another; in the second condition they represent more than themselves. A rich value economy that is civilizational in character guides them. This economy allows differentiation, disparateness, controlled contrast, and refutation between the caste Hindu and the Untouchable, but neither total opposition nor annihilation of one by the other.

However, contextual distinctions are "transcended" only by certain ultimate cultural postulations and principles (e.g., as *Puruṣa* would transcend the *varṇas* and *jātis*; *śūṇya* or nirvana would transcend all "worldly" states and statuses; and the Brahman would surpass moral dualism as well as amoral nondualism). It also means that all human social values, expressions, and experiences ought to remain "open" to this process of cultural transcendence. Put another way, voluntary effort, value correction, social reform, and a pursuit of social justice must remain feasible even within Indic ontology.

6. Postface, this study has tried to maintain discussion of empirical and analytic concerns at a level that would make the three frames of covarying cultural reference communicate with one another. It has also meant that I have returned again and again to a common set of analytic issues, but each time with a different import. There are no mere repetitions.

Conclusion: Aspects of significance

1. The purpose of such an explanatory device is to uncover linkages among selected Indic categories and principles about unequal and incomplete oppositions. The Western counterparts developed insightfully by Derrida under "erasure," "deconstruction," and "dissemination" are heuristically significant. Though Derrida's exercise is rooted in a whole segment of Western philosophical tradition (e.g., Rousseau, Nietzsche, Freud, Heidegger, Husserl, Lévi-Strauss, and Lacan; see Spivak 1976: ix–lxxxix), I discover a symbolic and ideational convergence between this genre of thinking about self and society and the Indic epistemic procedures about "deconstructing" the everyday reality (*sṃvṛtti*) of the world. The Untouchable thinker's schemes described before depend on the latter procedures (see also n. 3, this chapter).

Nonetheless, the purpose of such allusions (for they are no more than that), here as well as elsewhere in this study, should be clear, especially to my Indianist colleagues. It is, most of all, neither to divert nor hybridize nor disperse a sociological discussion in a seemingly alien and unusual direction. Rather, it is to open esoteric Indic schemes to a comparative consideration that is symbolically significant and anthropologically unavoidable.

2. Such a perspective discourages one to consider caste as the *only* ordering axis for the Indic cosmos, self, and society. The caste order is opened up to complementing and competing principles from the system as a whole. The larger proportions and perspectives take over. For example, the inherently cyclical model of the Indic cosmos takes over and "rounds out" (i.e., deconstructs) the "top" and "bottom" of the linear caste-ranking scale. An ethos of *ultimate* equality pervades and envelops all crucial relations within this model.

3. Like all paradoxes, this one also "packs a surprise" that, once *analyzed*, resolves into different sets of competing civilizational values. A case of "veridical paradox" (to use the term of W. V. Quine 1976: 9), it could be contrasted to "antinomy," which also "packs a surprise" but "can be accommodated by nothing less than a repudiation of part of our conceptual heritage." The Untouchable's paradox is discovered in his ambivalence toward the caste Hindu.

The nature of the Untouchable's moral ambiguity packs its own surprises. His ambivalence, perhaps a product of the civilizational approach to (i.e., of open-ended unity between) the "internal" and "external" states of human existence, nurtures hope as well as despair. It yields for the Untouchable an "eternal margin," a condition that keeps boons in abeyance but enforces curses (just as in the case of the mythic Triśaṇku). It is a condition of endless restlessness. The Untouchable ascetics, reformers, charismatic leaders, and protesters are all examples of such individuals who, to use Victor Turner's (1980: 23) phrase, represent a "creative destructuration of . . . [the] order. The intent of individuals in antistructural liminality is not to produce chaos but to realize a new and more effective integration of the components of experience."

But the Untouchable's paradoxical ambiguity is not incidental to Indic thought. It is treated as a function of illusion (*māyā*) and ignorance (*ajñāna*). Their removal helps to uncover reality; some stock examples are utilized to illustrate it (e.g., "rope taken for a snake"). Although there is no need to go into the Indian epistemological procedures involved in such cases (e.g., see Prasad 1958; Matilal 1971, 1977), both the *pramāṇa* and *prasanga* schools of philosophical debates are known to handle ambiguity, liminality, and "deconstruction" to argue their goals. Untouchable thinkers often utilize the *prasanga* form of argument, systematically refuting the opponent's position. Their argument involves strong reduction, deconstruction, and tests. As Matilal (1977: 19) observed, "Strong reduction [could be compared] with 'deconstruction-tests' of the engineers and physicists to determine the usefulness of metals, etc." It is like "the threshing operation by which chaff is separated and discarded and grain is collected."

4. This concern here has drawn attention to several questions of perspective and analysis for an Untouchable study: For example, has the Indian Untouchable been sufficiently approached for what he himself thinks? Has his version (verbal and nonverbal) been fully examined on its own basis – for studying his structures of meaning and significance? Could it be that our understanding of the Indian Untouchable (textual and contextual) has suffered because the literate segment of the Untouchables (tiny in size, but persistent nevertheless) has remained unattended? Though we know that the ordinary Indian still gets trapped in seeing only (or largely) what he has been used to, how does an investigator reliably pierce this limitation? How can the investigator seriously approach the genuine worth of what the Untouchable consciously says or does to controvert the dominant position of the caste order?

Robert Miller's (1966) study may be, in principle, as instructive in the preceding background as Moffatt's (1979), but for two very different reasons and with two different analytic assumptions. If the first proceeded in the right direction but could not go far enough to establish the case, the second one clearly outmaneuvered itself from a fuller inquiry. It "discovered" in the field (pace the investigator who endured himself *sans peur et sans reproche*) only that Untouchable who verified its theory (i.e., the obligingly "consensual"). Though Moffatt's opening and closing disclaimers enclose his argument in a disarming reasonableness (1979: 4, 6; 303–4), the disclaimers in fact could not reduce the crippling constraints to which he had to surrender to reach a totally caste-won picture of the Indian Untouchable. Our study warns us to be cautious in taking a "closed" view of the Untouchable.

5. Obviously, such a characterization is a deliberate simplification of certain Indian philosophical ideas. But since my purpose is to articulate a view that is sociologically useful, I find such a simplification conducive to our exercise. A total exclusion of the discussion of "self" distinctly weakens, I submit, a sociological explanation of Indian society. A distortion will persist in the formulation and comprehension of the "caste person" and the Hindu society as long as we do not evolve a comprehensive scheme to account for the vital Indic constructs, orders, and experiences of moral individuation.

6. To the Indian specialist this is a popular way of correctly stating more profound transformations between the Indic conceptions of "self" (i.e., of *bhūtātmana* or *śarīra ātman*) and Self (*prajñātman*). The Indic individuation is *not* an exercise only about thinking of or for "ego" (i.e., *ahaṃkāra*); it is about a part that becomes the harmonious locus for comprehending the social Whole, and vice versa.

Coomaraswamy (1978) widely characterized aspects of this issue. As he wrote about spiritual authority and temporal power, he noticed how the "ego" (the outer person) communicates (and "consummates") with the Self (the inner person). In this communication the individual gets conjugated with its collective counterpart, privation with abundance, ignorance with knowledge, "want" with "will," heteronomy (*anya-rāj*) with autonomy (*svarāja*), Regnum with Sacerdotium, existence (*esse*) with essence (*essentia*), self-control (*ātmasaṃyama*) with "Self-government" (the polysemous *svarāja*), and rule with ruliness. Actually, if we carefully go over the cultural language we have already recorded (whether on a Ravidas temple's verandah, or at a Chamar's shoe shop, or before an itinerant ascetic), we may discover several formulations illustrative of the preceding markers of the Indic system. The lesson is clear: We cannot afford to overlook the Indic ways of individuation and their symbolic orders and values of transformation, for in them may be the key to understanding many sociological issues in India.

7. A cultural analysis could be creative in such a circumstance exactly because it gives us necessary freedom to examine from alternative directions and at several levels the sociologically assumed. It raises different questions and reaches wider interpretations. A cultural analysis brings forward the civilizational placement of the Untouchable, commenting on both sides – the civilization as well as the

Untouchable's supposed definiens, the caste Hindus. Finally, such an analysis, by its premises and procedures, fosters multiple (multistranded) orders of significance, implication, and suggestion, *without* rejecting (though it may refute and adjust) the worth of alternative explanatory schemes. It contributes toward a better explanation without claiming too much, and without a need to trap itself in a theoretical corner. Cultural analysis follows the ever-adapting social reality, putting in context even the ultimate systems of cultural values.

Bibliography

The following is a two-part presentation of the works cited or consulted during the course of this study. Part A lists relevant books and pamphlets, mostly by Untouchables, published in Hindi by Janata's Welfare Publications (a pseudonym; henceforth JWP) in Lucknow. In using a pseudonym I depart from the established scholarly norm for offering documentary evidence. However, I decided to do so to honor the insistent request of the present management of this publishing house that I use a pseudonym, given current political sensitivities. Because most of the works listed are still available in Lucknow, one could verify the essential sources without much difficulty. Part B offers the remaining citations.

When known, the date of original publication of titles given in Part A is indicated in brackets. Ambedkar's translated works in Hindi are listed here, and works published in English appear in Part B. I use this system because *both* versions have often been useful in this study for different reasons.

Part A

Ambedkar, B. R. 1972a[1936]. *Jātibhéda kā Ucchéda* (Annihilation of caste). 6th Hindi ed. Translated into Hindi by Srivardhana and Sunderlāl Sāgar. Lucknow: JWP.

1972b [1966]. *Śūdron kī Khoja?* (Who were the Shudras?). 3d Hindi ed. Translated into Hindi by "A downtrodden Indian soul." Lucknow: JWP.

1973 [1949]. *Achchūta kaun aur kaiśe?* (The Untouchables). 3d Hindi ed. Translated into Hindi by Bhadanta Kausalyāyana. Lucknow: JWP.

1975 [1972]. *Bhārat mein Jātivāda* (Caste in India). 2d Hindi ed. Translated into Hindi by Dayārāma Jain. Lucknow: JWP.

Baṛgotyā, Srī Lālchand. n.d. *Bhīma Cétāvanī* (Bhīma's [Ambedkar's] warning). Poem. 4th ed. Lucknow: JWP.

Harihar, Srī 108 Swāmī Achchūtānandaji. 1975. *Ādi-vaṃśa kā Daṅkā* (Pronouncements of Ādi-vaṃśa). 10th ed. Lucknow: JWP.

Jādava, Lalaī Singh. 1971 [1961]. *Śoṣitoñ par Dhārmika Dakaitī* (Religious dacoity on the exploited). 3d ed. Kanpur: Sasta Press Jhinjak.

Jigyāsu, Chandrikā Prasād. 1965. *Nirvāṇaprāpta Bhadanta Bodhānanda Mahāsthavira* (Late Bhadanta Bodhānanda Mahāsthavira). Lucknow: JWP.

ed. 1965. *Bābā Sāhéb ké Upadeśa-Ādeśa* (Baba Saheb's precepts and teaching), part 2. Lucknow: JWP.
1968a. *Santapravara Ravidās Sāhéb* (Eminent Saint Ravidās Sāhéb). 2 vols; vol. 1 in 4th ed. Lucknow: JWP.
1968b [1960]. *Srī 108 Swāmī Achchūtānandji: Jīvanī, Siddhānta, Bhāṣaṇa, and Kavitāyen* (Srī 108 Swāmī Achchūtānandji: Life, principles, speeches, and poems). 2nd ed. Lucknow: JWP.
1968c. *Triratna-vandana, Paritrāṇa-patha tathā Jayamangala Attagāthā* (Triratna prayer, Paritrāṇa recital, and eight tales of Jayamangla). Pamphlet. Lucknow: JWP.
1969. *Nitya-Pūjā-Vandanā-Paritrāṇa-Mañgla Pātha* (Daily worship-prayers-salvation-welfare recitals [for Buddhist householders]). Lucknow: JWP.
ed. 1971[1965]. *Bābā Sāhéb ké Pandrah Vyākhyāna* (Fifteen speeches of Baba Saheb [Ambedkar]). 3d ed. Lucknow: JWP.
1972a [1956]. *Bhārtīya Carmakāron va Mahāron kī Utpatti, Sthiti, aur Janasaṃkhyā tathā unké sambandh mein Bābā Sāhéb Dr. Ambedkar ke vicāra* (Origin, status, and population of Indian Chamars and Mahars, and thoughts of Dr. Ambedkar on these). Pamphlet. 4th ed. Lucknow: JWP.
ed. 1972b [1965]. *Bābā Sāhéb kī Bhaviṣyavāṇī* (Baba Saheb's predictions [on Indian republic, Congress party, foreign policy, and Kashmir policy]). Pamphlet. 4th ed. Lucknow: JWP.
1973a [1961]. *Bābā Sāhéb kā Jīvan Saṃgharṣa* (Life struggle of Baba Saheb [Ambedkar]). 7th ed. Lucknow: JWP.
1973b [1966]. *Lokaśāhī banāma Brāhmaṇśāhī* (Democracy alias Brāhman rule). 4th ed. Lucknow: JWP.
n.d. *Bhartīya Republican Party hī kyon āvaśyaka hai?* (Why is the Republican party alone necessary?). Pamphlet. Lucknow: JWP.
Kabīrpanthī, Mahant Bansūdās. 1977 [1954]. *Viśvagurū Sadgurū Kabīr Sāhéb kā Mānava-Saṃdeśa* (Humane message of Kabir Sahib). 5th ed. Lucknow: JWP.
Lāl, Añgné. 1973 [1968]. *Ādivaṃśa Kathā* (Story of *Adivamsa*). 3d ed. Lucknow: JWP.
1975 [1972]. *Bauddha Dīkṣā* (Precepts of Buddhism). 2d ed. Lucknow: JWP.
Lomoṛa, G.R., ed. 1975 [1972]. *Bābā Sāhéb kā Upadeśa aur Ādeśa* (Baba Saheb's [Ambedkar's] precepts and teaching). Pamphlet, pt. 1. 2d ed. Lucknow: JWP.
Lucknawī, Rāshtrakavī "Prakāsh," and Avadhbihārī "Avdhésh." 1977. *Harijan Gohār aur Chchūta-Chattīsī* (Call to the Harijan and thirty-six [Savaiyā]). Poem. 10th ed. Lucknow: JWP.
Maṇi, Premkumār. 1975. *Manusmṛti: Eka Pratikriyā* (*Manusmṛti*: A reaction). Pamphlet. Lucknow: JWP.
Prasād, Gajādhar. 1972 [1969]. *Aryanīti kā Bhandāphoṛa* (Exposure of Aryan policies). 4th ed. Lucknow: JWP.
Praśānt, Gayā Prasād. 1974. *Achchūta kaon aur kyon?* (Who is Untouchable and why?) 6th ed. Lucknow: JWP.
n.d. *Bhīma Gītāwalī* (Lyrics [dedicated to] Bhima [Ambedkar]). Pamphlet. Lucknow: JWP.
Sāgar, Sunderlāl. 1973 [1965]. *Hindū Saṃskṛti mein Varṇa Vyavasthā aur Jāti bhéda* (*Varṇa* order and *Jāti* distinctions in Hindu culture). 4th ed. Lucknow: JWP.
Sāgar, Sunderlāl, and Chandrikā Prasād Jigyāsu, trans. and ed. 1977 [1966]. *Gandhi-Ambedkar Vivāda* (Gandhi-Ambedkar controversy). Pamphlet. 4th ed. Lucknow: JWP.
Saraswatī, Srī Swāmī Devānand et al. 1970. *Jāti Toṛo* (Demolish Caste: Five speeches by Saraswati, Bharati, Jigyasu, Santrama, and Habiba Bano during "All Indian

Congress on Caste Demolition." [Given in Lucknow, April 1966]). Lucknow: JWP.
Sen, Yogendra. 1974 [1970]. *Bhārat mein Sāmājika Viṣamatā kyon?* (Why is there social inequality in India?). Pamphlet. 2d ed. Lucknow: JWP.
Shāstri, Śaṁkarānanda. 1977 [1946]. *Poona Pact banāma Gandhi* (Poona Pact alias Gandhi). 8th ed. Lucknow: JWP.

Part B

Agarwal, C. B. 1934. *The Harijans in Rebellion*. Bombay: Taraporevala.
Aiken, Henry D. 1956. *The Age of Ideology: The 19th Century Philosophers*. New York: Mentor Books.
Aiyappan, A. 1944. *Iravas and Culture Change*. Madras: Government Press.
1965. *Social Revolution in a Kerala Village*. Bombay: Asia Publishing House.
Ambedkar, B. R. 1917. Castes in India. *Indian antiquary* XLVI: 81–95.
1945. *Annihilation of Caste, with A Reply to Mahatma Gandhi*, ed. Bombay: Bhusan Press.
1946. *Who Were the Shudras*? Bombay: Thacker.
1948. *The Untouchables*. New Delhi: Amrit.
Anand, Mulk Raj. 1970. *Untouchable*. New Delhi: Orient Paperbacks.
Anonymous. 1972. *Bhajanasamgrah* (Collection of devotional songs [Hindi]). Gorakhpur: Gita Press.
Apte, Vaman Shivram. 1965. *The Practical Sanskrit-English Dictionary*. Rev. ed. Delhi: Motilal Banarsidass.
Babb, Lawrence A. 1972. The Satnamis – political involvement of a religious movement. In *The Untouchables in Contemporary India*, ed. J. Michael Mahar. Tucson: University of Arizona Press.
Bailey, F. G. 1957. *Caste and the Economic Frontier*. Manchester: Manchester University Press.
1960. *Tribe, Caste, and Nation*. Manchester: Manchester University Press.
1969. *Stratagems and Spoils: A Social Anthropology of Politics*. New York: Schocken Books.
Béteille, André. 1965. The future of the backward classes: The competing demands of status and power. *Perspectives, Supplement to the Indian Journal of Public Administration* xi: 1–39.
Bhagat, M. G. 1935. The Untouchable classes of Maharashtra. *Journal of the University of Bombay* IV:1–45.
1976. *Ancient Indian Asceticism*. Delhi: Munshiram Manoharlal.
Bhajan Saṃgraha. 1972. 26th Hindi ed. Compiled by Viyogi Hari. Gorakhpur: Gita Press.
Bhaktamāla. 1969. 5th Hindi ed. Compiled by Nabhadasa, with commentaries in poetry and prose by Priyādāsa and Bhagwan Prasad Rupakala. Lucknow: Teja Kumar Press.
Bhandarkar, R. G. 1950. *Some Aspects of Ancient Indian Culture*. Madras: University of Madras.
1965. *Vaisnavism, Saivism and Minor Religious Sects*. Varanasi: Indological Book House.
Bouglé, Celestin. 1971. *Essays on the Caste System*. Trans. D. F. Pocock. Cambridge: Cambridge University Press.
Bourdieu, Pierre. 1977. *Outline of a Theory of Practice*. Cambridge: Cambridge University Press.

Brass, Paul. 1965. *Factional Politics in an Indian State*. Berkeley: University of California Press.

Briggs, G. W. 1920. *The Chamars*. Calcutta: Association Press.

Burke, Kenneth. 1954. *Permanence and Change: An Anatomy of Purpose*. Indianapolis: Bobbs-Merrill.

Burridge, Kenelm. 1979. *Some One, No One*. Princeton, N.J.: Princeton University Press.

Census of India. 1931. Ādi-Dharmi. Sec. 4, Chap. XI, App. III, vol. XVII, *Punjab*, Pt. I, *Report*. Lahore: Government Printing Press.

1931. United Provinces, vol. XVIII. Ed. A. C. Turner. Allahabad: Superintendent Printing and Stationery.

Cohn, Bernard S. 1955. The changing status of a depressed caste. In *Village India: Studies in the Little Community*, ed. McKim Marriott. Chicago: University of Chicago Press.

1959. Changing traditions of a low caste. In *Traditional India: Structure and Change*, ed. Milton Singer. Philadelphia: American Folklore Society.

Concise Oxford Dictionary. 1976. Oxford: Oxford University Press (Clarendon Press).

Coomaraswamy, Ananda K. 1978. *Spiritual Authority and Temporal Power in the Indian Theory of Government*. Delhi: Munshiram Manoharlal.

1979. *The Bugbear of Literacy*, 2d ed. Middlesex: Perennial Books.

Crooke, W. 1903. Chamars. In *Census of India*, 1901, vol. I. *India: Ethnographic Appendices*, ed. H. H. Risley. Calcutta: Superintendent of Government Printing.

Culler, Jonathan. 1979. Jacques Derrida. In *Structuralism and Since: From Lévi-Strauss to Derrida*, ed. John Sturrock. Oxford: Oxford University Press.

Dahrendorf, Ralf. 1968. *Essays in the Theory of Society*. Stanford, Calif.: Stanford University Press.

Das, Veena. 1977. *Structure and Cognition*. Delhi: Oxford University Press.

Derrida, Jacques. 1976. *Of Grammatology*. [Original French edition was published in 1967.] Baltimore: Johns Hopkins University Press.

Deussen, Paul. 1966. *The Philosophy of the Upanishads*. New York: Dover.

De Vos, George, and Hiroshi Wagatsuma. 1967. *Japan's Invisible Race: Caste in Culture and Personality*. Berkeley: University of California Press.

District Gazetteers of the United Provinces. 1904. *Lucknow*, vol. XXXVII. Compiled and edited by H. R. Nevill. Allahabad: Government Press.

Douglas, Mary. 1980. *Evans-Pritchard*. Glasgow: Fontana Paperbacks.

Dumont, Louis. 1960. World renunciation in Indian religions. *Contributions to Indian Sociology*, no. IV: 33–62.

1965. The modern conception of the individual. *Contributions to Indian Sociology*, no. VIII: 13–61.

1980. *Homo Hierarchicus*. Complete revised English edition. Chicago: University of Chicago Press.

Farquhar, John Nicol. 1917. *Modern Religious Movements in India*. London: Macmillan.

1967. *An Outline of the Religious Literature of India*. Oxford: Oxford University Press; Delhi: Motilal Banarsidass.

Feuer, Lewis S. 1975. *Ideology and the Ideologists*. Oxford: Blackwell Publisher.

Galanter, Marc. 1972. The abolition of disabilities – Untouchability and the law. In *The Untouchables in Contemporary India*, ed. J. Michael Mahar. Tucson: University of Arizona Press.

Galston, William A. 1980. *Justice and the Human Good*. Chicago: University of Chicago Press.

Gazetteer of the Province of Oudh. 1877. *Lucknow*, vol. II, 312–97. Lucknow: Oudh Government Press.

Geertz, Clifford. 1973. *The Interpretation of Cultures*. New York: Basic Books.

1983. *Local Knowledge*. New York: Basic Books.

Ghurye, G. S. 1964. *Indian Sadhus*. Bombay: Popular Prakashan.

Gokhale, Gopal Krishna. 1903. Elevation of depressed classes. In *Speeches and Writings of Gopal Krishna Gokhale*, vol. III. Ed. D. G. Kaine and D. V. Ambedkar. Bombay: Asia Publishing House.

Gombrich, Richard. 1978. On being Sanskritic: A plea for civilized study and the study of civilization. An inaugural lecture delivered before the University of Oxford on October 14, 1977. Oxford: Oxford University Press (Clarendon Press).

Gonda, J. 1970. *Visnuism and Sivaism: A Comparison*. London: Athlone.

Hardgrave, Robert L. 1965. *The Dravidian Movement*. Bombay: Popular Prakashan.

1969. *The Nadars of Tamilnad: The Political Culture of a Community in Change*. Berkeley: University of California Press.

Harper, Edward B. 1968. Social consequences of an "unsuccessful" low caste movement. In *Social Mobility in the Caste System in India: An Interdisciplinary Symposium*, ed. James Silverberg. The Hague: Mouton.

Heesterman, J. C. 1964. Brahmin, ritual and renouncer. *Wiener Zeitschrift für die Kunde Süd- und Ostasiens* VIII: 1–31.

1971. Priesthood and the Brahman. *Contributions to Indian Sociology*, n.s. 5: 43–50.

1981. Householder and Wanderer. *Contributions to Indian Sociology*, n.s. 15 (1, 2): 251–71.

Hirschman, Albert O. 1970. *Exit, Voice, and Loyalty*. Cambridge, Mass.: Harvard University Press.

Holck, Frederic. 1969. Some observations on the motives and purposes of asceticism in ancient India. *Asiatische Studien* 23: 45–57.

Iyer, Raghavan N. 1973. *The Moral and Political Thought of Mahatma Gandhi*. New York: Oxford University Press.

Kane, Pandurang Vaman. 1941. *History of Dharmasastra*, vol. 2, p. II. Poona: Bhandarkar Oriental Research Institute.

Keer, Dhananjay. 1962. *Dr. Ambedkar: Life and Mission*, 2d ed. Bombay: Popular Prakashan.

Khare, R. S. 1970. *The Changing Brahmans*. Chicago: University of Chicago Press.

1973. One hundred years of occupational modernization among Kanya-Kubja Brahmans: A genealogical reconstruction of social dynamics. In *Entrepreneurship and Modernization of Occupational Cultures in South Asia*, ed. M. Singer. Duke University Program in Comparative Studies on Southern Asia, Monograph 12. Durham, N.C.: Duke University Press.

1976. *Culture and Reality*. Simla: Indian Institute of Advanced Study.

1978. The one and the many: Varna and jati as a symbolic classification. In *American Studies in the Anthropology of India*, ed. Sylvia Vatuk. New Delhi: Manohar Publications.

1979. The untouchable elite: Aspects of changing cultural ideology and leadership among the Lucknow Chamars. Mimeo. Rev. October 1979. University of Virginia.

Kumaraswami, T. J. 1923. The Adi-Dravidas of Madras. *Man in India*, vol. 3, pp. 59–64.

Langer, Susanne K. 1974. *Philosophy in a New Key*. 3d ed. Cambridge, Mass.: Harvard University Press.

Larson, Gerald J. 1980. Karma as a "sociology of knowledge" or "social psychology" of process/praxis. In *Karma and Rebirth*, ed. Wendy D. O'Flaherty. Berkeley: University of California Press.

Laski, Harold J. 1934. *A Grammar of Politics*. London: Allen & Unwin.

Lukes, Steven. 1973. *Individualism*. New York: Harper & Row [Harper Torchbooks].

Lynch, Owen M. 1969. *The Politics of Untouchability*. New York: Columbia University Press.

Macpherson, C. B. 1964. *The Political Theory of Possessive Individualism: Hobbes to Locke*. Oxford: Oxford University Press.

Marriott, McKim. 1968. Caste ranking and food transactions, a matrix analysis. In *Structure and Change in Indian Society*, ed. Milton Singer and Bernard S. Cohn. Chicago: Aldine.

1976. Hindu transactions: diversity without dualism. In *Transaction and Meaning*, ed. Bruce Kapferer. Philadelphia: Institute for the Study of Human Issues.

Matilal, Bimal Krishna. 1971. *Epistemology, Logic and Grammar in Indian Philosophical Analysis*. Paris: Mouton.

1977. The logical illumination of Indian mysticism. An inaugural lecture delivered before the University of Oxford on May 5, 1977. Oxford: Oxford University Press [Clarendon Press].

Mauss, Marcel. 1979. *Sociology and Psychology: Essays*. Trans. Ben Brewster. London: Routledge & Kegan Paul.

McGavran, D. A. 1939. *India's Oppressed Classes and Religion*. Jubbulpore: Mission Press.

Mencher, Joan P. 1972. Continuity and change in an ex-Untouchable community of South India. In *The Untouchables in Contemporary India*, ed. J. Michael Mahar. Tucson: University of Arizona Press.

1974. The caste system upside down, or the not-so-mysterious East. *Current Anthropology* 15: 469–93.

Merleau-Ponty, Maurice. 1964. *Sense and Non-Sense*. Trans. H. L. Dreyfus and P. A. Dreyfus. Chicago: Northwestern University Press.

Mill, J. S. 1974. *On Liberty*. Ed. with intro. Gertrude Himmelfarb. New York: Penguin Books.

Miller, Beatrice. 1972. The man inside. In *The Untouchables in Contemporary India*, ed. J. Michael Mahar. Tucson: University of Arizona Press.

Miller, Robert J. 1966. Button, button . . . great tradition, little tradition, whose tradition? *Anthropological Quarterly* 39: 26–42.

1967. They will not die Hindus: The Buddhist conversion of Mahar ex-Untouchables. *Asian Survey* VII: 637–44.

Miller, Robert J., and Pramodh Kale. 1972. The burden on the head is always there. In *The Untouchables in Contemporary India*, ed. J. Michael Mahar. Tucson: The University of Arizona Press.

Moffatt, Michael. 1979. *An Untouchable Community in South India: Structure and Consensus*. Princeton, N.J.: Princeton University Press.

Nikhilananda, Swami. 1963. *The Upanishads*. New York: Harper & Row [Harper Torchbooks].

O'Flaherty, Wendy D. 1980. *Karma and Rebirth in Classical Indian Traditions*. Berkeley: University of California Press.

Ouwerk, Louise. 1945. *The Untouchables of India*. Oxford: Oxford University Press.

Parry, Jonathan P. 1979. *Caste and Kinship in Kangra*. London: Routledge & Kegan Paul.

Potter, Karl H. 1965. *Presuppositions of India's Philosophies*. New Delhi: Prentice-Hall of India.

1980. The karma theory and its interpretation in some Indian philosophical systems. In *Karma and Rebirth*, ed. Wendy D. O'Flaherty. Berkeley: University of California Press.

Prasad, Jwala. 1958. *History of Indian Epistemology*. Delhi: Munshiram Manoharlal.

Quine, W. V. 1976. *The Ways of Paradox and Other Essays*. Rev. and enl. ed. Cambridge, Mass.: Harvard University Press.

Rajah, Rao Bahadur M. C. 1925. *The Oppressed Hindus*. Madras: Huxley Press.

Ramaswamy, Uma. 1974a. Scheduled castes in Andhra: Some aspects of social change. *Economic and Political Weekly* 9 (29): 1,153–58.

1974b. Self-identity among scheduled castes: A study of Andhra. *Economic and Political Weekly*, 9 (47): 1,959–64.

Rao, M. S. A. 1978. *Social Movements in India*. New Delhi: Manohar Publications.

1979. *Social Movements and Social Transformation*. Delhi: Macmillan of India.

Rawls, John. 1971. *A Theory of Justice*. Cambridge, Mass.: Harvard University Press.

Report of the Commissioner for Scheduled Castes and Scheduled Tribes. 1977. *Twenty-Fourth Report*. 1975–76, 1976–77: Part I. New Delhi: Government of India Press.

Rose, Horace Arthur. 1919. *Frontier Provinces*, based on the census report for the Punjab. Lahore: Superintendent of Government Printing.

Rudolph, Lloyd I., and Susanne H. Rudolph. 1967. *The Modernity of Tradition: Political Development in India*. Chicago: University of Chicago Press.

Ryan, John. 1935. *Distributive Justice*. New York: Macmillan.

Sahlins, Marshall. 1976. *Culture and Practical Reason*. Chicago: University of Chicago Press.

Sayaji Rao III, Maharaja. 1928. *Speeches and Addresses of His Highness Sayaji Rao III Maharaja of Baroda*. London: Macmillan.

Schneider, D. M. 1976. Notes toward a theory of culture. In *Meaning in Anthropology*, ed. K. Basso and H. Selby. Albuquerque: University of New Mexico Press.

Sigrist, Christian. 1971. The problem of "Pariahs." In *Max Weber and Sociology Today*, ed. Otto Stammer. New York: Harper & Row [Harper Torchbooks].

Singer, Milton. 1961. Review of *The Religion of India*. *American Anthropologist* 63: 143–151.

Sinha, Surajit, and Baidyanath Saraswati. 1978. *Ascetics of Kashi: An Anthropological Exploration*. Varanasi: N. K. Bose Memorial Foundation.

Spivak, Gayatri Chakravorty. 1976. Translator's Preface. In *Of Grammatology*, by Jacques Derrida. Baltimore: Johns Hopkins University Press.

Srinivas, M. N. 1962. *Caste in Modern India and Other Essays*. Bombay: Asia Publishing House.

1966. *Social Change in Modern India*. Berkeley: University of California Press.

Srinivas, M. N., and André Béteille. 1965. The Untouchables of India. *Scientific American* 213 (December): 13–17.

Stevenson, Mrs. Sinclair (Margaret). 1930. *Without the Pale: The Life Story of an Outcaste*. Calcutta: Association Press.

Thakkar, A. V. 1945 (?). *Aboriginals Cry in the Wilderness: Their Education and Representation in Legislature*. Bombay: A. W. Thakkar, Servants of India Society.

Thapar, Romila. 1981. Householders and renouncers in the Brahmanical and Buddhist traditions. *Contributions to Indian Sociology*, n.s. 15 (1, 2): 273–98.

The Laws of Manu. 1964. *Sacred Books of the East*, vol. 25. Trans. G. Bühler. Delhi: Motilal Banarsidass.

Toulmin, Stephen E. 1970. *An Examination of the Place of Reason in Ethics*. Cambridge: Cambridge University Press.

Turner, Victor. 1980. The ambiguous individual: Liminality and morality. Mimeo. University of Virginia.

Uberoi, J. P. S. 1967. On being unshorn. In *Transactions of the Indian Institute of Advanced Study* (IIAS). Simla: IIAS.

Wadia, Sophia. 1932. *Theosophy and Untouchability*. Bombay: Servants of Untouchables Society.

Walzer, Michael. 1983. *Spheres of Justice: A Defense of Pluralism and Equality*. New York: Basic Books.

Warnock, Mary. 1978. *Ethics Since 1900*, 3d ed. Oxford: Oxford University Press.

Weber, Max. 1958. *From Max Weber: Essays in Sociology*. Trans. and ed. with intro. H. H. Gerth and C. Wright Mills. New York: Oxford University Press.

1963. *The Sociology of Religion*. Trans. Ephraim Fischoff. Boston: Beacon Press.

Westcott, G. H. 1953. *Kabir and the Kabir Panth*. Calcutta: Susil Gupta.

Whitehead, A. N. 1927. *Symbolism: Its Meaning and Effect*. New York: Macmillan.

Zelliott, Eleanor. 1966. Buddhism and politics in Maharashtra. In *South Asian Politics and Religion*, ed. Donald E. Smith. Princeton, N.J.: Princeton University Press.

1969. Dr. Ambedkar and the Mahar Movement. Ph.D. diss., University of Pennsylvania, Philadelphia.

1970a. Learning the use of political means: The Mahars of Maharashtra. In *Caste in Indian Politics*, ed. Rajni Kothari. New Delhi: Allied Publishers.

1970b. The nineteenth century background of the Mahar and non-Brahman movements in Maharashtra. *Indian Economic and Social History Review* VII: 397–415.

1972. Gandhi and Ambedkar: A study in leadership. In *The Untouchables in Contemporary India*, ed. J. Michael Mahar. Tucson: University of Arizona Press.

Index

Absolute (the), 31
Achchutananda, 16, 38, 55, 74, 81–7, 91, 98, 100, 108, 115, 119, 120, 131, 143, 149, 162 n8, 163 n2; ideology of, 82, 84, 85
accommodation, 138–9, 147
accountability, 3–4, 55, 59, 60, 127, 128, 131, 135, 137–42, 144, 151, 166 n6; comparative, 110; competing, 63; and evaluation, 129–30; positive, 62, 129; pragmatic, 91
action, 3, 91, 125, 142
ādi-Hindu ideology, 6, 17, 74, 82, 83, 85, 87, 96, 120
ādi-Hindu movement, 83, 84
All-Worker, 30, 76, 81, 90, 148
Ambedkar, B. R., 2, 6, 10, 17, 23, 32, 71, 72, 81, 83, 88, 89, 97, 115, 131, 156 n6; as ascetic, 168 nl; influence of, 38; language of social bias, 120; neo-Buddhist alternative, 31; painting of, 136; role of, 143–4; *Who Were the Shudras*, 143
ambiguity, 35–6, 51, 86, 145–8, 171 n3; of Ambedkar, 143–4
Anantananda, 55, 163 nl
articulation, 3, 91, 93–110, 111, 119
Arya Samaja, 82, 83, 150
ascertaining (*jānanā, patā lagānā*), 130
ascetic(s), 40, 51, 94, 95–6, 148; as All-Worker, 30, 81; as ambivert mediator, 68, 78; "awakened," 95–6; cultural constraints on, 31–4; cultural positions of, 25–6, 81; effecting social change, 35–6; ideal, 40–50, 56–8, 90; ideological linchpin of Untouchables, 23–4, 80; low-caste, 11, 12, 96–104, 130, 133, 134; medieval, 32–4, 37, 40, 48; as model, 36–7, 58; "monist," 11; participation/nonparticipation in society, 68, 69, 73–4, 75; position of, 101, 102, 103–4; Protestant, 68; Ravidas as, 44, 45; as representation of individuality, 55, 58, 166 n4; resident, 90; role of, 32, 79–80, 95–6, 108, 148; sectarian, 32; spiritual line of descent of, 33–4; spiritualist, 36–8; spurious, 76; *see also* householderlike ascetics; protesting ascetic; radical ascetic; reformist ascetics; worldly ascetic
ascetic–Brāhman axis, 26–9, 30, 39, 47, 160 n3, 164 n6
ascetic–mystic distinction, 21–2, 25, 35, 68
asceticism, 7, 21–4, 34, 67, 68, 76, 145, 159 nl, n2; ambiguity in, 36–7; ascetic–Brāhman axis, 26–9; and Chamar ideologist, 24–6; essential, 25–6; individuality in 63; lo-